D1568496

STAGING STRIKES

WORKERS' THEATRE AND THE AMERICAN LABOR MOVEMENT

In the series

Critical Perspectives on the Past

edited by

Susan Porter Benson,
Stephen Brier, and
Roy Rosenzweig

STAGING STRIKES

WORKERS' THEATRE AND THE AMERICAN LABOR MOVEMENT

COLETTE A. HYMAN

TEMPLE UNIVERSITY PRESS PHILADELPHIA

Temple University Press, Philadelphia 19122
Copyright © 1997 by Temple University. All rights reserved
Published 1997
Printed in the United States of America

⊛ The paper used in this book meets the requirements of the
American National Standard for Information Sciences—
Permanence of Paper for Printed Library Materials, ANSI Z39.48-1984

Text design by Will Boehm

Library of Congress Cataloging-in-Publication Data
Hyman, Colette A., 1958–
    Staging strikes : workers' theatre and the American labor movement /
Colette A. Hyman.
        p.   cm. — (Critical perspectives on the past)
    ISBN 1-56639-504-6 (cloth : alk. paper).

    1. Workers' theater—United States—History—20th century.   I. Title.
II. Series.
PN3307.U6H96   1997
792' .022—dc20   96-24739

For John Campbell, *mensch*

CONTENTS

ACKNOWLEDGMENTS

The experience of seeing a play is profoundly collective; it involves interpretation and participation at many levels and is shaped by the political, physical, and social environment in which the performance takes place. Because scholarship is equally collaborative, *Staging Strikes* reflects the environment in which the book developed.

This project has followed me around the country since graduate school; in each location I developed new relationships that had a profound effect on my work. On my many research trips friends welcomed me into their homes and helped me keep my work in perspective. I am especially grateful to Grey Osterud and Patricia Haines and her family in Ithaca; Sandra Van Burkleo, Edward Wise, and Bill Bryce in Detroit; Elizabeth Nagy Masters in Washington, D.C.; Jessica and David Rozenson in Boston; Julie Talen in Los Angeles; and my family in New York City.

The project began as a graduate school seminar paper at the University of Minnesota, developed into a dissertation, and finally evolved into this book. I am indebted to the professors who believed that this project was feasible and provided invaluable encouragement and suggestions along the way. Rudolph Vecoli's comments on the original seminar paper and my discussions with Lary May about movies, with George Lipsitz about resistance and cultural theory, and with Sara Evans about organizing and citizenship have all found their way into the final product. Working with Sara since then on other projects has rewarded me with insights about how this research is, at its heart, connected to most other academic and political endeavors in my life, despite appearances to the contrary.

The help I received from Richard Strasberg and the excellent staff at the Labor-Management Documentation Center, Martin P. Catherwood Library, Cornell University School for Industrial and Labor

Relations, made me wish I could do all my research there. But then I would not have had the opportunity to work with the knowledgeable staff of the Archives of Urban and Labor Affairs, Walter Reuther Library, Wayne State University, or with Debra Bernhardt and the staff of the Tamiment Library at New York University, who gave me access to materials that were still being sorted and catalogued.

My research would have been thwarted without the assistance of the dedicated people in the interlibrary loan departments of the libraries at the University of Minnesota, the University of Arizona, and Gustavus Adolphus College. Helen Neavill and Roy Smith, the interlibrary loan staff at Winona State University's Maxwell Library, merit special thanks for their five years of thoroughness, patience, and good humor. I will probably never know all they did to help me finish this project.

Friends and colleagues inside and outside "the academy" contributed tremendously to the substance of this work while keeping me grounded in the realities and pleasures of everyday life. Lauren Lenzen, Lynnda Lenzen, Sandy Touba, Barb Davis, and Jackie Urbanovic provided necessary distractions from graduate school; Eve Harris and Holly Gayle Baumann saw me through the most intensive periods of writing in Tucson; and JoAnn Thomas and the wonderful women at the Women's Resource Center in Winona reminded me that studying social change is not enough and helped me put my principles into action.

I thank Joy Lintelman, Richard Chapman, Angel Kwolek-Folland, Anton Rosenthal, Catherine Preston, Elizabeth Faue, Grey Osterud, Roger Horowitz, Peter Rachleff, Sherry Linkon, Miriam Frank, Dorothy Fennell, Joyce L. Kornbluh, Jonathan Bloom, Lynn Mally, Kathryn Oberdeck, and Eric Lott for comments on dissertation chapters, conference papers, article drafts, and book chapters. Gary Gerstle and Bucky Halker read my dissertation and suggested how I might turn it into a book manuscript, and Roy Rosenzweig read my manuscript and suggested how I might turn it into a better book. Marilyn Urion perused the manuscript with a writer's eye. Beth Cherne, whose work as a theatre historian overlaps my own, gave me renewed enthusiasm for my research and writing when I needed it most. The support of my colleagues in the History Department at Winona State University made it possible for me to continue my research and writing while teaching and serving on committees. Lori Beseler, the department secretary, transcribed almost two dozen interviews. Michele Huling translated the manuscript into the appropriate format for the press. I am particularly indebted to Janet Francendese and Joan Vidal at Temple University Press for their patience, understanding, and talent throughout the process of producing this book. Finally, students and colleagues in the Women's Studies Program helped me identify the pedagogical implications of my writings.

The women and men involved in the theatre ventures of this study are much more than just historical actors; they are individuals who shared a part of their lives with me. I am very grateful to Perry Bruskin, Rose Green, Lionel Davis, Carl Ross, Shaun Nethercott, Milt Reverby, and the late Wilbur Broms for sharing their memories and contacts with me. I thank the scholars—including Paul Buhle, Jonathan Bloom, Rita Heller, and Mary Frederickson—who put me in contact with workers' theatre participants they had encountered in their own research.

This project would not have been possible without a University of Minnesota Dissertation Special Grant and J. Putnam McMillan Fellowship; American Historical Association Albert J. Beveridge Travel Grant, the Henry J. Kaiser Family Foundation Grant that provided a trip to the Walter Reuther Library at Wayne State University; funding from the National Endowment for the Humanities and Winona State University's College of Liberal Arts; and a 1993 summer stipend from Winona State University, which allowed me to visit the National Archives and attend the fifteenth annual Great Labor Arts Exchange in Washington, D.C.

My daughter, Raizl Ambler Campbell, came into this world as I was in the final stages of the manuscript; the realization that she might read the book herself in a few years renewed my enthusiasm for completing the project.

My final thanks go to John Campbell. Because there are no words to thank him adequately for all he has contributed to my life and my work, I dedicate this book to him.

STAGING STRIKES

WORKERS' THEATRE AND THE AMERICAN LABOR MOVEMENT

1. BACKDROP

Workers' Theatre and Organized Labor

Man: They found Lefty . . .

Agate: Where?

Man: Behind the car barns with a bullet in his head!

Agate (*crying*): Hear it boys, hear it? Hell, listen to me! Coast to coast! HELLO AMERICA! HELLO, WE'RE THE STORMBIRDS OF THE WORKING-CLASS. WORKERS OF THE WORLD . . . OUR BONES AND BLOOD . . . [*To audience*] Well, what's the answer?

All: STRIKE!

Agate: LOUDER!

All: STRIKE!

Agate and others on stage: AGAIN!

All: STRIKE, STRIKE, STRIKE!!![1]

With those words, the audience jumped onto the stage and poured into the street, moved to a labor demonstration by a play produced in one of the most venerable theatrical venues in New York City. According to one observer, *Waiting for Lefty* quickly became "the most produced play in the entire repertory of the social theatre, playing in almost a dozen cities simultaneously" five months later.[2]

This historic performance at the Civic Theatre on January 6, 1935, began as one of a series of Sunday night showcases sponsored by the New Theatre League, an organization dedicated to promoting "theatre as a weapon" in class struggle, or, more concretely, theatrical productions as vehicles for educating audiences about labor issues, sustaining militant unionism, and supporting organizing campaigns and strikes. These Sunday New Theatre Nights usually attracted a coterie of dedicated left-wing theatre activists, but these women and men took the plays featured there to a broader public in union halls, at rallies, and at labor schools.[3]

Waiting for Lefty is one of the most prominent productions of a movement that involved men and women across the country in different kinds of settings, in theatrical productions aimed at advancing and supporting the labor movement. This workers' theatre movement was part of the left-wing political and cultural milieu of the 1930s, when writers, artists, musicians, and labor educators, Communists, Socialists, and trade unionists believed that collective leisure-time activities—whether sports, musical performances, classes in labor history, or theatrical productions—could be used to develop and sustain among working people and their allies the solidarity necessary for bringing about social and political transformation.

The workers' theatre movement was, then, among other things, a nationwide effort, organized at the local level, to use working people's leisure hours as a terrain for political education. It represents a particular approach to labor organizing, and for many, workers' theatre provided significant contact with and information about the labor movement, as well as a network of friendships and alliances that sustained their political work. Labor plays taught explicit lessons about unions and movement building; they also created empowering images of working-class people; finally, they gave workers and their allies a tool for disseminating the lessons of organized labor. For women and men who would not have attended a union meeting or workers' education class, attending performances of labor plays or participating in their production offered access to the labor movement, its past, its struggles, and its vision for a more just society. Workers' theatre did not always prompt participants and audiences to join picket lines—though often it did—yet it exposed them to the central issues facing the labor movement both locally and nationally.

Workers' theatre also led participants and audiences to others like themselves who were seeking entertainment that was relevant to their lives and politics and a place to become involved in the burning issues of their day. Workers' theatre could meet the needs of the labor movement for educating and politicizing its constituencies and the needs of young people for entertainment and community because of the nature of theatre and the theatrical experience. In the words of theatre historian and cultural critic Raymond Williams, theatre presents "the dramatic possibility of what might be done within what is known to have been done."[4] Plays about successful worker militancy gave a certain reality to scenarios of working-class action and, in so doing, awakened the optimism of audience members who were already moving toward worker insurgency.

Didactic, polemical theatre has been part of many insurgent and revolutionary social movements in the twentieth century, precisely because it is able to present scenarios of empowerment in which marginalized, disenfranchised social groups can see themselves otherwise. The theatrical productions that emerged within revolutionary movements in Latin America in the 1960s, for instance, were conceived as practical exercises in learning about the process of social transformation and as encouragements to public participation in political action.

Like the leaders and theorists of the workers' theatre movement in the United States in the 1930s, Augusto Boal, the most prominent theorist of Latin American political theatre, believed in the great power of this art form as "a weapon of liberation."[5] He attempted to develop theatrical forms that would move participants to challenge conventions and authorities and to work for social change. Accounts of political theatre performances in revolutionary movements in South America confirm the significance of theatre in mobilizing and inspiring audiences. According to Diana Taylor, a scholar of Latin American political theatre, "theatrical performances also became acts of collective affirmation and group definition."[6] Judging from spectators' responses to labor plays in the 1930s in the United States, this process was at work there, too.

Accounts of workers' theatre productions in the United States in the 1930s frequently emphasize the enthusiasm and boisterousness of audiences. Indeed, workers' theatre exploited theatre's innate ability to (as Williams says) "express and test the many versions of reality which are possible" by constituting working-class and left-wing audiences already predisposed to its messages of activism and militance.[7] By carefully selecting and "organizing" its audiences, workers' theatre created performances that promoted the desired effect. The power of workers' theatre, the vigorous responses it generated from audiences, and the attraction it held for those participating as writers, directors, designers, or actors resulted not so much from the quality of the scripts or production values as from the entire context of performance and production. The enthusiastic reactions of audiences at plays such as *Waiting for Lefty* or satirical skits on labor themes reflected a shared interpretation and political orientation among those producing and those attending the plays.

A play in performance involves interpretation at multiple levels. Each aspect of the production—direction, acting, set design, lighting, costumes, and so on—adds shades of meaning, intended and unintended, to the dramatization of the play's words. The physical and cultural attributes of the theatrical venue itself, including the layout of the performance space, publicity for the performance, and its location, shape audience reception. A play performed in a venerable downtown theatre, for example, elicits expectations from the audience that differ from those evoked by a performance in a loft or a storefront in a funky neighborhood.

The audience itself has its own assumptions and outlooks and actively engages with the performance.[8] Would the audience of *Waiting for Lefty* at a national theatre festival that included dignitaries from the worlds of art and politics have had the same response to the play or drawn the same meanings from it as factory workers watching it in their union hall?[9] Audiences interpret the action on the stage according to their own experiences, bringing to bear "recollection of past action or anticipated future ones" and contemplating relationships between what is taking place in performance and what is taking place outside it, in the theatre or in the city.[10] Workers' theatre cannot be understood either as a political movement or as an artistic or aesthetic movement without a consideration of the full context in which its plays were developed and performed.

Consequently, *Staging Strikes* is simultaneously a social history, a cultural history, and an institutional history of the workers' theatre movement, which blossomed in the 1930s and persists, in different ways, to this day. This study explores the experiences, values, attitudes, and outlooks of the women and men involved in workers' theatre and, to the extent possible, the composition and responses of their audiences. It also looks at the understanding of and assumptions about theatre that guided productions and efforts to "constitute" audiences. Finally, *Staging Strikes* juxtaposes the histories of various groups that have produced workers' theatre, comparing, on one hand, the approaches that different institutions and organizations have taken in producing labor-oriented theatre and, on the other hand, the experiences of the people in those productions.

On the whole, this work steers clear of assessing the flaws and virtues of the theatre it studies qua theatre; such evaluations are better left to drama critics and others with the requisite knowledge and background. Nonetheless, embedded in this analysis of workers' theatre are certain assumptions about what makes "good" or "effective" workers' theatre. "Good" workers' theatre teaches about activism, animates participants with a vision of social change, and leads them to question and challenge, in thoughts, in words, and in deeds, existing structures of social relations. Good workers' theatre is optimistic and imbued with a sense of possibility in working for social justice.

Most often, theatre that meets these criteria has been produced by local, small-scale, grassroots organizations that have the flexibility to respond to the concerns of those involved and that invite substantive contributions to the final production from all participants. Such organizations have tended to be democratic, participatory, and able to set their own political and aesthetic agendas. All the groups in this study hold some of these characteristics; few have them all. Nevertheless, groups such as the Brookwood Labor Players in the

1920s and 1930s; the Dram Group of Local 65, United Wholesale and Warehouse Employees, in the 1930s and early 1940s; and, since 1983, Workers' Lives, Workers' Stories demonstrate that workers' theatre groups can educate audiences while stimulating those involved in the productions; can develop and promote political analyses and strategies in ways that satisfy participants and audiences alike; and can, finally, sustain a culture—however narrow its territory within the wider society—that challenges the status quo and advances an attainable vision of social justice.

Like all scholarship, *Staging Strikes* relies on the contributions of others, in particular those in the fields of theatre history and labor and working-class history. In 1965, theatre historian Douglas McDermott published an article entitled "The Theatre Nobody Knows: Workers' Theatre in America, 1926–1942."[11] Since then, theatre scholars have worked assiduously to rescue workers' theatre from behind the curtain of obscurity that fell rapidly at the close of the 1930s. We now know much more about the major organizations that produced theatre on labor and other political themes, about the dramatic theories underlying workers' theatre productions, and about how they embodied different models of drama.[12] Concerned about recuperating a moment in the history of theatre in the United States, these scholars have created a solid base not only for understanding the place of workers' theatre in the larger sweep of theatre history but for exploring how this theatrical movement, which defined itself by its relationship to workers and the labor movement, construed and acted on that relationship.

The present study builds as well on the work of a generation of labor historians who have explored the diverse paths taken by working people and unions since the 1920s. The past two decades of scholarship on the 1930s and the rise and subsequent decline of the Congress of Industrial Organizations (CIO) and its affiliated unions have provided the historical data and analyses necessary for reinserting workers' theatre within the history that, I believe, participants saw themselves writing. *Staging Strikes* relies on the accounts and interpretations of major themes in labor and working-class history from the 1920s to the present that scholars such as Lizabeth Cohen, Elizabeth Faue, Gary Gerstle, Robin Kelley, and Peter Rachleff have richly elaborated.[13] At the same time, it adds another dimension to this scholarship by demonstrating the role and significance of theatre, and cultural and social activities more generally, in the labor movement and the life of unions.

The men and women who wrote, directed, performed, and attended plays and skits produced to promote the cause of working people and organized labor needed no proof of the significance of this work. Their commitment to a vision of social relations and a vision of theatre kept them going despite daunting adversity. Their optimism, energy, and enthusiasm have enriched both the history of theatre and the history of labor; *Staging Strikes* restores them to their rightful roles in the political and social history of the United States in the twentieth century.

2. PROLOGUE

New Playwrights and
Worker-Students in the 1920s

On March 5, 1926, at the Labor Lyceum in New York City, an enthusiastic crowd of six hundred applauded a program of three one-
act plays: *Peggy,* by Harold Williamson; *The People,* by Susan Glaspell;
and *A Dollar,* by David Pinski. Performing the plays were the Brookwood Players, working people studying to become union organizers
at Brookwood Labor College in Katonah, sixty miles away. Of the
three plays performed, only one—*The People*—directly addressed the
labor movement. The other two focused on the problems underlying labor struggles: the unequal distribution of wealth and power in
a society dominated by private property and the profit motive.[1]

One year later, on March 2, 1927, John Howard Lawson's play
Loudspeaker opened at the 52nd Street Theatre in New York.[2] It too
presented a stinging critique of contemporary society, focusing on
political corruption and the threats posed by modern technology.
Loudspeaker was in itself not terribly successful, but it constituted the
inaugural production of the New Playwrights Theatre, organized by
a group of middle-class, professional writers and theatre artists who
set out to establish a repertory theatre company that would allow
them to experiment both artistically and politically.

Many observers and scholars of the workers' theatre movement
of the 1930s have seen in the Brookwood Labor Players and in the
New Playwrights Theatre the antecedents of that movement.[3] These

theatre groups undeniably prepared the soil for the blossoming of workers' theatre in the subsequent decade, but their work also remains significant for the 1920s because of the challenge it posed to the conservatism of that decade. While organized labor and the left succumbed to the rightward pressure of public opinion and politics in the 1920s, the labor-oriented theatre of Brookwood Labor College and the New Playwrights Theatre maintained a vocal critique of contemporary social and economic problems. These two theatre groups directly defied the short-sighted boosterism characteristic of mainstream entertainment and provided compelling explanations for the experiences of those Americans whose efforts had not yielded increased economic security or social status.

Despite their common roots and shared concerns, however, the New Playwrights Theatre and the Brookwood Labor Players offered strikingly contrasting visions of things to come: where New Playwrights plays reinforced liberal middle-class despondency over the rightward swing of public opinion and public policy, the optimism of Brookwood plays suggested a bright and attainable light at the end of the tunnel. These differences highlight the diversity of concerns and visions that existed within workers' theatre, but they point as well to factors beyond playscripts that shaped workers' theatre productions. Comparing the work of the two major producers of labor-related theatre in the 1920s emphasizes the importance of such factors as audience and performance venue in determining the experience of workers' theatre and its role in the labor movement, in that decade and subsequent ones.

*   *   *

Theatre production at Brookwood began in the fall of 1925 with the arrival of new faculty member Hazel Mackaye, who had acquired a widespread reputation for her women's suffrage and women's rights pageants in the 1910s and early 1920s.[4] Experienced in the use of dramatic presentations for promoting political struggles, she had clear views on theatre's potential for "quickening . . . the spirit animating the labor movement." Under her direction, students wrote their own pieces and performed in nearby New York and Philadelphia as well as on the Brookwood campus itself.[5]

Mackaye did not return to Brookwood after the spring of 1926, but theatre remained a popular activity at the school, and faculty made changes in the schedule to accommodate this new component of Brookwood's two-year curriculum. Following Mackaye's departure, Brookwood hired Jasper Deeter, the founder and director of the Hedgerow Theatre, an influential repertory theatre outside Philadelphia. Under his guidance, students at Brookwood continued to write short plays. They also produced contemporary "art theatre" plays such as *The Hairy Ape* by Eugene O'Neill, the rising star of the Provincetown Players.[6]

After Deeter's two-year tenure at Brookwood, responsibility for labor dramatics was shared by various members of the faculty until 1934, when the school once again hired a drama instructor. By then, theatrical work had become thoroughly integrated into the activities of Brookwood students, and the college sponsored yearly Labor Chautauqua tours that performed varied programs of skits and songs.[7] Play production at Brookwood was intended to create positive, affirming images of working-class Americans while developing among the worker-students new techniques for organizing co-workers and neighbors into unions.

Deeter's presence at Brookwood linked the college's theatrical productions to contemporary efforts in the arts and politics to challenge dominant values and cultural norms. As a member of the Provincetown Players, Deeter was part of the fertile Greenwich Village bohemia that critiqued and rejected what it saw as the dehumanizing effects of industrial capitalist society. This assemblage of writers, artists, social reformers, and militant left-wing activists made possible the famous Paterson Strike Pageant of 1913, staged in New York City's Madison Square Garden to publicize a strike of silkworkers.[8] Several key Provincetown Players took part in this large-scale production, which demonstrated the potential of an alliance between politics and art.

Yet the Provincetown Players themselves on the whole proved leery of exploring such an alliance. The Provincetowners, as they were called, were writers who performed their own plays, united by a belief in the spiritually redemptive and socially instructive value of theatre rather than its political potential.[9] Eugene O'Neill, for instance, made theatre history with his frank dramatizations of family relations, but he denied the critical implication of plays such as *All God's Chillun's Got Wings*, about the love-hate relations between a black man and a white woman.

Nevertheless, by substituting plays that directly addressed social problems for the usual commercial theatre fare of formulaic melodramas, lighthearted farces, and dazzling revues, the Provincetown Players opened the door to the more explicitly political dramatization of social issues. The Provincetowners wrote and premiered plays that were subsequently produced by workers' theatre groups such as the Brookwood Players: not only *The Hairy Ape* but *The People* and *A Dollar* also had their first performances through the Provincetown Players. Moreover, several Provincetowners besides Jasper Deeter later worked toward developing a more politicized theatre in the 1920s and 1930s.

Mike Gold, for instance, is perhaps best known for his autobiographical novel *Jews without Money* and for his contributions to the left press over several decades, but his career as writer and cultural critic also took him to the Provincetowners, who produced three of his one-act plays.[10] A visit to the Soviet Union in 1925 convinced him of the need for a more politically engaged theatre than the Provincetown Players would ever be, and, with Provincetowners Ida Rauh, Emjo Basshe, and Jasper Deeter, as well as other artists, he founded the Workers' Drama League, which was dedicated to the production of plays that were "revolutionary in character."[11] In May 1926, the league, which proclaimed itself "the first workers' theatre in America," produced Gold's script, *Strike!* a mass recitation about the textile workers' strike taking place at the time in Passaic, New Jersey.[12] The Workers' Drama League produced one other play and seems to have folded shortly thereafter, owing to personality clashes, policy differences, and, no doubt, the financial straits that habitually hound fledgling theatre groups. Undeterred by the league's rapid demise,

Gold and his colleagues embarked on another theatrical effort to "get close to the earth, the fields, factories and mass life of America."[13] To mark their departure from their origins in the Provincetown Players and the Playwrights' Theatre (which this troupe had established in Greenwich Village), they called the new venture the New Playwrights Theatre.

The new theatre group experimented with both form and content. In his script for *Processional,* for instance, John Howard Lawson (who had joined Gold in the Workers' Drama League) used jazz, vaudeville, and "constructivist" sets to highlight social tensions over a looming strike. The sets, which emphasized mechanical functions over naturalistic reproduction, supported the script and music in guiding audiences' attention to the structures and constraints underpinning American society. Where Gold had been moved by the political content of the theatre he witnessed in the Soviet Union, his colleagues sought to reproduce the technical and aesthetic innovations of Soviet theatre.[14]

The New Playwrights' and the Brookwood Labor Players' shared interest in dramatizing the experiences and concerns of working people led the two groups to select scripts with similar themes. Their plays criticized both the impact of technological improvements on the lives of ordinary Americans and the dominant ideology of upward social mobility. In 1927, the New Playwrights Theatre produced Paul Sifton's *The Belt,* in which a factory's assembly line takes center stage, and Brookwood produced *R.U.R.,* a play that gave modern civilization the word "robot" and that still resonates ominously sixty years later.

In Sifton's play, The Belt's unrelenting drive wears down all who live within its orbit, not only those working directly on the assembly line. In the words of theatre historian Ira Levine, "the Belt looms larger than life, a mechanized monster seemingly self-sufficient and feeding off the lifeblood of its workers."[15] A young woman works at the office of the company, and she is as exhausted by her work as her father and lover, both of whom work on The Belt; she too seems driven by its relentless pace, as if the accelerated production of cars also

speeds up her output as secretary. The Belt's inescapable presence
on the stage forces audiences to experience its rhythmic motion and
sound (see photograph).

The theme of the machine's domination and destructive influence on individual lives appeared frequently in the literature as well
as the theatre of the 1920s, beginning with Elmer Rice's *The Adding
Machine,* first produced in 1923 by the Theatre Guild.[16] In this play,
the main character, Mr. Zero, loses his accounting job to an adding
machine on the twenty-fifth anniversary of his employment with the
same firm. Later in the decade, Sophie Treadwell's *Machinal* interpreted a sensational murder trial as a case study of how the pace of

"It's The Belt makes them get this way" (Paul Sifton, *The Belt*
[New York: Macauley Co., 1927], p. 119). *Billy Rose Theatre Col-
lection, The New York Public Library for the Performing Arts; Astor,
Lenox, and Tilden Foundations.*

life set by mechanization corrupts and ultimately destroys the individual.

The Belt, in contrast, places the machine squarely in the factory and the lives of working-class people highlighting the impact of industrialism on collectivities, not just individuals. Moreover, where *The Adding Machine* and *Machinal* voice doubts about the benefits of technological progress in general, *The Belt* makes a concrete statement about the power relations embedded in technology. Machines like The Belt allow the ruling class to dominate ever more thoroughly the lives of working people. The chronic weariness it creates in workers leaves them vulnerable to the blandishments of The Company, which knows exactly how to exploit this weariness. In the opening act of the play, the "Old Man"—a transparent rendition of Henry Ford—and his entourage of assistants and photographers invade the home of the main character to award him a pin for ten years of loyal service.[17] It is nine o'clock at night, and the family is just getting ready to retire. Ten years on the job and a long day on The Belt have made Jim Thompson incapable of seeing through his employer's stratagem for maintaining his loyalty.

The class dimensions of mechanization are drawn with equal clarity in *R.U.R.,* which students performed at Brookwood. The play, translated from the Czech, is set at some point in the future when Rossum's Universal Robots have replaced humans in most manufacturing and service jobs. The engineer Rossum has developed the best worker "from a practical point of view: . . . the one that is the *cheapest,* the one whose requirements are the *smallest.*"[18] The action takes place at the R.U.R. factory, where managers pride themselves on the advantages of robots over flesh-and-blood "robots": they don't have emotions that get in the way of efficiency, and they don't organize. The situation changes, however, when a new batch of robots instigates mass revolt among the mechanical workers, who, trained to fight humans' wars, take over the world and kill its human inhabitants. The play rules out the possibility that mechanization can work to the benefit of humanity, as long as its development is driven by the profit motive. Harry Domin, the company's general manager, envisions a world in which "the dreadful and humiliating labor that man had to undergo" is eliminated. He wants to do away with poverty by producing goods so cheap that all can afford them. The more realistic Alquist, however, the "head of the Works Department," reminds him that such a vision is not compatible with that of the company's shareholders: "They dream of dividends, and their dividends are the ruin of mankind."[19]

As *R.U.R.* points out, delusions concerning the innocence of technology obfuscate the true power relations embodied in machines in a capitalist society. Belief in the benefits of technology makes those who are enamored of new inventions the unwitting accomplices of a system that is constantly on the lookout for more ways to maintain existing power relations. In this vein, John Dos Passos's play *Airways, Inc.,* produced by the New Playwrights in 1928, demystifies the magic of the airplane. Elmer, one of the main characters, is a flying hero who also works on perfecting airplane technology. He is as gullible as he is in love with flying, and he naively accepts the promises of entrepreneurs about a new airline they are planning.[20]

In the meantime, however, a strike is under way in the background, literally and figuratively. (Stage directions indicate picketing and demonstrating behind the sets representing homes and open space.) Elmer is hired to drop anti-union leaflets on the strikers, and when police begin shooting into the crowd, the plane is struck and crashes, permanently paralyzing the young pilot. The entrepreneurs renege on their promises to Elmer, citing his inability to fly, and he is condemned to spend the rest of his days delirious from pain, with little assistance from the company responsible for his condition.

In the context of the mass frenzy and admiration surrounding Charles Lindbergh's flight across the Atlantic in 1926, *Airways, Inc.* paints a sobering picture of how easily ruling-class interests appropriate marvelous feats of skill and technology. The staging of the play, which foregrounds the flyer's exploits and keeps the strike, for the most part, offstage, reflects a public mood in which attention is focused on the achievements of the few while the masses' attempts to claim just compensation for their efforts are hidden from view and doomed to failure.

All the promises of technology, the play indicates, cannot free Americans from their class status. Elmer had hoped to soar above his working-class origins, just as he was soaring above his striking, working-class neighbors. But like them, he remains under the control of elite-dominated technologies—the police who shoot at Elmer's plane no doubt injure or even kill strikers as well. Escape is not the answer to the deprivations of working-class youth.

Upward social mobility is also denied to Peggy, the eponymous protagonist of the one-act play that Brookwooders produced as part of their program in New York City in 1927. The daughter of tenant farmers, she dreams of escaping through a job in town and marriage to the planter's son. (The script is ambiguous about whether his flirtation with Peggy is her fantasy or his cruelty.)[21] Peggy's hopes for a better life are dashed when her father dies (from overwork and the inability to afford medical care) and the landowner evicts the remaining family members. Jed, a young tenant farmer in love with Peggy, offers the only way out of homelessness: if she marries him and works with him on the land, her mother and brother can remain in their run-down shack. Thus Peggy is condemned to follow in her family's footsteps. Although the play presents no efforts on the part of tenant farmers to improve their lot, it warns against looking for easy ways out of one's class status. Working-class Americans must understand that only others like themselves can offer them the support necessary for survival.

In a decade marked by a rising standard of living based on technological "advancements" and dominated by an ethos of self-improvement and self-realization, plays such as *Peggy, Airways, Inc., The Belt,* and *R.U.R.* called attention to the harsh realities of contemporary social relations that popular culture vigorously sought to obfuscate. The plays of the New Playwrights Theatre and the Brookwood Labor Players demonstrated the vacuousness of the promises held out by "labor-saving" devices and self-help manuals. Instead of distracting audiences from the oppressiveness of class relations and technological modernization, these productions confirmed the realities of spectators' lives. The plays of the two groups parted ways, however, in their outlooks for the future.

The overall vision of social relations and of things to come conveyed by theatrical performances is constructed at many levels beyond the playscript: in addition to the direction, the acting, the set design, the lighting, and the costumes, the theatrical venue itself and the life experiences of the audience help shape the interpretation of plays. Thus a play such as *The Belt*, which ends with the leader of a nascent strike promising to continue the struggle, could seem pessimistic when staged by the New Playwrights Theatre and full of promise when performed in the context of vigorous labor organizing activities.

The New Playwrights Theatre saw its function as "mirroring the color and tone of life around us [and] crystallizing rebellion" and lowered its ticket prices to attract working-class audiences.[22] Nevertheless, it failed to draw a following among working people, and its audiences were made up primarily of members of the middle class with liberal and left-wing sympathies. Such audiences would have been aware of and dismayed by the government repression of the left, employers' assaults against unions, and the internal disputes within the left and organized labor occasioned, at least in part, by the founding of the Communist Party in 1919. Such audiences also made up the readership of the *Modern Quarterly*, where V. F. Calverton wrote in 1929 that "nowhere is there light or hope," and read the liberal press's analysis of social and economic conditions. As Richard Pells notes, however, the leading liberal journals "confined themselves to probing beneath the prosperous surface of American life in an effort to uncover the roots of ultimate collapse," without articulating any platform for change.[23]

Entering the theatre with the gloomy outlook of disempowered dissenters, New Playwrights' audiences would see in *The Belt* a confirmation of the hopelessness of resistance in the face of mechanization and its control in the hands of powerful and deceitful capitalists. While audience sympathies are clearly intended to be with the women and men whose lives are ruled by The Belt, their boss has problems of his own: shrinking orders and bulging warehouses, which will require him to close down production. When workers in his plant confront him about the announced layoffs, he explains that the problem is even bigger than he is: "I can't help it. The country's crazy! They don't know what they want! . . . It's the bankers. . . . They hold the money. . . . The old car ain't good enough. . . . Gotta give 'em a new one that costs so much they can't pay for it. . . . Now the whole market's gone to smash. . . . Too many cars, that's what they say."[24] Under such circumstances, workers' resistance would be futile, and though Bill, the radical organizer, pledges, "I'll be back!" as he is being taken away by the police for leading the disruption on The Belt, an audience of disillusioned liberals might have found this difficult to believe. Four years later, when unionists and left-wing activists had begun organizing among working-class Americans, audiences attending a production of *The Belt* by the Rebel Players of Los Angeles no doubt left the performance with much more certainty about Bill's eventual return.[25] For the bourgeois audiences of the New Playwrights in the late 1920s, however, there was little cause for optimism.

By the same token, the conclusions of audiences at the Brookwood Labor College production of Karel Capek's *R.U.R.* were probably different from those of audiences at the production of the same play by the Theatre Guild, a prominent professional art theatre.[26] The focus of *R.U.R.* on the dangers of a mechanized labor force clearly resonated with contemporary skepticism regarding "the machine," and Theatre Guild patrons might have dwelt on the dangers of excessive mechanization. Yet the play can also be read as a satire of how industry treats its human operatives. An audience of labor activists might have seen in *R.U.R.* a parable of the humanizing power of collective action and resistance to industrial authority. For although the revolt of the robots results in the death of their human masters, it also opens the way for a labor force with emotions and visions that extend beyond the assembly line. In the closing scene, a male and female robot have fallen in love and go off together, while the sole remaining human being renames them "Adam-Eve."[27] Out of the revolt is born a new race of caring, loving human beings.

Such an optimistic reading of a play about machines displacing workers in a period when anti-labor forces decisively held the upper hand might seem dissonant if not self-deluding for workers were it not for the vitality of the workers' education movement in the same years. During the "lean years" of the 1920s, labor colleges kept alive the vision and ideals of the labor movement and nurtured in activists the skills they would need when organized labor was once again given a voice in both negotiating working conditions and setting public policy. Indeed, many of the key organizers of the new unions that would form the Congress of Industrial Organizations in the mid-1930s were alumni of schools such as Brookwood.

During the 1920s, nearly every large and medium-sized city in the country boasted a labor college. Brookwood itself was founded in 1921 as a residential institution with a two-year curriculum designed to "develop labor power and labor intelligence."[28] Two years later, the Bryn Mawr Summer School was established to address the specific educational and organizational needs of working women, the first of several such summer schools founded in the 1920s.[29] In 1925, a year-long residential program was established at Commonwealth College in Mena, Arkansas, and 1932 saw the founding of the Highlander Folk School, the only one of these institutions to endure, shifting its focus in the post–World War II years from labor issues to civil rights and, more recently, grassroots community organizing.[30] Brookwood, like other independent workers' education institutions, was always vulnerable to dissension within the left and the labor movement and to right-wing attacks from outside, but its supporters remained convinced that working people equipped with the right kinds of knowledge and analysis could bring about a more just social order.[31]

This belief in the power of education flowed easily from, on one hand, the roots of the workers' education movement in the Socialist and immigrant left of the decades surrounding the turn of the century and, on the other hand, the ties that existed between workers' education and Progressive education. In every major urban area, left-wing immigrants developed their own educational and cultural institutions, which, like the Workmen's Circle, or Arbeiter Ring, on New York's Lower East Side, promoted a social vision in which working men and women, confident in their knowledge of social, economic, and political processes, could liberate themselves, individually and collectively, from the oppression of existing class relations.[32] Among the founders of Brookwood Labor College were such labor leaders as Fannia Cohn of the International Ladies Garment Workers Union— a tireless promoter of workers' education, inside and outside her union—and Joseph Schlossberg of the Amalgamated Clothing Workers of America, whose roots in Jewish labor circles had endowed them with an equal commitment to the visionary and the practical potential of education for creating a more just social order.[33]

In the labor colleges of the 1920s, this political idealism was bolstered by the pragmatic goals and convictions of Progressive education. Faith in education as a tool of social reform can be traced back to Horace Mann's efforts to design school systems that would best serve the needs of the emerging system of industrial capitalism, but in the early twentieth century the Progressive education movement, inspired by the work of John Dewey, held out the promise of transforming formal education. The educational process could be a liberating experience in which the student would be encouraged to ask questions and propose and test various answers rather than being conditioned to adjust to existing structures. Central to Dewey's conception of education was the function of the school in developing students' "interest in community welfare, . . . an interest . . . in perceiving whatever makes for social order and progress, and for carrying these principles into execution."[34] Formal education was to develop both individual skills and community spirit and to prepare students to play an active role as citizens in their society.

The Brookwood curriculum, and workers' education more generally, was designed to serve such purposes among the working class and had the support of prominent Progressive educational theorists. Dewey himself sat on the advisory board of Brookwood Labor College, and when the school came under attack from the American Federation of Labor in 1928, he forcefully spoke out on its behalf, arguing that Brookwood's philosophy and programs should find their way into public school curricula.[35] Eduard Lindeman, another prominent Progressive education theorist, was for many years a member of the board of directors of the Affiliated Schools for Workers, an umbrella organization for labor schools. In addition, educators at these schools frequently drew on the works of Progressive education theorists in explaining their goals and methods; several had taught at Progressive elementary and secondary schools and wrote for *Progressive Education*, the journal of the Progressive Education Association.[36]

The influence of Progressive educational theory on the workers' education movement played a key role in shaping workers' theatre at labor colleges. First, the emphasis on "learning by doing" gave dramatic activities a place of honor at workers' schools; and second, the belief in the ability of ordinary citizens to effect social change infused theatrical productions at workers' schools with a sense of possibility that was largely absent from the productions of the New Playwrights Theatre. For workers' educators and Progressive educators alike, drama helped students understand the world around them and their place in it. As the editor of the journal *Progressive Education* noted in an issue devoted entirely to dramatics in education, "dramatic activities offer a singularly fruitful synthesis of all the arts, an integration of intellectual, emotional and physical aspects of experience."[37]

For teachers at workers' schools, labor dramatics prepared students to take action in their communities, in their unions, and at their jobs. Worker-students creating and performing skits could integrate what they learned in classes about unions and labor organizing with their own experiences. In participating in such projects, students could develop self-confidence and public-speaking skills while they explored problems of labor relations and labor organizing.[38]

The whole raison d'être of workers' schools was to equip students with the tools necessary to bring about a particular vision of social relations. As a result, the plays that students themselves wrote were frequently lessons for social change, suggesting possible solutions to the problems they dramatized. Unlike the skeptical and demoralized middle-class New Playwrights, organizers and activists of Brookwood saw in the current state of affairs opportunities for action and change.

One of the ways Brookwood students' plays asserted that change was possible was to contrast working-class heroes' commitment to their communities with the narrow and judgmental self-interest of those who try to thwart their efforts. In the play *Miners,* written by Brookwood student Bonchi Friedman in 1926, the two main characters, Martha and Peter, defy threats of violence to maintain miners' support for an ongoing strike.[39] Friedman's naming these characters is noteworthy, for the local civic leaders aligned against the workers are identified only by their roles in the conspiracy: the "All-Devouring Capitalist" is assisted by "three detectives," "a judge," "a priest," "a kleagle," and "a wholesale business man." These caricatures are two-dimensional characters whose power is "cut down to size" by the parody they embody. Martha and Peter are much more fully developed: they have children and parents and friends and neighbors whom they are fighting for and who love and respect them. Such scripts suggest that the power of the established social order shrinks when confronted with groups of individuals whose very humanness empowers them to act on the behalf of themselves and others like themselves.

Although workers in these scripts are often killed because of their commitment to their communities, such deaths are not in vain. Martha is shot by police officers and Klansmen; her death becomes a rallying cry for the miners and their families to continue the strike, and Peter, her widower, takes up her role, promising the crowd, "Yes, I will lead you in the strike."

The image of the striker dying so that the struggle may continue was taken up more humorously in another play that Bonchi Friedman wrote a few months later with fellow Brookwooder Stanley Guest. In *Shades of Passaic,* a striker is beaten to death by a police officer on the same day as the owner of the factory against which he is striking dies of overeating.[40] The two meet in Purgatory, where they await their assignment for the eternal life. Saint Peter, the Lord High Remodeler, sends the capitalist to Hell "for boiling down," but he gives the striker the choice of going to heaven or going back to earth. He describes heaven as "like your very best dreams" but clarifies that

24   *Chapter 2*

going there means giving up the fight. The striker decisively opts for continuing the struggle: "I was in on it from the first. I'll see it through." As he starts back to Passaic, "strains of 'the Internationale' are heard: his pals in Passaic calling him back."

Plays such as *Shades of Passaic* were realistic in their outlook on workers' struggles in the 1920s: strikers faced strong, corrupt, and united allies. They also faced death. The 1920s witnessed powerful alliances of financial and political interests, and the Passaic textile strike of 1926 was one of the bloodiest in the decade. Nonetheless, this play, like other Brookwood plays, remained immersed in possibility, both the possibility of continuing struggle and the possibility of ultimate victory.

*   *   *

Like all theatre at some level, labor-oriented theatre presents a certain social and political analysis; it also addresses the possibility of challenging the status quo. For the New Playwrights Theatre, such a possibility was quite dim; the young people of Brookwood Labor College, however, were preparing for direct engagement in campaigns to improve the lives of working people, and they therefore created scenarios for change. What the New Playwrights could offer a labor movement intent on challenging the powers of employers and the state was a comprehensive analysis of social and economic relations. The Brookwood Labor Players offered analysis and action: definitions of the problem, tangible strategies for addressing it, and encouragement to those undertaking the struggle to eliminate it.

As the 1920s drew to a close, the curtain fell on the New Playwrights Theatre as well. Incapable of attracting its intended audience of workers, the group was also unable to compete with commercial entertainment for middle-class theatregoers. Theatrical production at Brookwood, in contrast, thrived as the school participated in and contributed to the rise of the labor movement in the following decade. Brookwood Labor College in the 1930s would belong to a labor movement that saw in artistic and recreational activity important opportunities for educating and organizing and would play an active part in a theatre movement closely tied to the labor organizing campaigns of its day. This movement would include not only working-class theatre troupes like Brookwood's but groups of middle-class artists and intellectuals who exchanged the despair of the 1920s for the conviction that their work as performers and writers was part of building a better society. The New Playwrights Theatre, a symptom of its times, passed from the scene with the 1920s; the Brookwood Labor Players, a harbinger of things to come, helped make workers' theatre a part of a revitalizing labor movement.

3. ACT I

A Movement Grows across the Nation

The August 1929 issue of *New Masses* ran an article, "Did the New Playwrights Theatre Fail?" in which John Dos Passos reviewed the strengths and weaknesses of the eight plays the group had produced. Concluding with a bland observation about the difficulties inhering to playwrights producing their own plays, he also noted that, "the fact that [the New Playwrights] existed makes the next attempt in the same direction that much easier."[1]

Dos Passos's words proved prophetic, as in that year, numerous workers' theatre groups around the country began to organize and announce their existence through the labor and left-wing press. Indeed, according to Michael Gold, Dos Passos's New Playwrights colleague, there were "at least fifty small workers' theatre groups functioning in American cities and towns" by 1929. Yet these theatres were, in key ways, hardly following "in the same direction" as the experiment in which Dos Passos had participated. Rather than taking the New Playwrights' path of cynicism, disillusionment, and despair, the plays of the new workers' theatre groups emulated Brookwood's productions, dramatizing possibility, victory, and empowerment for working people.

The flowering of workers' theatre belonged to the entire reawakening of labor and the left at the close of the 1920s. In the next decade, the successes of labor organizing campaigns revitalized the labor movement and inspired the development of a rich "movement culture," to use Lawrence Goodwyn's phrase, which, in turn, lent a distinctive energy to the movement.[2] The sense of possibility generated by the victories of labor infected activists and their allies, who went to work in diverse ways to build and maintain the momentum of organizing campaigns and labor unions themselves.

In workers' theatre, this vitality was translated into productions that affirmed the potential of workers' collective action. It was also translated into strong convictions regarding the efficacy of theatre for advancing the cause of labor. Moreover, for spectators as well as performers, the plays of the workers' theatre movement reinforced the idealism, the optimism, and the enthusiasm generated by the victories of organized labor. Buoyed by such passion, workers' theatre groups developed among themselves the informal and formal networks that would allow them to expand their field of work and create for the labor movement a shared vision of social transformation.

Through shared personnel, shared scripts, and a national organization, individual groups scattered in neighborhoods, union locals, and labor schools, around New York City and across the country, coalesced into a discernible movement. Indeed, many in these workers' theatre groups drew inspiration and encouragement from the work of other groups like their own. This chapter focuses on how these disparate groups wove themselves into the fabric of a movement. In order to understand the nature of this movement, however, we must also understand how young people in the 1930s made theatre part of their political and social life as performers, producers, and spectators of workers' theatre.

*   *   *

The economic dislocation of the Great Depression provided fertile ground for planting new seeds of activism, in rank-and-file organizing as well as in policy making, and when Franklin Delano Roosevelt was elected president, organizing efforts among working people took on new life. Unions that had languished through the 1920s viewed the renowned Section 7(a) of the 1933 National Industrial Recovery Act (NIRA), which protected workers' rights to collective bargaining, as a veritable invitation to union recognition strikes and campaigns, and workers took ample and enthusiastic advantage of this apparent deliverance from the tyrannical and unbridled powers of employers.[3]

Even before the passage of the NIRA, however, the Socialist and Communist parties had begun looking for ways to channel into effective action the discontent of working people disempowered by employers' workplace and welfare strategies and disillusioned by government policies that ignored all but the rich and powerful. Communists and Socialists alike sought to organize the unemployed, and in 1929 the Communist Party (CP) sent organizers to work with striking millworkers in North Carolina and started organizing militant unions to challenge the complacency and conservatism of the American Federation of Labor.[4]

Among those motivated by the combination of rapidly deteriorating economic conditions and ineffectual policy making were young radicals who saw theatre as an arena in which to explore contemporary economic and political issues and to urge action. One such group of radicals established the Workers' Laboratory Theatre (WLT), which would become a sparkplug for a whole movement that saw in theatre vast potential for advancing the cause of social justice. The Workers' Lab originated with a group of activists developing skits for events sponsored by the CP-affiliated Workers' International Relief between 1928 and 1930. Some of the WLT's first members had also worked with the short-lived Workers' Drama League, and some were close to the Proletbuehne, a German-language group inspired by the political theatre experiments of Weimar Germany.[5]

New York City rapidly emerged as the center of workers' theatre under the dual influence of left-wing political and intellectual activity and Broadway, the Great White Way. Numerous theatre professionals took detours from their Broadway careers to work in labor-oriented theatre, and some, like those who formed the Theatre Union, explicitly challenged the dominance of Broadway by developing new opportunities for producing serious, class-conscious drama. Broadway and New York's theatrical culture also attracted aspiring actors and playwrights who found greater opportunity, along with political congeniality, in workers' theatre groups than on Broadway.[6] Finally, adding to the apparent inevitability of New York as a center for left-wing theatre was the presence of well-developed ethnic communities with lively theatrical traditions, in particular the popular Yiddish theatre, which brought romance, melodrama, and tragedy in the *mamaloshn*—mother tongue—to the lives of eastern European Jews crowded into Manhattan's Lower East Side.[7]

New York City and its surroundings came alive after 1930 with a profusion of labor-oriented and left-wing theatre groups that shared scripts and audiences, that split off from one another and came together for festivals, conferences, and political rallies, each very clear about its distinctiveness and all eager to exchange information, techniques, and teachers. The Workers' Laboratory Theatre soon shared the spotlight with the Theatre Collective (formed by Workers' Lab members who wanted to produce full-length plays), the Theatre Union (which produced workers' theatre with professional artists and technicians), the Brooklyn Labor Theatre, the Newark Theatre Collective, the Suitcase Theatre based in Harlem, and many more who have left little but a name in the historical record. These independent groups were joined by others, such as the Brookwood Labor Players, that were sponsored by labor schools, and by still others that were organized within unions, including the International Ladies Garment Workers Union (ILG), the International Fur and Leather Workers Union, and Local 65, United Wholesale and Warehouse Employees. Later in the decade, when the Works Progress Administration's Federal Theatre Project (FTP) established its central office in New York, it would absorb a good number of women and men from these groups and, along with them, their left-leaning politics, which ultimately made the FTP a favorite target of anti-Communists and led to its closing at the height of its activity and success.[8]

Labor-oriented political theatre also appeared in the languages of working-class immigrants and in their communal organizations. The Bronx Hungarian Workers' Club, for instance, ran a circulating library, organized lecture series and dances, sponsored sports teams, and issued "a monthly publication of general interest, *Spartacus,* . . . featuring articles both in English and Hungarian."[9] In addition, the organization ran an impressive drama program that produced mass recitations and short plays in Hungarian as well as in English. In 1930 and 1931, the club produced five plays, including *The Belt,* and took two of them on tours through Pennsylvania, New Jersey, Connecticut, and Maryland and throughout New York City.[10]

The best known and most highly regarded of the foreign-language workers' theatre groups was probably the Artef (Arbeiter Teater Farband), which started in 1926 as a theatre studio where working-class Jews attended evening lectures on theatre art by Jewish professionals in the field. Beginning in 1928, it developed a repertory theatre made up of workers trained by Artef staff and performing revolutionary plays in Yiddish. While hewing closely to Communist ideology, Artef plays, directed by veterans of Moscow's art theatres of the 1920s, also experimented with new styles of performance and stagecraft.[11]

The Artef remained in existence until 1938, attracting Yiddish- and non-Yiddish-speaking audiences. It belonged to a strain of the Communist movement that sought to keep alive constituents' ethnic cultures and languages. The growing numbers of American-born sons and daughters of immigrants eager to identify themselves as American and a Communist Party eager to identify Marxism as "twentieth-century Americanism," however, placed groups such as the Artef and the Hungarian Workers' Club in a precarious position.[12] In 1934, the New York Competition of Foreign Language Workers Theatres included groups performing in Yiddish, German, Ukrainian, Turkish, and Esperanto.[13] After 1935, when the CP adopted a Popular Front ideology and promoted itself as all-American, the workers' theatre movement became almost exclusively an English-language movement, though ethnicity and ethnic culture remained central to the plays it produced.

Although New York groups dominate the history of left-wing theatre in the 1930s, the workers' theatre movement was truly national in scope. In the early 1930s, the Solidarity Players in Boston entertained audiences with satires of liberal and left-wing politics. Later in the decade, the New Theatre of Boston performed at charitable institutions and for meetings of textile workers in Lowell.[14] The New Theatre of Philadelphia offered theatre classes for children and adults, in addition to producing "social plays, vigorously and truthfully concerned with the historic struggles surrounding contemporary life."[15] The touring productions of the Brookwood Players brought workers' theatre to industrial cities and towns throughout the Northeast and into the South and Midwest.

In midwestern industrial centers, labor activism and left-wing politics made for eager audiences for workers' theatre, as well as highly dramatic scenarios for playwrights, amateur and professional. According to Paul Sporn, whose research has unearthed a lively workers' theatre scene in 1930s Detroit, at least five plays drew their inspiration from autoworkers' efforts to establish collective bargaining in their workplaces. The works were produced by such groups as the Detroit Contemporary Players and the New Theatre of Detroit, founded by the local John Reed Club.[16] Even in smaller cities such as Omaha, political theatre found its way into struggles for better working conditions and union recognition. There Tillie Olsen (then Tillie Lerner) and other members of the Young Communist League performed among meatpackers and other industrial workers.[17]

In the South, workers' theatre seems to have been sparked largely by labor schools. At the Highlander Folk School in Tennessee, students—union members and labor activists—spent a good amount of their time in various cultural activities, including music and folk dancing as well as drama. Under the direction of former Highlander student Zilphia Horton, students wrote their own scripts, which the school made available to other interested groups. Like Brookwood, Highlander also organized chautauqua tours that included students' plays, puppet shows, and songs.[18]

The Southern Summer School for Working Women in Industry also used theatre to teach students the analytical and practical tools necessary for becoming effective activists. As a result, the school and its alumnae brought workers' theatre to communities throughout the South. Instructor Hollace Ransdell, who had also worked at Brookwood Labor College, coached students as they developed pieces that specifically addressed their situation as women and as members of the southern working class. Beginning in 1931, the Summer School sent Ransdell to work with union locals and with former students to establish labor drama groups.[19]

One of these students was Mary Lee Hays, who had moved to Pritchard, Alabama, to organize her fellow and sister textile workers. In 1934, Ransdell helped Hays begin a labor dramatics club, which performed for strikers from the local textile mills and for a newly organized local of fishermen and cannery workers. The club also picketed with striking waitresses in Mobile and donated part of its ticket sales to the waitresses' cause.[20]

Meanwhile, in Mena, Arkansas, Commonwealth College also developed a program of labor dramatics. Unlike the majority of workers' theatre productions, which focused on the plight of industrial workers, labor dramatics at Commonwealth addressed the concerns of rural agricultural workers. One of the first plays produced at the college, in 1932, was *Can You Hear Their Voices?* in which a group of impoverished, drought-stricken farmers become politicized by their encounters with banks, government relief agencies, and the Red Cross. Throughout the 1930s, Commonwealth maintained a strong interest in farmers' movements and, after 1935, recruited students from and worked with the Southern Tenant Farmers' Union.[21]

Finally, workers' theatre made its way to the West Coast. The Rebel Players of Los Angeles undertook several ambitious productions, including *Gods of the Lightning*, about the conviction and execution of Nicola Sacco and Bartolomeo Vanzetti, and Paul Sifton's *The Belt*. Political theatre even took root in the backyard of the motion picture industry, as the New Theatre of Hollywood staged several plays with labor themes.[22] In San Francisco, students at the California Labor School learned to use theatre in their unions and communities.[23]

These groups were certainly not uniform in their political affiliation, institutional structure, or performance format; they reflected various political, aesthetic, and cultural orientations and responded to local issues and concerns. These groups also left very different traces on the historical record: some kept meticulous records that were deposited in libraries, and others are known to us only through a flyer, an announcement in the *Daily Worker,* or a reference in a union local's newsletter.

The differences that existed among these disparate groups did not preclude high levels of contact and interaction among them, however. Participants became aware of one another's existence and productions as they moved across town or across the country; ran into each other at CP events, workers' education programs, or union conventions; and attended one another's performances. They also read about one another in the left-wing press, and beginning in the early 1930s, they read magazines and joined organizations dedicated to the particular task of promoting workers' theatre and sustaining efforts in the field.

One of the earliest attempts at promoting contact among workers' theatre groups was Michael Gold's appeal in the pages of *New Masses.* In "A Letter to Workers' Art Groups," published in September 1929, Gold noted with pride the burgeoning numbers of workers' theatre groups, film clubs, choral societies, and education projects of various sorts. According to Gold, many turned to *New Masses* for more information and materials for their work. "Every week in the office of the *New Masses,*" he wrote, "we receive at least a dozen letters asking us to suggest suitable one-act workers' plays, short movies, recitations and choral pieces."[24] To address this evident need, he proposed to begin the work of organizing workers' art groups by opening the pages of the magazine to them. Over the next few years, *New Masses* regularly published a "Workers' Art" page, which usually contained several letters from theatre groups describing their activities and needs.

In April 1931, the appearance of a two-hundred-copy run of a mimeographed magazine calling itself *Workers' Theatre* signaled a new phase in the growth of the workers' theatre movement. The publication was the work of members of the Workers' Laboratory Theatre, who themselves collaborated with the German-language Proletbuehne and who believed that the growing numbers of workers' theatre groups would benefit from shared information. According to Ben Blake, an early chronicler of the workers' theatre movement (and, under his given name, Bernard Reines, a member of the WLT), "*Workers' Theatre* within its own range was an instantaneous success. Its pages were alive with discussion and controversy as the necessary task of establishing the theory and practice of the workers' theatre went on month after month."[25] The magazine also published workers' theatre scripts and kept readers abreast of developments in political theatre in Germany, the Soviet Union, Japan, and England, as well as in California, New York, and points in between. So successful was *Workers' Theatre* in promoting its message that within one year, circulation rose to almost one thousand.[26]

The new publication appeared just when the rapid growth of workers' theatres made regular communication among them necessary. *Workers' Theatre* would, along with its successors *New Theatre* and *New Theatre and Film*, be a catalyst in the growth of the left-wing theatre movement. It brought attention to numerous experiments in labor-oriented political theatre, provided a forum for debate on the theory and technique of workers' theatre, and by the mid-1930s came to rival the staid *Theatre Arts Monthly* as an organ of the contemporary theatre.[27]

Buoyed by the response to *Workers' Theatre,* the Proletbuehne and the Workers' Lab continued to organize workers' theatre groups. In the summer of 1931, they set up the Dramatic Bureau as a clearinghouse for scripts and information on workers' theatre. In the following year, the bureau held the first National Workers' Theatre Festival and Conference in New York. Twelve dramatic groups, some coming from as far as Chicago, attended, and participants voted to establish the League of Workers' Theatres, which took over and expanded the publication of *Workers' Theatre* and the functions of the Dramatic Bureau.

Though most members of the league were workers' theatre groups in and around New York City, it clearly designed its role for a national stage: in 1934, the National Workers' Theatre Festival was moved to Chicago, making it more accessible to enthusiasts from the Midwest and the West. Indeed, groups from Portland, Seattle, and San Francisco formalized their ties to the league in order to attend the festival, and the Progressive Art Club of Toronto was given a place on the program. The festival attracted 120 delegates from the league's more than three hundred affiliated organizations; reports estimate that three thousand people attended performances each day.[28]

In 1935, the League of Workers' Theatres, which was close to the Communist Party, changed its name in order to appeal to a wider audience—and to keep in line with the CP's turn to a Popular Front strategy of cooperation with liberals and other anti-fascists. In existence through the end of the decade, the New Theatre League encouraged "that type of theatre which actively participates in the social struggles of the day," by publishing *New Theatre,* publishing and distributing plays, organizing conferences, and managing the New Theatre School.[29] The league also ran a booking service for groups and individuals to perform at meetings and on picket lines and dispatched directors trained at the New Theatre School to newly formed theatre groups requesting assistance. At its peak, the organization counted a membership of forty to fifty theatres around the country and several in Canada. New Theatre Nights, which the league organized as fund-raising events for itself, played the important role of introducing new short plays that other groups could perform.[30] It was at one of these Nights that Clifford Odets's *Waiting for Lefty* burst onto the stage and into the street, becoming a landmark in the history of political theatre in the United States.

According to Ben Irwin, executive director of the New Theatre League for three years, the majority of the theatre groups joining the organization were "not actually trade union groups." Rather, they were "socially minded theatres" interested in producing plays about the important political and social issues of the day.[31] Nonetheless, the league remained especially interested in producing plays within trade unions. In the later years of its existence, 1940 and 1941, it organized the short-lived Trade Union Play Directors' Group and sponsored trade union play tournaments.[32]

Although no more than a small proportion of the nation's workers' theatre groups joined the New Theatre League, the organization reached many more, directly and indirectly. Zilphia Horton, for instance, who directed the labor dramatics program at Highlander Folk School, studied at the New Theatre School. Among the faculty members were George Sklar, a member of the Theatre Union who taught playwriting, and Margaret Larkin, the Theatre Union's executive secretary, who taught courses on theatre management and organization.[33] Unions such as the International Fur and Leather Workers Union and the United Wholesale and Warehouse Employees' Local 65 competed in league-sponsored tournaments without being members of the organization.[34]

When groups joined the league, they gained access not only to its resources and services but to its wider audiences as well. When Brookwood Labor College joined in 1936, for instance, it identified its theatre group with the kind of theatre represented by the New Theatre League. The league also began publishing scripts developed by students at Brookwood.

By associating themselves with the New Theatre League, theatre groups joined a growing national movement and shared an expanding body of playscripts and technical skills. Yet workers' theatre groups usually performed on a local stage and needed to be credible in the eyes of local labor and left-wing organizations. The Workers' Laboratory Theatre, for instance, maintained its contact with the Communist Party in New York City through individual members who were in the party and through performances and benefits for CP organizations (see photograph).[35] Political theatre groups in New York, Philadelphia, Pittsburgh, Detroit, Buffalo, and Hartford sought and received endorsements and support from union locals and their cities' central labor councils. The New Theatre of Philadelphia got the United Mine Workers Union to endorse its production of *Black Pit*, a play about coal miners, and received financial assistance from the stagehands' union.[36]

Daily Worker picnic promises entertainment by several groups, including the Workers' Laboratory Theatre performing *World Fair* (see Chapter 6). Daily Worker, *July 27, 1933*

The Minneapolis Theatre Union provides a good example of how labor-oriented theatre groups were woven into the local political scene at the same time as they belonged to the nationwide network of workers' theatre centered in New York City. The Minneapolis Theatre Union included an assortment of Farmer-Laborites, trade unionists, CP activists, liberal Unitarians, and less politicized young people looking for a good time. The organization itself joined the Farmer-Labor Association, a membership organization that controlled the Farmer-Labor Party in Minnesota, drafting platforms, endorsing Farmer-Labor candidates, and conducting electoral campaigns.[37] The group contributed to building a Popular Front coalition in Minneapolis by bringing together people of varied political views as performers and as spectators. When Ruth Shaw wrote to the Theatre Union in New York for assistance, she described the individuals who met to set up the Minneapolis Theatre Union as "members of the Farmer-Labor Party, members of the Socialist Party, the Socialist Labor Party and the Communist Party. All of them have connections to the labor movement. . . . We wanted to draw in others so as to assure a wide united front theatre."[38]

Through Ruth Shaw, the Minneapolis Theatre Union maintained an active correspondence with the Theatre Union in New York; she and others in the Minneapolis organization were sufficiently familiar with the Theatre Union's first play, *Peace on Earth,* to want to produce it themselves, but they had to change their plans when a professional theatre received permission to produce the play in a downtown theatre. (It was, no doubt, with a certain satisfaction that Janet Ross, a moving force in the Minneapolis Theatre Union and the wife of a CP organizer, wrote to the Theatre Union that this production "was poorly attended because the prices were so high that very few could afford them.")[39] Nonetheless, the Minneapolis Theatre Union eventually produced three other plays written for the New York organization, as well as *Take My Stand,* written by a Brookwood Labor College instructor and first produced at the college, and the ubiquitous *Waiting for Lefty.* The Minneapolis Theatre Union's existence spanned three years and nine productions. The organization owed its longevity and success to its ability to draw simultaneously on local political networks for personnel, audiences, and financial support and on cross-country relations for artistic material and technical assistance.

Groups such as the Minneapolis Theatre Union could become credible political actors because the women and men of the workers' theatre movement were, for the most part, committed as much to political activism as to theatre. With the exception of the Theatre Union in New York, which made a special point of demonstrating that it was possible to produce professional theatre—paying Equity wages—that addressed workers' struggles, workers' theatre groups were made up of young people for whom theatre was, at least at that point in their lives, much more a form of political expression and entertainment than a career choice. Enthusiasm and commitment frequently took the place of technical proficiency and professional experience. Though workers' theatre attracted aspiring performers and playwrights with few other options in an economic depression, far more came to it animated by the conviction that they were educating, organizing, and politicizing their audiences—though among these activists there frequently lurked an attraction to the stage.

Each group incorporated many different points along the political and theatrical spectrum. The Theatre Union began with discussions among groups of writers, activists, playwrights, and actors of various liberal and left political persuasions and of no particular political

orientation. The original members of the Workers' Laboratory Theatre were more homogeneously Communist or attracted to left-wing
politics, but their experience with theatre varied from practically nil,
to participation in settlement house productions, to undergraduate
degrees in theatre. The Minneapolis Theatre Union included the
members of an already existing amateur theatre group, political activists with little or no theatre experience, and some transplanted radical New Yorkers who had seen productions of the Theatre Union and
wanted to do the same thing in Minnesota.

Though serious about politics and/or theatre, participants in
such groups were also looking for affordable amusement. Unmarried
and unburdened by family responsibilities, the women and men who
found their way into political theatre were, for the most part, on the
prowl for opportunities to have fun with minimal financial invest-
ment. Most members of the Workers' Lab had started college but,
because of the depression, were unable to continue; others in the
group had finished high school and were working to support themselves and contribute to their families' incomes. Ole Fagerhaugh, of
the Minneapolis Theatre Union, had been involved in theatre productions in high school and afterward had been active in a variety of
cultural activities, including a Norwegian folk dance group. By all accounts a charming and gregarious young activist, he put as much energy into creating entertainment for himself and others as he did
into union organizing. So pleased was he with his theatrical achievement with the Minneapolis Theatre Union that he invited his high
school drama teacher to attend one of the theatre's productions.
(She dismissed it as "sheer propaganda.")[40]

Workers' theatre also provided restless young people opportunities to leave behind the dreariness and grimness of the depression
and create a new life with others like themselves. Lucy Kaye, a member of the WLT, was the only wage earner in her family after her father lost his job in millinery. What kept her motivated to make the
long subway ride from Brooklyn into Manhattan several times a week
was the sense of collective effort she found in the Workers' Lab. "It
was an extraordinary experience," she later recalled.[41] The core

members of the group lived in a large apartment where they debated politics and planned, wrote, and rehearsed their productions.[42] In the WLT, Kaye found young people sharing not only a home but, more important, a set of goals and the commitment to working to achieve them. For many young people, cooperative and communal projects became havens from the disconcerting and disorienting economic dislocation of the Great Depression.[43]

Theatre, by virtue of its collaborative nature, lent itself particularly well to cooperative experimentation. Like the Workers' Laboratory Theatre, the Theatre Collective and the Theatre Union were organized along principles of shared decision making and demonstrated their commitment to creating a new social order by replacing the individual authority of the producer, artistic director, or playwright with committees that selected plays and shaped them to fit their collective vision.[44] Ironically, the theatre organization that best represents the this collective spirit, the Group Theatre, was careful to dissociate itself from workers' theatre, even though some of its most prominent members, among them Elia Kazan, worked closely with the Workers' Lab and the Theatre Collective. Nevertheless, as the memoir of one Group member makes clear, what gave excitement and passion to the Group's work was its members' commitment to being, well, a group.[45]

Joining the Workers' Laboratory Theatre, the Theatre Collective, or the Group Theatre also meant becoming part of a cultural scene. "After a while, people got to know each other," as Frank Drucker, an active member of the Brooklyn Labor Theatre, put it fifty years later.[46] The matter-of-fact quality of Drucker's statement should not obscure its importance. Workers' theatre provided friends, lovers, and co-conspirators as much as it offered opportunities for artistic expression and political action.

Like the members of any urban subculture or counterculture, young people in workers' theatre frequented specific commercial establishments in particular neighborhoods. One such watering hole was Stewart's Cafeteria, where artistically and theatrically inclined leftist youth whiled away nights over coffee and cigarettes. Clifford Odets reputedly spent many such nights with members of the Workers' Lab and others, developing along the way the scenario that would become *Waiting for Lefty*.[47] Lucy Kaye and many others who came to the WLT after the group had begun performing entered via such venues, learning as much about the Lab over coffee and drinks as at performances. Looking for new ideas and excitement, Kaye had gravitated to 14th Street in Manhattan because "that's where the action was," as she later explained.[48] There she met members of the Workers' Lab and became part of its evening troupe. When she lost her job, she joined the theatre full-time, doing the office work that was often neglected when the eager young (male) actors rushed to perform on picket lines and at strike meetings.

For Earl Robinson, the path to the WLT led from Seattle to Union Square, the hub of New York City's left-wing political life. He came to New York to study music at Julliard, but as he tells it, he never made it there once he started hanging around Union Square. He soon fell in with the Workers' Lab, moved into the collective apartment, and became a central writer and performer for the troupe.[49]

Outside New York City, young people interested in political theatre found one another through different political and cultural institutions; in Minneapolis it was the Farmer-Labor Association and the Unitarian Center, and in other cities it was through John Reed Clubs, CP-affiliated organizations promoting labor-oriented and left-wing artistic production. Toby Cole, for one, began her lengthy association with workers' theatre when she went to a meeting of the local John Reed Club in Newark, New Jersey.

Cole had grown up in a working-class family in Newark and was, in her own words, "always a very political being, almost from the day of my birth," and "always interested in theatre." Through the John Reed Club, she found she could blend her interests in theatre and politics and have a lot of fun along the way. For several years, she performed with the Newark Theatre Collective in union halls, at parties and picnics, and at other events sponsored by labor and left-wing organizations. She eventually moved to New York City to attend the Theatre School of the New Theatre League. She became active in workers' theatre groups in New York and in the late 1930s married Ben Irwin, director of the NTL.[50]

The experiences of individuals such as Cole and Robinson and Kaye, who each found in workers' theatre a community that sustained them personally, artistically, and politically, were not unusual. Yet they should not be taken as evidence of overarching harmony and homogeneity among the young people involved in workers' theatre. The collective nature of theatre production and the self-conscious collectivism of many workers' theatre groups certainly encouraged a strong degree of artistic and political consensus among members of individual workers' theatre groups; however, attempts at collaboration among individuals of divergent interests and priorities also sometimes resulted in fractious working relations. Toby Cole was fortunate to find, both in Newark and in New York, others who shared her dual commitment to theatre and left-wing politics. For others in workers' theatre, the acculturation between theatre and politics, or between differing political visions, was a more gradual and incomplete process.

For individuals who came to the movement from an interest in theatre, the connection between theatre and politics was not always obvious. Several of the young people involved in the Minneapolis Theatre Union, for instance, had little or no interest in politics, but they stayed in order to pursue their theatrical ambitious. Along the way, however, they certainly "got an education." According to Ole Fagerhaugh, the Minneapolis Theatre Union had hired one "theatre man," Tom Russell, "because he was a professional." When the group produced Clifford Odets's *Till the Day I Die*, about Nazi repression of Communists, he seemed completely unaware of what was going on in Germany. "Could it really be that this sort of thing was going on?" Russell would ask.[51]

Young people coming into labor-oriented theatre with an interest in dramatics did not always remain isolated from the politics surrounding them. Because of the living and working arrangements of the Workers' Laboratory Theatre, new members sooner or later adopted the group's politics and perspectives. Oscar Saul came to the WLT because he had written a poetic drama that he wanted to see performed and his sister told him this group might be open to his work. They never read his work, but they asked him to write lyrics for a piece they were putting together to support a taxi drivers' strike then in progress. From then on, he was a central member of the Workers' Lab. Looking back after several decades, Saul, who later became a producer at Columbia Pictures and a novelist, was far more critical than other WLT veterans of the quality of the theatre they produced. Nevertheless, in his years with the Workers' Lab and afterward, he threw himself wholeheartedly into workers' theatre, as one of the main writers in the Workers' Lab and later as a contributor to politically oriented plays and musical revues.[52]

Surviving members of the Workers' Laboratory Theatre speak with great fondness for the group several decades later, remembering that the WLT enthusiastically welcomed newcomers into the bosom of its collective working and living arrangements. Though these memories have, no doubt, expunged the more painful moments of shared lives, participants frequently point to the WLT's apartment as the source of the group's longevity, vitality, and congeniality. The cooperative living arrangement, though not including all participants in the Workers' Lab, generated a core of activists committed to one another and experienced in working out personal and other differences that arise in the day-to-day life of persons sharing a home. Members of the WLT stayed together for five years, and when the group—by then rechristened Theatre of Action—decided to disband in 1935, it was, by all accounts, without acrimony or grievance.

If Workers' Lab veterans are eager to reminisce fondly about the trials and tribulations of sharing living quarters and expenses, they seem far less willing to discuss another factor that helps explain the consensus among them: the group's relationship to the Communist Party. The Workers' Laboratory Theatre was first formed as part of the Workers' International Relief, a Communist-affiliated organization, and throughout its existence, it performed at events sponsored by the CP for causes supported by the party. According to WLT member Perry Bruskin, one party official frequently sat in on the group's discussions of new productions.[53] Although membership

in the CP was not a prerequisite for participation in WLT productions, the group's visible ties to the party suggest that those who
could not accept that political ideology or identification did not stay
around very long. Thus a general agreement on political views and
partisan affiliation helped sustain the work of the WLT and the ability of its members to live together.

Unlike the WLT, the Theatre Union in New York actively and
self-consciously sought out individuals of different political orientations for its Executive Board. As a Popular Front organization, the
Theatre Union proclaimed its political diversity in order to appeal to
broader audiences. It also presented itself as a model of coalition politics, asserting by its very nature that liberals and leftists of different
stripes could work together on the problems that really mattered: fascism, racism, the labor movement, among others. In answering a letter inquiring about the group's makeup and functioning, executive
board member Margaret Larkin noted, "We have two communists,
two socialists and a member of the American Workers' Party on our
Executive Board," suggesting that they worked together amicably.[54]

The unity the Theatre Union sought to project, however, did
not always exist. Victor Wolfson, who had worked with the Socialist
Party–affiliated League for Industrial Democracy but claims that
"politics were not [his] forte," knew that Communists and Socialists each discussed Theatre Union matters among themselves.
Samuel Friedman, a Socialist Party member who was staunchly anti-
Communist, later learned that he and Mary Fox had been recruited
to the Theatre Union's board of directors by the Communist members of the organization in order "sell the Theatre Union as a non-
Communist, nonsectarian group . . . to the regular [non-Communist]
labor movement."[55] He felt used and duped by those in the Theatre
Union he identified as Communists and remained bitter about the
experience for many years. Under such conditions, the survival of
the Theatre Union for three and a half years, through eight full-scale
productions, never far from the brink of bankruptcy, is most impressive and testifies to the commitment of the executive board to producing professional-quality theatre for and about working people.

Young people came to workers' theatre with a wide range of aesthetic, political, and personal needs and goals. Theatre professionals, aspiring theatre professionals, left-wing activists, trade unionists, and young people in search of adventure found ways of working together to achieve individual goals as well as collective ones. What ultimately kept them together, though, was a forceful conception of theatre as a potent tool for effecting social transformation.

When theatre artists placed their work at the disposal of the labor movement, and when unions and political activists turned to theatre to promote their causes and campaigns, they were acknowledging the power of theatre to establish bonds of communication between performers and spectators and to persuade. Workers' theatre groups frequently used the slogan "Theatre Is a Weapon," suggesting a fairly naive and blunt understanding of the impact of dramatic performances on audiences; yet these groups clearly saw themselves as engaged in an ideological struggle that was as important as the physical ones being waged on picket lines. Theatre in itself was political, they believed, and underlying all theatre was the attempt to sway audiences to a particular point of view. As Margaret Larkin of the Theatre Union put it, "all plays are propaganda for something."[56]

In the spring of 1935, the movie *Black Fury* appeared on screens across the nation, setting off a discussion of the nature of propaganda in, of all places, the *New York Times*. Criticized because the movie portrayed miners as stool pigeons and drunkards, and mine owners as the epitome of fair play, the author of the screenplay asserted, "We were not trying in any way to generalize conditions by our portrayal of a slice of a miner's life." In an article entitled "What Is Propaganda?" which appeared in the *Times*, Theatre Union member Albert Maltz characterized the movie as anti-labor propaganda and argued that, whatever the dramatist's intention, "an author is a propagandist by what he says or fails to say. He is a propagandist for one cause or another, directly or indirectly, by the very nature of the 'slice of life' he selects or fails to select."[57] Rejecting the conventional wisdom that politics and art do not mix, Maltz and the workers' theatre in general embraced propaganda as an inherent characteristic of theatre, which they intended to use to its full potential.

Set designer Mordecai Gorelik, whose association with labor-related theatre went back to the New Playwrights Theatre, succinctly summed up the premises underlying workers' theatre when he wrote, "Theatre is a weapon, but it is a weapon for both sides."[58] Where conventional theatre promoted "bourgeois" values, workers' theatre, in contrast, used theatre as "propaganda" for the labor movement. Hyam Shapiro, a founding member of the WLT, outlined this position in an article published in *Workers' Theatre*. Shapiro noted that "religious theatre" was intended to "propagate" religion, that "folk theatre" celebrated marriage and market festivals. In his analysis, "bourgeois theatre" was designed to "keep the mind of the worker steeped in bourgeois sentiment." In contrast, the aim of "proletarian theatre" was to develop "the class-conscious revolutionary worker."[59]

Participants in workers' theatre endowed theatre with almost mystical powers. They believed not only that theatrical performances could transform the consciousness of spectators but that theatre could move them to action as well. According to Margaret Larkin, whereas bourgeois theatre lulled its audiences into complacency, workers' theatre had the ability to "awaken to class consciousness leading to organization" and indeed had the responsibility to place the power of theatre at the service of workers' movements. "A workers' theatre," she wrote, "should serve as a means of drawing unorganized workers into militant struggle."[60]

As many observers—and participants, with several decades of hindsight—have pointed out, however, few minds were changed by such performances, because most of those attending were predisposed to agree with the plays' point of view. Charles R. Walker, a founder and influential member of the Theatre Union, noted that his organization "had discovered a large untapped audience of left theatre goers." When a new Theatre Union production opened in the spring of 1937, the magazine *New Theatre and Film* proclaimed that "only through the trade unions, fraternal and other mass organizations can *Marching Song* find its real audience and in sufficient numbers to make the play the success it deserves to be and which the social theatre needs."[61] What these writers were implicitly acknowledging is that the transformative powers of workers' theatre were limited, if they even existed at all. Labor-oriented theatre could bring about a metamorphosis only among "its real audience," that is, men and women already receptive to the influence of workers' theatre.

The workers' theatre movement thus worked with a double-edged notion of the effectiveness of theatre: on one hand, theatre could bring about profound transformation in the consciousness of audiences, but, on the other hand, it could do so only with appropriate audiences. Although this analysis seems limiting, the weakness of workers' theatre became its greatest strength: workers' theatre cultivated a close relationship between audience and performers. Workers' theatre groups in the 1930s, whether in unions, at workers' schools, or in legitimate theatres, feasted on the masses mobilized by unions and left-wing activism. But it was not a passive relationship: at both the theoretical and the practical level, workers' theatre reached out and shaped audiences that would be most receptive to its work.

Whatever its political or aesthetic orientation, theatre exists for audiences, or, as Erwin Piscator, whose work greatly influenced political theatre in the United States, put it, "There is no theatre without an audience."[62] At the same time, assumptions and premises about the designed impact of theatre on audiences and about the role of audiences in theatre vary. Where the genteel "legitimate" theatre that emerged in the second half of the nineteenth century sought audiences "of refined attention rather than of eager interest," the "happenings" of the 1950s and 1960s actively challenged distinctions between spectators and performers and manipulated putative audiences into participating in the "performance."[63]

Although labor-oriented theatre rarely challenged contemporary theatrical conventions, it was highly self-conscious in its rapport with audiences. Participants considered how to write for particular audiences in order to achieve the desired impact. According to one student of the movement, "the playwright was of this time and place and wrote his plays for the purpose of communicating to, altering, and changing the views and actions of an audience."[64] In mapping out the aesthetic territory of "revolutionary theatre," Theatre Union member Michael Blankfort asserted that "a great deal of what we have to say to the playwright depends on what we find in the audience. It is an essential, if not the most essential, ingredient of the 'revolutionary theatre.' "[65]

In 1936, John Howard Lawson, a central figure in the New Playwrights Theatre, the Workers' Drama League, and the Theatre Union, published a thick tome entitled *The Theory and Technique of Playwriting*. After a survey of European dramatic theory "from Aristotle to Zola" and an overview of contemporary dramatic writing, Lawson focused on how to develop conflict and action in dramatic texts. Devoting nearly three hundred pages to how to write credible and engaging situations and characters, he concluded with a brief "Postscript on the Audience" that cast his previous discussions in an entirely new light. He argued that "the audience is the ultimate necessity which gives the playwright's work its purpose and meaning,"[66] implying that the nature of the audience for whom the playwright is writing shapes the substance of the play. The audience influences the play's development, and, when the play is performed, determines whether it succeeds in communicating the playwright's views and ideas. "The playwright's interest in his audience is not only commercial, but creative: the unity [between playwright and audience] which he seeks can only be achieved through the collaboration of an audience which is itself unified and creative." If the playwright has not achieved this "unity," has not "persuade[d] the audience to share his intense feeling in regard to the significance of the action," the playwright has not succeeded in achieving what Lawson sees as "the purpose of drama."[67]

Lawson developed his ideas by observing the work of the Theatre Union, the Workers' Laboratory Theatre, and countless other groups in the workers' theatre movement. Their productions were intended to outrage and galvanize audiences, to inculcate in them principles of mass action, and to convey the necessity of unified struggle. Whether any of these productions led to sustained militance among audience members is all but impossible to demonstrate, but workers' theatre groups made arduous efforts to ensure that audiences at their performances would yield the kind of collaboration with the playwright that Lawson believed to be the pinnacle of the playwright's experience; some focused on bringing audiences to their performances, and others brought performances to their audiences.

Several decades after the fact, Earl Robinson gleefully recounted how calls for Workers' Lab performances would come in day and night from striking workers. WLT members would pack up their musical instruments and a few props and perform on a picket line to keep up morale. "A strike was a sacred event," emphasized Robinson. "In the middle of the night, we'd pick up a tambourine or whatever and head for where the strike was, wherever they happened."[68] The WLT's "Shock Troupe" also made frequent planned appearances for unions, for workers' clubs, wherever they could find space, and if the workers requesting their services were on strike, the WLT waived its nominal fee.

The troupe's efforts spread the WLT's reputation. Tireless self-promoters, members set up performances on street corners and advertised widely in the Communist Party's *Daily Worker*. They performed in Labor Day parades, at left-wing parties and benefits, and at left-wing summer camps. Wherever workers and radicals gathered, the Workers' Laboratory Theatre was there, with its minimalist props, costumes, and scripts.

Organizations performing "stationary" theatre also found various ways to sell their shows. In addition to advertising in the labor and left-wing press, they frequently sent out speakers to other organizations to publicize upcoming productions, even when the organizations were not in full sympathy with the theatre's point of view. Ole Fagerhaugh, a founding member of the Minneapolis Theatre Union, recalls going with other MTU members to a meeting of a truck drivers' union local to perform scenes from the play they were working on, in order to generate interest and sell tickets. The Trotskyist leaders of the local refused to admit the members of the theatre group, several of whom had close CP ties, but the rank and file clamored for the performance and overruled the leadership. Ole also recruited his sister-in-law, Dorothy

Fagerhaugh, who was not otherwise involved with the MTU, to sell tickets through her garment workers' union local.[69]

Such strategies for audience recruitment ensured not only sympathy between spectators and performers but also the presence of spectators. In order to fulfill its goal of producing political theatre of professional quality at prices that working people could pay, the Theatre Union in New York needed to sell voluminous numbers of tickets. The responsibility for attracting large audiences fell largely to Sylvia Regan, whose familiarity with Yiddish theatre had taught her the value of organizing theatre parties. Under Regan's direction, the Theatre Union set out to recruit audiences through unions, workers' clubs, and political organizations.[70] Members of the Theatre Union met with leaders of various political organizations and addressed their meetings in order to interest their members in the Union's current production. To encourage ticket sales, the Theatre Union offered discounts for blocks of tickets which allowed organizations to raise funds for their own purposes.[71]

Not all groups that took advantage of this opportunity were political or workers' organizations. In fact, the Theatre Union derived satisfaction from the diversity of the organizations that such arrangements drew to its plays. The Dentists' Wives Society bought tickets, as did at least one college fraternity, one church, and one synagogue. Still, the bulk of the audiences was made up of groups from labor unions and political organizations, including the Socialist Party, the Communist Party, the International Labor Defense (a CP relief and advocacy organization), and the Committee for Progressive Labor Action, made up of labor leaders and educators advocating industry-wide labor organizing. Based on the success of its first production, *Peace on Earth,* the Theatre Union had an advance sale of 138 theatre parties, some thirty thousand seats, for its second production, *Stevedore,* guaranteeing a six-week run. The next production, *Sailors of Cattarro,* opened with a guaranteed nine-week run.[72]

Contemporary observers, almost in spite of themselves, admired the Theatre Union's ability to attract its intended audience. "The success of its audience organization is perhaps the most important achievement of the theatre, since it establishes that a social theatre can exist financially," wrote one critic.[73] The Theatre Union's successes demonstrated not only that working-class Americans and their left-wing allies would support theatre, but also that, given affordable prices and content that bore some relevance to their lives, working people would take a prominent place among theatregoers.

Workers' theatre cultivated sympathetic audiences beyond large metropolitan areas by taking their productions on tours. For example, the Rebel Players of Los Angeles gave eleven performances in ten cities on a thousand-mile tour of California.[74] Under such circumstances, the need to plan ahead for performance venues and ticket sales required advance contact with groups likely to support labor-oriented performances; these contacts could then become the basis for continuing activism after the performances.

The value of a touring labor theatre was clear to one energetic and creative labor activist working with Rhode Island textile workers. In 1936, Larry Spitz, an experienced union organizer, was recruited into the leadership of the Independent Textile Union in Woonsocket, Rhode Island. As a member of the executive board of the ITU, he developed a broad plan of cultural activities to support the union's militance, and in the second half of the 1930s, the union sponsored choral groups, a drama group, sports teams, outings, and dances that attracted large numbers of union members.[75]

Before his arrival in Woonsocket, Spitz had functioned as impresario and road manager for a tour through northeastern mill towns of *Let Freedom Ring,* a play about textile workers. He was first approached by Albert Bein, the author of the play, after it had completed a successful run in New York sponsored by the Theatre Union.[76] After a well-received performance by the New York cast in Woonsocket, Spitz, anticipating the value of this play for promoting unionism among textile workers, agreed to organize a tour of the show on behalf of the United Textile Workers, whose executive committee sent out calls to its locals urging them to book the show.[77]

Let Freedom Ring dramatized the struggles and eventual successes of textile workers who form a union and go on strike. Publicity for the play highlighted the UTW local sponsoring the performance, and during the intermission, Spitz told spectators whom to contact about local activities. In some cases, the performers took part in strike activities and in boycotts of businesses supporting scabs. Audiences received the play with enthusiasm, and Spitz believed the tour gave a boost to organizing efforts among textile workers in the communities it visited. "It resulted in contacts," he later affirmed. "In some instances, [the tour] gave people more courage to move and made them more open when organizers went talking to them."[78]

The tour of *Let Freedom Ring* was assisted by Brookwood Labor College, which lent a bus to transport cast and props, as well as its considerable expertise in running tours of workers' theatre productions. Brookwood had been organizing theatrical tours since 1932, and in the following year, it had inaugurated its Labor Chautauqua, a traveling educational program that included short plays, songs, and a pitch for unionism, workers' education, and Brookwood Labor College.[79]

The chautauqua became an integral part of the Brookwood course of training.[80] After the close of each academic year, two or three groups of students and faculty traveled north through New England, as far south as South Carolina, and as far west as Minnesota. The local community guaranteed lodging (usually in homes) and its share of travel expenses. The local sponsor distributed publicity supplied by Brookwood and split profits with the school.[81]

By 1936, the year of the *Let Freedom Ring* tour, Brookwood had accumulated substantial experience in planning and carrying out theatrical tours and finding audiences for them. Journals kept for the 1936 tours indicate that performances usually attracted one hundred fifty to three hundred spectators; some drew as many as eight hundred.[82] Because local arrangements were made through unions, Socialist Party branches, or interested liberal organizations, "we had a sympathetic audience right from the start," as Dominic Gianasi, Brookwood alumnus and chautauqua tour organizer, put it.[83]

On tour or at home, workers' theatre performances evoked intense emotions in audiences: spectators applauded and cheered

workers and booed bosses and their cronies every time their presence darkened the stage. Doug Hanson, who worked behind the
scenes of Minneapolis Theatre Union productions, remembered
that audiences were powerfully affected by the group's plays, and it
was not uncommon for spectators to be moved to tears.[84] The Brookwood Labor Players also received warm welcomes from audiences.
Writing to Brookwood after a performance, Cecil Crawford, who had
arranged the chautauqua's visit to Barre, Vermont, noted that the
show was "a huge success." The audience was smaller than hoped for
but "very enthusiastic about the whole show."[85]

Reviewers in the liberal and mainstream press frequently commented on the active responses of the spectators and the emotional
sincerity of their cheering, laughing, and hissing.[86] More sympathetic observers clearly understood the role of the audience in
heightening the impact of a play. A *New Republic* article about workers' theatre remarked that "nearly every performance is giving to the
playwrights and actors the invaluable discussion and support of a participating audience, under whose stimulus the production tends
steadily to gain power."[87]

This enthusiasm was evident even when the play's producers
were not particularly labor-oriented. The first production of the
Group Theatre was Paul and Claire Sifton's *1931–*, a play about the
effect of the depression on a young working man and his fiancée. The
Group Theatre saw its audience as conventional theatregoers rather
than the more politicized, working-class audience that the Theatre
Union and the Workers' Lab sought; nevertheless, the subject matter
attracted the same boisterous crowds. According to Harold Clurman,
a founding member of the Group who was not particularly sympathetic to workers' theatre, "the audiences at *1931–* were far more
taken with the play than the press. We couldn't fail to notice a kind
of fervor in the nightly reception of *1931–* that was intense with a
smoldering conviction uncharacteristic of the usual Broadway audience. All the business we did, however, was balcony business." For the
last performance, the theatre was packed and the audience lively.
During a curtain call, some yelled from the balcony, "Long live the

Soviet Union!" to which one of the actors responded from the stage, "Long live America!" "Both outcries," Clurman noted in his memoir of the period, "might be described as irrelevant, but evidently there was something in the air beyond theatrical appreciation."[88]

For the participants in and supporters of workers' theatre, there was little mystery about the "something in the air beyond theatrical appreciation." Audience members recognized themselves on the stage, identifying with the working-class and activist characters, and were drawn into the action. As Wilbur Broms, a Young Communist League leader in Minnesota who participated in several labor-oriented performances, put it, audiences "felt involved."[89] Broms's friend Ole Fagerhaugh recalled union leaders' praise for Minneapolis Theatre Union productions, especially their closeness to the experiences of working people. After an MTU performance of *Black Pit,* a play about mineworkers, Fagerhaugh was told by the head of one union local, "This is what we need. . . . Now you're giving Minneapolis something about real life as it is!"[90]

Frequently, actions on the stage paralleled actions that audience members were involved in or planning. Audiences of union members were particularly vocal, for instance, during plays that included strikes. Dominic Gianasi recalls that when the Brookwood Labor Players came to the end of one piece in which the characters had resolved to go on strike, audiences in towns with strong unions always gave them "a very enthusiastic response."[91] As Freddie Paine, an ILG member and activist in the 1930s, said regarding one show she attended, "This is us. This is the way we do it. . . . Your work is glorified and you feel good about it."[92]

As the daughter of a liberal lawyer in Saint Paul, Minnesota, Dorothy Broms, who became active in local CP affairs, "saw all the theatre that came through Saint Paul." The labor plays of the Minneapolis Theatre Union, however, "had an aliveness, an immediacy that conventional theatre didn't have." At performances of the MTU, for instance, there was no "awe" for the actors. When actors such as Katherine Cornell performed, "you sat and listened and were respectful . . . whereas [at MTU performances] you felt you were in it and the rest of the audience obviously felt that [they] were in it too," she recalled.[93] This identification between performers and spectators was palpable to those on both sides of the footlights. Looking back on the chautauqua performances she participated in as a member of the Brookwood Labor Players in 1935, Edith Berkowitz Parker noted, "Wherever we went, [audiences] adored us. All the plays were oriented toward the kind of lives they led. And we could do it well because we weren't removed from it."[94]

The plays of the workers' theatre movement took the reality of the workplace and the neighborhood and heightened it to suggest to audiences alternative, empowering scenarios. Such performances affirmed the experiences of audience members and, at the same time, told them they could make real changes in their lives and the conditions around them. Judging from the responses it received, the Theatre Union play *Stevedore*, which dramatizes the conditions of African American dockworkers, was a particularly powerful example of the impact of workers' theatre on its audiences. For this production, the Theatre Union made serious efforts to recruit African American performers who would be familiar to African American audiences, attracting the latter by advertising in publications such as the *Amsterdam News* and by organizing special previews to encourage African American organizations to buy blocks of seats. Even before the play opened, the Theatre Union caught attention by announcing that it would give equal treatment to blacks and whites at the box office. According to Sylvia Regan Ellstein, Theatre Union sales manager, the box office attendant was instructed to give blacks the best seats available instead of following the accepted Broadway practice of seating them in distant corners of the balcony.[95]

Consequently, when *Stevedore* opened, it "appeared not as a play at all, but as an emotional experience," according to the reviewer for the *New York Sun*. For Robert Garland of the *New York Telegram*, "it [was] almost as if the on-lookers were taking part in [the action on the stage], as if the forbidding barrier of the footlights had been magically removed."[96] As audiences responded to the play with loud cheers and applause, they became part of the performance that the critics reviewed. Some critics in the mainstream press found the experience refreshing and welcomed it as a valuable challenge to the finicky sensibilities of jaded theatregoers. Gilbert W. Gabriel, reviewing the play for the *New York American*, noted that *Stevedore* gave off "a smell of genuine long-grown anger, of scorn sweat-drenched . . . and it is a smell which should sharpen the nostrils of even that most inveterate sniffer, the casual theatre-goer." Yet Gabriel, while gently mocking "the casual theatre-goer," warns such a spectator of the play's ominous implications. The "smell" he describes is that of "a righteous cause pushing its big black fist at last up out of the ooze of defeatism and servility."[97] Although he seems to approve of the emotional honesty and directness of the play, he also suggests that it has sinister, threatening potential.

Some of Gabriel's colleagues were distinctly more direct in identifying the threat of such emotional performances. For Percy Hammond, reviewing the play for the *New York Herald Tribune*, "if there had been a rope in the mildly infuriated audience, a lynching might have occurred."[98] Willella Waldorf, who clearly disagreed with the play's politics, nevertheless had a grudging admiration for the production's ability to move its audience. The play, she wrote, "sticks with uncommon persistence to a single purpose—which is to inflame the passions of its audience and to sweep that audience forward on a wave of fighting hate. . . . *Stevedore* becomes an incitement to riot of the first order."[99]

Waldorf was not the only one to see *Stevedore* as a call to riot. A year after it opened in New York, the Gilpin Players of Cleveland, a respected African American theatre company that was not aligned with the workers' theatre movement, announced its own production of the play. Protest instantly arose from various corners, including the charge that *Stevedore* contained "indecent language." In addition, the sudden discovery of problems with the theatre building required that immediate and extensive repairs be made. Both the protest and the need for repairs seem politically motivated: the Players had presented other plays that contained profane language, and the theatre had been in constant use, with regular inspections, for several years. Cleveland audiences saw the play only after a vociferous campaign by liberal and left-wing supporters of free speech.[100]

In cities across the country, local officials sought to prevent workers' theatre performances, using obscenity laws as shields for political repression. Such attempts at silencing labor and the left frequently backfired, however, as supporters of workers' theatre mounted successful campaigns to lift bans on plays such as *Stevedore*. As a result, the targeted productions received far more publicity than they would have otherwise. In addition, the attacks gave the left new opportunities to raise the very American issues of freedom of speech and constitutional rights. Finally, bans on workers' theatre prompted people in the movement to build a coalition with mainstream theatre artists. In 1935, the National Committee Against Censorship of the Theatre Arts was formed, bringing together not only actors, directors, and writers associated with workers' theatre but performers such as Fanny Brice and drama critics such as Brooks Atkinson of the *New York Times*. The committee documented local efforts to ban labor plays in the pamphlet *Censored!* which it published with the assistance of the New Theatre League and the American Civil Liberties Union.[101]

Censorship thus made workers' theatre, in some ways, more "respectable": it attracted the support of prominent public figures and organizations as well as the attention of a wider public. When the police chief of New Haven, Connecticut, for example, issued an order prohibiting the performance of *Waiting for Lefty* anywhere in the city, the *Bridgeport Sunday Herald*, a newspaper in an adjoining town, printed the entire text of the play, inviting readers to make up their own minds about it.[102]

If censorship brought workers' theatre into the mainstream, it also attributed a certain power and efficacy to its productions. Local crusades to prevent the performance of labor plays suggest that theatre could indeed transform docile workers into riotous revolutionaries. At the very least, labor and left-wing movements had found in theatre a medium that threatened the confidence and complacency of local power structures. Undeterred and even encouraged by attempts to thwart workers' theatre, left-wing political parties and organizations, workers' schools, and labor unions drew on the strengths and accomplishments of the workers' theatre movement to mobilize their constituencies.

*   *   *

From the late 1920s to the mid-1930s, the number and visibility of theatre groups performing plays by and about working people grew dramatically. Although most of these groups were formed to advance and support other social and political causes, they rapidly constituted their own movement with its own culture, stresses, and challenges. Workers' theatre groups became gathering places for energetic young people of diverse backgrounds and outlooks. Inevitably, the richness that such diversity lent to workers' theatre also resulted in tensions and inconsistencies. Art and politics, Socialists and Communists did not always cohabit constructively, and the shared commitment to theatre as a weapon in political struggles resulted in a somewhat contradictory notion of the power of theatre.

In the first half of the 1930s, though, the workers' theatre movement was still establishing its identity and figuring out how best to deliver its lessons. Individual theatre groups labored to find their own form and forum while attempting to produce stimulating theatre for audiences and shape a stimulating community for writers, performers, and activists. Rarely did they succeed at both. The full-scale, professional productions of the Theatre Union attracted broader attention than the quick skits of the Workers' Laboratory Theatre, but by all accounts, the latter did a better job with congeniality and personal satisfaction.

Similarly, the movement found that its goals of promoting theatre as a political tool and mobilizing audiences for political action were not always compatible. Workers' theatre groups saw themselves as building other political movements, primarily the labor movement, but labor had separate goals and visions. The contributions of workers' theatre to the labor movement would not necessarily be reciprocated.

4. INTERLUDE

Unionism and Militance in the Plays of the Workers' Theatre Movement

If workers' theatre was as powerful as right-wing censors believed, *Stevedore* made an appropriate target for their efforts. In the final scene of the play, after considerable violence on and off stage, black and white workers join together to fight off a vicious, racist white mob; Binnie, an African American woman, shoots down the mob's ringleader and shouts exultantly: "I got him! That red-headed son-of-a-bitch, I got him! I got him!" A cry of triumph arises from the interracial crowd on the stage, and a few moments later, the final curtain falls.[1] The action transgressed all the norms that censors and their allies sought to maintain to promote social stability: animosity between blacks and whites, the silencing of women, and fear and passivity among workers. Judging from the play's extended run and animated spectators, the vision of social transformation enacted in *Stevedore* met with strong approval from audiences, black and white.

What moved *Stevedore*'s audiences so powerfully, and scared censors, was that audiences recognized themselves on the stage. Working-class audiences accepted the vision of collective working-class power that *Stevedore* and other workers' plays fashioned because it affirmed their own assumptions and, in some cases, their prejudices. Far from presenting a utopian dream of a harmonious working class in which black and white, male and female link arms and ignore real tensions among themselves and the social roles in which they have historically been cast, the play, like many in the workers' theatre repertoire in the 1930s, drew heavily on pervasive ideas and ideals about gender, race, and ethnicity. At the same time as the plays portrayed working people's realities and world views, however, they also drafted blueprints for changing them.

Although the plays of the workers' theatre reveal a great deal about working-class culture, they remain the creation of playwrights, producers, and performers dedicated to using theatre to promote social change. The scripts of this theatrical movement molded dominant values and attitudes into a vision of working-class militance and grassroots unionism that drew in all members of working-class communities. Because this vision reflected contemporary assumptions about gender, ethnicity, and race, however, it was also limited by such assumptions.

*   *   *

However lofty their goals, workers' theatre groups were chronically plagued by inadequate resources. It is perhaps for this reason that, aside from *The Belt*, few plays take place inside industrial workplaces, requiring sets depicting heavy machinery. Yet even *The Belt* is staged for the most part outside the factory, demonstrating how the relentless assembly line reached into every corner of workers' existence. Similarly, most workers' theatre plays are set in working people's homes and in outdoor spaces in their communities, showing that working-class activism is nurtured in all aspects of life, not exclusively on the shopfloor among co-workers. Labor plays translated the necessity of low-budget productions into the virtues of community-based, grassroots organizing.

One play that vividly conveys the personal and communal dimensions of effective working-class action is, ironically, staged in a work setting: John Howard Lawson's *Marching Song*, premiered by the Theatre Union in 1937, takes place in an abandoned factory building.[2] No longer functioning as a factory, providing jobs and income for the community, the building has become home to unemployed and transient men and an evicted family. In this space, husband and wife prepare their next move, lovers rendezvous, leaders plan actions, and the unemployed make a home for themselves. Emphasizing how industrial capitalism has ravaged working-class families, this dilapidated industrial site is transformed into both home and town "green." The setting blurs boundaries between public and private, knitting the problems of individuals and their families into issues facing the community as a whole.

The setting of workers' plays in communal spaces outside the workplace highlights the importance of community-based activism in the 1930s. Whether it was among white textile and garment workers in Rhode Island or Minneapolis, African American steelworkers and sharecroppers in Alabama, or the racially and ethnically heterogeneous workforces in meatpacking plants and steel mills in Chicago, much of the brass-tacks work of labor organizing took place through informal networks.[3] New supporters were recruited through conversations on street corners, in bars, and in kitchens as often as on shopfloors, and workers' plays frequently dramatized these kinds of casual exchanges.

Both *All for One* and *In Union There Is Strength,* created by Fannia Cohn and the Education Department staff of the International Ladies Garment Workers Union in the early 1930s, take place in workers' homes and feature family members and friends discussing the importance of unionism in order to win over one or more recalcitrant characters.[4] To establish realism, the introduction to *All for One* assures the reader that "this play . . . is drawn from the actual daily life of our members in their unions." Cohn, a veteran union activist and labor educator, knew that relatives and friends played an important role in recruiting members, and the settings of her plays reflect her experiences as an organizer. But because the scripts are didactic, we also have to see them as promoting this kind of organizing.

Everyone had a role to play when labor organizing was defined as a community-wide project, but since labor plays reflected the values of their creators, the "worker" remained a gendered figure. Although women as well as men in the plays perform paid labor, only men are identified as "workers" outside the factory and the mine; women are mothers, sisters, wives, lovers when they are not at their jobs in mills, sweatshops, and offices. The relentlessly male identity of workers emerges most unambiguously in the skits of the Workers' Laboratory Theatre. Its short productions dramatized the same labor conflicts as the proletarian prose promoted by male CP intellectuals in the early 1930s.[5] Both the plays and the novels reflect Communist ideology's neglect of women's participation in the labor force and adhere to a rigid gender distinction between work and family.[6] In the Workers' Lab skit *The Miners Are Striking,* for example, "generic" characters—Worker, Woman, Priest, Capitalist—discuss working conditions and class relations. The character Worker attacks the Capitalist for the deadly working conditions and low pay, the immediate concerns of male miners and other workers, whereas the character Woman, representing the concerns of families, decries the poor living conditions and women's inability to feed their children.[7]

The cast of another WLT skit, *Tempo, Tempo!* which dramatizes industrial workplace conditions, includes an employed female character who is identified as "woman worker," confirming the assumption that the normative gender of the worker is male; it also creates a place for the female workers: at work.[8] Unlike the (male) "worker," who retains this appellation and identity wherever he goes, the female of the species reverts to "woman" once she leaves the workplace. Thus despite the occasional presence of female workers (even female labor leaders, as in the case of *Shop Strife,* written by two male students at Brookwood Labor College)[9] "women workers" remained strictly on the shopfloor.

So pervasive was this construction of gender that women as well as men accepted and promoted it. Indeed, it appears as well in scripts developed at the summer schools organized specifically for working women. Thus, in *Bank Run,* written by dramatics instructor Hollace Ransdell with her students at the Southern Summer School for Working Women in Industry in 1932, the character Worker is a "working man in his thirties, a machinist perhaps."[10] Similarly, in the pageant produced at the Bryn Mawr Summer School for Women Workers, *Who Are the Workers?* the speaking chorus opens with the lines: "I am the working man, the inventor, the maker of the world's food and clothes."[11]

Nonetheless, students at the Southern Summer School also staged a skit about female tobacco workers; and in spite of opening with a distinctly masculine voice, *Who Are the Workers?* illustrates the conditions facing garment workers, cigarette makers, jewelry makers, and other all-female groups of "workers." The women writing these skits thus reconciled their experiences as women workers with the image of "the worker" as male by distinguishing the "generic" worker—male—from workers in specific industries whom they knew to be women like themselves.

In plays set outside the workplace, however, though women might be identified as employed in a factory or a mill, their role definitions remain strictly female and reproductive. In another Southern Summer School script, *On the Picket Line*, the main character, "Ma" Simpson, is described as a "spinner, old and lively," but her role in the developing action is purely female and maternal: as the skit opens, she is "bending over the fire stirring a big kettle boiling there."[12] She is making stew to feed the picketers. Though Ma Simpson is one of the "workers," she stands outside the mill and therefore loses her identity as a worker.

It is interesting to note that at the margins, in the workplace, women could move between their roles as nurturers and as workers, but men could not. In *Mill Shadows*, written by an instructor at Brookwood Labor College, Roy, one of the male textile workers, loses his wife to illness. Recognizing that he cannot be both father and mother to his infant daughter, Roy turns her over to Grannie, the play's main character.[13] By divesting himself of any maternal responsibilities, the man can remain fully a "worker." Roy understands that his parental role requires him to provide for the material well-being of his family, while the physical and emotional caretaking is the province of women, all women, regardless of their life-cycle status. He also understands that family needs cannot supersede community needs, and were he to attempt to raise his daughter himself, he would become far less effective in the struggle for a union in the textile mill.

Black Pit, by Albert Maltz, also pointed out to audiences the necessity of placing community and family in the proper perspective. Joe Kovarsky, the main character, betrays his co-workers in order to keep his job at the coal mine, justifying this act on the grounds that he must look after the welfare of his wife and newborn son.[14] His betrayal results in the death of two miners and the failure of their organizing campaign, and when the other coal miners learn of his duplicity, Joe is exiled. He must leave behind wife and son, who, we are to believe, will be provided and cared for by male workers and female nurturers who are better able than Joe to maintain the appropriate balance between family needs and community needs.

What these plays suggest is that men somehow lose their strength as workers—their virility, perhaps—when they take on excessively nurturing concerns. Women, in contrast, can provide material and moral sustenance to *all* the members of the extended family of working people without losing any of their effectiveness as community leaders. Indeed, familial appellations might even reflect special respect given female community leaders: "Ma" Simpson, "Grannie," and "Auntie" Flora (in Samuel Ornitz's play *In New Kentucky,* published in *New Masses*),[15] were more recent incarnations of itinerant activist Mary Jones who was known as "Mother" Jones.

The image of the strong, nurturing female in these scripts in many ways meets the conventions of 1930s iconography, but it also subverts those conventions. This image is Ma Joad (John Steinbeck's and, even more, John Ford's); she is also the "madonna of the fields," the wiry, burdened farm woman of the Farm Settlement Administration/Resettlement Administration (FSA/RA) photographs.[16] The Mas and Aunts and Binnies of labor plays part ways with Ma Joad and the madonnas of the fields on two significant points, however. First, they are nurturers to their entire community, where they are firmly rooted. Women in FSA/RA photographs, in contrast, are often shown isolated from their communities, surrounded only, if at all, by their children. Similarly, as *Grapes of Wrath* comes to a close,

Ma Joad is once again on the road, with the remnants of her family, uprooted again from a community of farm/workers. Second, the migrant mother of the FSA/RA photographs and Ma Joad are models of resignation, whereas the women of the labor plays are optimistic and energetic leaders who mobilize their constituencies, encourage their struggles, and even stand on the barricades, as Binnie does at the conclusion of *Stevedore*. These figures won't wait for assistance or insurgence from other quarters: they provide it themselves.

Strong female figures in labor plays derive their authority precisely from their ability to meet the spiritual as well as physical needs of the whole community, in times of struggle as well as in times of peace. In Ornitz's *In New Kentucky,* the character of Flora Richards is introduced as "a shriveled old woman . . . called Aunt Flora. She is the midwife of Coal Creek, also its undertaker, lay preacher, lay doctor and minstrel." All other members of the miners' community are depicted as weary, haggard, and at various stages of illness and despair, but she retains a spark of life: "She looks like a sleazy skin full of bones. But her walk is spry, her way eager, her look hopeful."[17] Indeed, it is she who mobilizes the miners' wives and leads them into the mine—violating all norms of separation between work and community space—in order to persuade the miners to stop working until the company agrees to pay them in cash instead of scrip.

The presence of the women inside the mine highlights the extent to which workplace issues are ultimately community and family issues: the women are galvanized into action by the realization that the prices at the grocery down the road are half what they are at the company store and that with cash they would be able to feed their families more adequately than with scrip. These characters belong to a venerable tradition of activism in which women, moved by "female consciousness" of their reproductive roles and their inability to fulfill them, engaged in food riots and other mass actions.[18] The plays of the workers' theatre movement, however, took the power of female consciousness one step further and argued that women's responsibilities in the realm of home and family could and should spark united action among working-class women and men, under the leadership of women.

In these plays, definitions of women's communal nurturing roles were wide enough to include women for whom social reproduction was a "productive" activity as well. In *Stevedore*, Binnie does not appear to be the mother (or any other relative) of any of the other characters; her feeding role occurs in the business she operates. Yet, like Ma Simpson and other maternal leaders, she provides moral support and encouragement as well as food. The fact that providing food is, literally, Binnie's job is immaterial.

African American women were generally more likely than white women to be employed outside the home, and in many cities they ran numerous small businesses catering to personal service needs such as food and lodging.[19] *Stevedore* told these women and their families that such activity did not disqualify them as nurturers and leaders for their communities. On the contrary, the play affirmed the centrality of the kinds of establishments black women owned and managed in the life and struggles of black communities. Moreover, for women in the 1930s who found themselves under attack from many different directions for taking jobs while their husbands remained unemployed, the character of Binnie, who seemed to derive her authority in the community from her work in the restaurant, provided a strong role model and confirmation that women's paid work would not rend the social fabric but actually could strengthen it (see photograph).

Binnie's restaurant, Ma Simpson's stew pot, and Grannie's caring for Roy's daughter all tie leadership to nurturing and assert women's central roles in their communities. These images reflect both the realities of women's contributions to maintaining working-class community institutions and the didactic vision of the plays' authors: working people, they told audiences, must value their women leaders and incorporate all their needs—not only workplace issues—in their struggles for better treatment. The plays of the workers' theatre movement reinforce women's familial and nurturing roles, but in doing so, they also make two different points about labor organizing: at a literal level, the plays insist that women, as family members and as leaders, must be part of all organizing efforts; more metaphorically, the plays note that the kind of leadership that women

"Run along and strut yo'stuff, white boy" (Paul Peters and George Sklar, *Stevedore: A Play in Three Acts* [New York: Covici-Friede, 1934], p. 91). *Billy Rose Theatre Collection, The New York Public Library for the Performing Arts; Astor, Lenox, and Tilden Foundations.*

represent, emphasizing the personal and emotional bonds among community members, is key to effective collective action.

Labor plays also addressed questions of ethnicity and race. If female characters became metaphors for describing effective leadership, the introduction of characters with different ethnic and racial identities suggested models for rank-and-file cooperation. Yet racial and ethnic differences also led to divergent forms of cooperation. Where white working-class characters of different European origins created a shared culture among themselves, black and white characters remained largely within their respective cultural and geographical spheres. The cooperation represented in the plays by the alliance of whites and blacks is limited to working together toward discrete goals that different groups hold in common, whereas cooperation among white workers of different European origins features full cultural and residential integration.

Frequently, cultural differences among white workers were indicated by their names or their language. In *Shop Strife,* written by two male students at Brookwood, for instance, Anna, the woman who leads the strike, is later identified as Anna Silverstein, and the presser who is fired also bears a typically Jewish name, Izzy; Joe Tomaine, a cutter, exclaims "Santa Marie!" denoting a Catholic, probably Italian, background.[20] Through these details, the writers conjured up realms of experience. They did not need to be more explicit about what it meant that these workers were Jewish or Italian, because they knew their audiences would know.

The authors of workers' plays, from professional playwrights to industrial wage workers, shared with one another and with their audiences the experience of growing up as sons and daughters of European immigrants.[21] In coming of age, they worked to integrate their ethnic identity with their emerging identity as Americans. At the same time, mass culture and mass consumption, combined with the economic dislocation of the depression, weakened the isolation of white European ethnic groups from one another and fostered the development of shared social spaces and outlooks.[22] This growing consciousness of being American and the increased interactions among young people of different European ethnic groups greatly facilitated the labor organizing campaigns of the 1930s.

When these young women and men attended workers' theatre performances, they understood the ethnic allusions to their own lives and to the lives of their peers of other European backgrounds. Labor plays populated by characters with distinct ethnic identities circulated widely and were warmly received by many different groups of working people. The references to ethnicity also served an instructional purpose, however, which is clearest in plays where ethnicity goes beyond name or language. In one of the key scenes in *Black Pit,* for example, the miners and their families gather to celebrate the birth of Joe Kovarsky's son. The people share music and dances, and the playwright describes two characters, Josef and Mary Anetsky, dancing "in native manner" as an old man plays an accordion; later, "two Slovak feller play Eyetalian game," counting in pidgin Italian.[23] The different traditions of the miners and their families have become part of a shared culture and the center of communal celebrations. Suggestions about ethnicity that are only veiled allusions in scripts such as *Shop Strife* are here writ large: individuals' ethnic background and identity can become the basis of shared experience, just as the sharing of dances and games creates a new culture within this community and binds its members to one another.

Ethnicity could be represented as a terrain of mutuality because, in many ways, it was. Race, in contrast, frequently remained a barrier, which the plays explicitly worked to tear down. The scripts did not portray black and white workers sharing their lives, because black and white working people most often did not. Beginning in the 1920s, residential segregation by race increased in urban areas. Mutual suspicion between African American and European American workers remained generally high.[24] Black workers were aware that whites had frequently excluded them from organizing drives, and many whites had seen blacks employed to break their strikes or undercut their wages.[25]

Workers' plays could draw on and reinforce existing commonalities among white workers, but they had to establish such shared ground between whites and blacks, and they did so in a variety of ways. Some plays bring black workers onto the scene, very literally, for the purpose of explaining to white workers the importance of working with African Americans. In Elizabeth England's *Take My Stand*, for instance, the elected committee of textile workers that confronts the mill owner is made up of one white man, one white woman, and one black man. The white man, Lem, is clearly the spokesman for the group; Mamie and Brig spend much of their time onstage exchanging fearful and puzzled looks. The mill owner tries to dissuade Brig from participating in the planned strike by promising to give jobs to "all the lik'liest niggers in Shantytown." Brig responds, "We larnin' we can't cure the black man's troubles by sickin' him on the poh whites's jobs,"[26] but white workers in the audience would not have missed the point: if you don't include African Americans in your organizing drives, employers will hire them to break your strikes.

The lesson is even blunter in *Let Freedom Ring,* also set among textile workers. When Kirk, the white workers' leader, announces that he's invited representatives from the packing room to the meeting to discuss a possible strike, all the white workers know that only African Americans work in the packing room and several threaten to leave the meeting. Kirk explains to them the importance of having African American workers in the union: "Thar's thousands o' black folk livin' in Leesville an' we mought as well use our haids an' make the first step linin' em up fer a fight side by side with us afore the mills does the hirin' o' blacks an' the linin' 'em against us."[27] Three black workers then enter the scene, "howdye's" are exchanged all around, the black workers introduce themselves and take a seat, and they are not heard from again. The white workers accept that their organizing efforts will succeed only if they include black workers but show little interest in hearing their perspectives on problems in the mill.

The contrast between rhetoric and action in this play is vividly illustrated in the staging. Attention is focused on a banner emblazoned with the union's slogan: "TEXTILE WORKERS BLACK AND WHITE ORGANIZE IN UNION" (see photograph). The black workers themselves are seated, almost in a slump, among the white workers, most of whom are standing. Though the black workers are clearly visible to the audience, they are visually overpowered by the white union brothers and sisters.

Even when labor plays confront head-on the racism that black workers encounter, they present it as part of capitalist oppression, avoiding any serious engagement with white workers' racist attitudes and assumptions; these productions also end up appealing to white workers' self-interest. In *Scottsboro!* a WLT skit performed to mobilize support for the defense of nine black youths accused of raping two white women, "workers" declaim:

> Will you let them murder nine Negro boys in Scottsboro?
> Will you deliver your fellow workers to the capitalist
>   murderers?
> Will you deliver yourselves to the capitalist murderers?[28]

"Textile Workers Black and White Organize in Union" (Albert Bein, *Let Freedom Ring: A Play in Three Acts* [New York: Samuel French, 1936]). *Billy Rose Theatre Collection, The New York Public Library for the Performing Arts; Astor, Lenox, and Tilden Foundations.*

The skit ties the accusations against the young men to white racism, but ultimately, the appeal is to white audiences' concerns for themselves: they can best safeguard their own rights by fighting on behalf of these black men. Despite the Communist Party's staunch anti-racist stance, members of the Workers' Lab, like others producing workers' theatre, were unable to conceptualize, and therefore to represent, African Americans as part of the same community of workers as whites.

African American poet Langston Hughes also wrote a short play about the "Scottsboro boys." Unlike the WLT's skit, however, Hughes's *Scottsboro, Limited* keeps the attention focused on the accused. This piece has them speak for themselves and renders their plight graphically: they walk onto the stage "chained by the right foot, and to the other," watched and harassed by the sheriff.[29] In the WLT skit, the characters are generic "workers," far removed from the incident: white workers have, in effect, silenced the black men by absorbing their cause into the struggles of white people.

Presenting the perspective of the black men did not require abandoning the vision of a unified and powerful working class. Hughes, who was at that time sympathetic to the Communist Party, concluded his play with a call to workers to take action—"Rise, workers, and fight!"—but he maintained a clear distinction between fighting employers and fighting racism. The final lines of the skit call on workers, "Black and White together," to put an end, once and for all, to both their shared oppression as workers ("greed and pain") and the oppression of African Americans as African Americans ("the color line's blight").[30] The WLT skit, in contrast, like most other workers' theatre plays, addresses the issue of racism as an outgrowth of social relations under capitalism and minimizes the experience of black people themselves.

The rare plays that focused on the experiences of African American working people emphasized, if anything, the social and cultural distances between black and white workers. *Stevedore*, which was written by two white playwrights, went the furthest in presenting race and class issues from the perspective of black people. The overt message of the play is that black and white workers can and should join forces, but what audiences saw of African American culture in the play reinforced the notion that African Americans could not dissolve into the great melting pot of American society in the same way as white Americans of various European ancestries could.

Paul Peters and George Sklar, the authors of *Stevedore*, honor African American culture by including black hymns in their script. These are heard, however, during an all-black event: the funeral of a man shot by white thugs.[31] The suggestion here is that African American culture cannot be shared with whites; in this way, it stands in stark contrast to the songs and games of different white ethnic groups. *Black Pit* could realistically portray European ethnic cultures as bases of commonality and exchange among white Americans, but to suggest the same exchange between whites and blacks would have violated the reality of race relations: African American culture remained quite distinct from white ethnic cultures even when it encountered the forces of mass culture and mass consumption that began to dissolve differences among white ethnic groups.[32]

The work that best reveals the contrasts between ethnicity and race in the labor plays is John Howard Lawson's *Marching Song*. At the center of the plot are Pete and Jenny Russell, who seek refuge in the abandoned factory building with their infant daughter. As the play develops, we learn that Pete took part in an earlier strike, lost his job as a result, and has been unemployed ever since. In their time of need, the Russells receive help from their neighbors, with names such as Zilitch, Malucci, and McGillicuddy. The Russells also meet a variety of unemployed men living in the building, among them Lucky. Through this character, we learn about the existence of a black community in another part of town and about the recruitment of African Americans from a nearby large city to work as strikebreakers during the strike in which Pete lost his job.

In this play, as in others, the white women and men of different ethnic groups work harmoniously together, defending one another against landlords, sheriffs, and employers. Interracial cooperation is more problematic, however, as Pete resists working with Lucky, especially once he learns that Lucky was one of the scabs in the last strike. Lucky, though not as hostile as Pete, is no less skeptical about the possibility of blacks and whites working together and reveals a deep-seated bitterness against white workers, who have "been scabbin' on the black man the whole o' your life."[33] In the end, Pete accepts Lucky as a brother worker, and Lucky, who has organized the members of the black community to join the strike, speaks on behalf of the whole community of white and black workers and their families in proclaiming the power of workers and their communities when united in their goals and actions. Yet the fragmentary and tentative nature of race relations remains: blacks and whites have a common political action, destined, it would appear, for success; nothing suggests that this unity will translate into shared cultural and social life.

Marching Song, one of the most polished and popular of the plays of the workers' theatre movement, combines lessons about different kinds of diversity. White workers who share the experience of immigrant backgrounds must continue to work together without forgetting one another's distinctiveness. Black and white workers must put to rest their antagonisms and recognize that whatever injustice white workers have done to black workers in the past, and whatever black workers' role has been in breaking strikes, they must work together for the good of their communities.

Indeed, *Marching Song* is very much a community-based play. What advances the plot, ultimately toward a general strike, is a family's eviction from its home and, soon thereafter, the death of the couple's infant daughter. The whole neighborhood comes to Pete and Jenny's assistance, and when one of the sheriff's deputies asks, "Who's running that crowd?" Bill, one of the leaders of the planned strike, answers, "A kid." "What kid?" Bill replies, "She's dead."[34] The workplace issues around which the autoworkers are preparing to strike are never made clear. What the workers and their families are fighting for is the integrity of their community and the chance to live decent lives without the obstructions of insufficient pay and corrupt politics.

Although this community has no single female leader comparable to Binnie or Ma Simpson, women—who, again, are not "workers"—play indispensable roles in the action. Mary McGillicuddy organizes the women in the community to prepare strike relief, and Rose, Jenny Russell's sister, runs the printing press and serves as the spokesperson for working-class solidarity. In her discussions with her sweetheart, Joe, Rose explains why working people must stand together, why they must give up daydreams of fame and fortune, if they are truly to succeed in making a better world for themselves. When Bill, the male worker-leader, is martyred by the sheriff and his henchmen, Rose continues her work, both moral and material, which results in a shutdown of the power plant and eventually the auto plant.

Rose's efforts would have been to no avail, however, without the help of her Irish, Slavic, Italian, and Jewish friends and neighbors, who join forces with African American workers and families, in the same way as the implied victory of the dockworkers in *Stevedore* required unity among black and white workers as well as Binnie's forceful and courageous leadership. Through the portrayal of interracial and interethnic relations on one hand and of gender roles on the other hand, these plays provided audiences with models of both leadership and solidarity. Working men and women attending these plays saw their own lives, concerns, and prejudices enacted on the stage and transformed into a vision of a powerful and effective working class that includes women and men, blacks and whites, Italians, Jews, Slavs, and others. This vision echoed the experiences of working-class audiences and offered the hope that, working together, they could overcome all obstacles to a better life.

The plays of the workers' theatre movement identify strategies for achieving this goal by defining leadership, community, and solidarity. Yet they frequently marginalize those institutions most concretely associated with workers' issues: labor unions. Unions may indeed have played only negligible roles in community-level organizing, but these blueprints for collective action write them out of the picture almost entirely. Frequently, the union is barely even mentioned or is dismissed as ineffectual or constricting. In *Black Pit*, for example, the miners who are in the process of organizing themselves raise the issue of securing a local charter in order to receive the material support of the international union. "When we're ready to strike, we'll strike," responds McCullough, who seems to be the most experienced in union matters. "The National Office'll hafta okay it."[35] This is one of the few allusions to the union, in a play about miners who organize themselves to demand safer working conditions.

In other instances, the union's effectiveness is highly questionable and certainly questioned. In *Stevedore,* the union, which has until now kept out black dockworkers, does not represent the interests of its white members either. In *Marching Song,* when Pete is asked by one of his neighbors, "Why don't your union get busy?" Pete replies,

"The union's got no money and no plans. They made a lousy settlement an' we're left holding the bag." Pete is now unable to get a job because, as one of the strike leaders, he has been blacklisted, and the union seems unable and unwilling to come to his assistance. In each case, the union, through poor judgment or its own prejudices, has abandoned its constituency.

Though implicitly and explicitly critical of existing unions and how they treat their members, the plays nevertheless suggest that, in the end, working people need unions, and the characters accept unionism as part of workers' struggles. Despite their earlier experience with an all-white union, the black dockworkers agree to work with sympathetic white dockworkers to build an interracial union. In *On the Picket Line,* Ma Simpson is the main character and leader of her community, but there is a union involved in the strike, represented by the character of the union organizer. This character speaks a few lines in an almost perfunctory appearance and then withdraws to the background. The juxtaposition of ineffectual or even obstructionist unions with highly militant and effective communities of working people suggests that unions can rescue themselves from irrelevance by emulating these inclusive, participatory communities of working people.

Judging from the images and actions in the plays of the workers' theatre movement, their creators and enthusiastic audiences wanted unions to involve all working-class men and women in the process of organizing and to represent them all at the bargaining table. If Rose, who is a woman and therefore not a "worker," can run the printing press that is so essential to the planned strike, aren't rigid definitions of "workers" irrelevant and, in fact, self-defeating? Moreover, if the question of who is a "worker" becomes moot in this form of working-class organizing, so do, by implication, divisions among workers. Because all working-class men and women should be members of an inclusive organization, so should all workers, regardless of job or skill level.

The true bases for working-class organizing, according to these plays, are family and community rather than craft or occupation, which had been the organizing model of the influential American Federation of Labor. In order for community-based organizing to be effective, however, constituencies must learn to address differences among themselves, the plays told audiences. Working people and their organizations need to acknowledge these differences, recognize them for what they are—potential bases for mutual exchange, or barriers to be taken down—and deal with them accordingly. What emerges from these scripts, then, is the model of an institution that welcomes all workers and their communities and can still promote the necessary unity among them.

The emphasis on community relations is heightened by the presence of central, nourishing female figures such as Binnie and Ma Simpson. These female leaders make two additional statements about the ideal vision of unions. First, as institutions emerging from the grass roots of working-class communities, working people's unions are to be led by members of these communities rather than by officials with no ties, either geographical or familial, to their constituencies. Second, the presence of female nurturers, who not only literally feed their community but also look after its shelter and emotional well-being, indicates that unions' concerns appropriately include more than workplace issues. Unions should involve themselves equally with their constituencies' needs for secure housing, sufficient food, and a satisfying personal and social life.

The contrast between Ma Simpson and the union organizer in the Southern Summer School skit *On the Picket Line* captures this vision's two key elements of vision of unionism: the person who leads the strikers is clearly the elder of the textile workers' community rather than the union organizer, who seems disoriented and is largely ignored, and this chosen leader offers food as well as wisdom regarding strike strategy. This vision of unionism and activism combined lived experience with desired goals. The creators and audiences of these productions no doubt were familiar with unions dominated by an absentee bureaucracy that prohibited admission of immigrants or African Americans and refused to organize unskilled workers. Conversely, they might have been affected by the organizing drives of the

Congress of Industrial Organizations in the mass production industries after 1935 and seen in industrial unionism a movement that not only organized the unskilled but welcomed immigrants and their American-born offspring, made special efforts to organize African Americans, and at the very least, did not bar women outright from participation. The authors and audiences of workers' plays might also have viewed CIO organizing as drawing on the strengths of workers' communities and existing institutions and fighting racism as well as workplace battles.

One can clearly read in the workers' plays of the 1930s a rejection of the exclusive, craft-based, bread-and-butter unionism of the American Federation of Labor and an embrace of CIO industrial unionism, which organized workers regardless of job classification and worked to build an inclusive, highly politicized labor movement. It would be a mistake, nonetheless, to interpret these scripts as unambiguous testaments of faith in the CIO. Rather, with these plays the workers' theatre movement served notice on new as well as existing unions that they should not become complacent about their constituencies' support. In their enthusiastic responses, workers' theatre audiences indicated quite clearly that they had little use for unions that could not meet their needs, both as workers and as members of families and communities.

*   *   *

Workers' theatre plays presented visions of optimism. By affirming the experiences and values of their audiences, the plays transformed the ordinariness of working people's everyday lives and struggles into the tangible possibility of successful collective action. The drawback to such a strategy, however, is that in valuing the lives and world views of the men and women they wanted to organize, workers' theatre groups also reinforced values and experiences that perpetuated the marginalization of certain groups of people. While working to weave an inclusive vision of labor activism, the plays were ultimately constrained by contemporary prejudices: women, white and black, were acknowledged as workers but remained tied to domestic and repro-

ductive realms; African Americans, male and female, were acknowledged as important participants in labor struggles but remained distinctly outside the communities of European Americans. The realism of the lives dramatized on the stage opened up the possibility
that audience members would see themselves as militant labor activists. At the same time, the close resemblance between performance and reality drew clear boundaries around the possibility for
change.

Like good organizers, the creators of labor plays started "where
they were at": instead of seeking to transform their audiences radi-
cally, the plays' producers echoed and affirmed working people's experiences and values. On one hand, this approach perpetuated limiting images of women as economic actors and marginalized people
of color—Latinos and Asian Americans are entirely absent from
these plays. On the other hand, the affirmation that radical social
change begins with the actions and gestures of everyday life gave
workers' theatre performances their edge, their excitement, and, ultimately, their power.

5. ACT II

Two Unions Take to the Stage

In the 1930s, new unions in previously unorganized industries and revitalized existing unions exemplified the kinds of unions that plays such as *Marching Song* called for: they organized across lines of craft, race, ethnicity, and gender, and they addressed members' concerns and needs far beyond the shopfloor. Unions offered housing, health care, and sick and death benefits and became schools and recreational centers for their members. Picnics, classes, sports leagues, and musical and theatrical activities were part of unions' efforts to build what Lizabeth Cohen calls a "culture of unity" among unionists. These activities brought together members and their families for entertainment, for education, and ultimately for developing the kind of solidarity necessary to sustain strong unions.[1]

The socials, classes, and performances that many began to associate with joining a union were also part of well-thought-out educational and organizing strategies that served the institutional needs of unions at the same time as they filled a certain space in the lives of members and their families. For union leaders, such educational and recreational activities could serve to advance their personal and political goals and the goals they set for the union. As a result, the myriad activites that constituted the so-called culture of unity within a union, far from being exclusively the site of rank-and-file consensus-building picnics and ball games, frequently became the grounds of contest between union leaders and union members. Theatrical productions—which combined the collective effort and performance involved in team sports, the entertainment of socials and picnics, and the more formal learning of classes in labor history and collective bargaining—were often at the center of union recreational and educational programs. Thus, an exploration of theatre is useful for illuminating how different constituencies within a union used the institution to advance their goals, both personal and political.

Not surprisingly, New York City, already a center of workers' theatre and of labor and left-wing activism, was also a center of union-sponsored theatre: union locals and internationals jumped on the bandwagon of workers' theatre and offered members labor dramatics classes, and members themselves formed their own workers' theatre groups. Among the countless unions that sponsored theatrical activities by and for their members, two in particular stand out in terms of the scope of their activities and their commitment to using theatre to promote unionism to their members and allies: Local 65 of the United Wholesale and Warehouse Employees and the International Ladies Garment Workers Union. Although no other union-sponsored production could match the visibility and professionalism of the ILG's Broadway hit *Pins and Needles,* Local 65's plays and musicals rapidly became the center of the social life organized by the union for its members and the focus of the entertainment that members provided one another in the union's spacious quarters. The plays and skits produced by Local 65 and the ILG's *Pins and Needles* brought members into contact with the workers' theatre movement and with members of other unions in the New York area—and in the case of *Pins and Needles,* union members around the country.

The ILG and Local 65 are interesting unions to study in tandem because, in the 1930s, they represented progressive unions at earlier and later stages of their institutional development. In the early 1930s, the ILG was coming out of a decade of fierce factional disputes marked by the decisive victory of social democrats over Communist insurgents. Beginning in the organizing campaigns of 1932 and 1933, the ILG solidified itself as a union dominated by a powerful bureaucracy and a powerful president.[2] Local 65, in contrast, owed its existence to Communist organizing in the 1930s and to the formation of the Congress of Industrial Organizations in 1935. While the ILG was fiercely anti-Communist, Local 65 was a "red union": the men—and women, after the mid-1930s—who held leadership positions were members of the Communist Party or sympathetic to it, and the union's political stands and coalition efforts closely followed CP lines.[3] Nevertheless, leaders of both unions held many of the same ideals: they saw themselves as heading democratic trade unions that were oriented toward the needs of the rank and file.

The ILG and Local 65 also appealed to similar constituencies. The young women and men who worked in the union shops, joined the ranks of their members, and participated in the union's theatrical activities had much in common with one another and, in fact, with the individuals who peopled the workers' theatre movement overall. They were young and in search of affordable entertainment; many were from upwardly mobile Jewish families and had had their ambitions of completing a college education dashed by the Great Depression. A significant number had preexisting interests in theatre.[4] Without these ambitious, educated young people, whose appetite for greasepaint was whetted by New York City's seductive theatre scene, neither union could have made dramatic activities so central to its social and recreational programs.

Parallels between ILG members and Local 65 members provide a control of sorts for looking at the place of theatrical activities and, more generally, educational and recreational activities in the life of unions. In bureaucratic, established unions as well as in younger, more militant unions, these activities expressed and furthered leaders' views of their union. In the more established unions, however, such programs also became terrains of contention between leaders and rank-and-filers, whereas in the younger unions, they served as a terrain of mutuality.

*   *   *

The International Ladies Garment Workers Union was founded in 1900 to represent the unskilled, mostly female, mostly immigrant garment workers ignored by the existing United Garment Workers of America. When union leaders saw that new recruits won during major strikes let their memberships lapse once contracts were signed, they turned to education as a means for ensuring garment workers' continued association with the union. Growing out of the Jewish socialist culture of New York's Lower East Side, the ILG modeled its activities on those of the Workmen's Circle and other social and political institutions that instilled in participants a socialist vision as well as pragmatic notions of how to achieve it.[5]

The ILG's militant Local 25, the shirtwaist makers' local, had provided leadership for the "Uprising of the 20,000," the massive strikes of garment workers in 1909 that had swelled the ranks of the union. Local 25 developed a wide array of programs that would be the benchmark of progressive unionism in the first decades of the century. Classes covered such subjects as history, literature, art, political theory, and parliamentary procedure. The local also sponsored lectures, concerts, and plays and in 1917 created a vacation center for its members at a rented house in the Pocono Mountains. In 1916, the union's General Executive Board, impressed with the achievements of Local 25's educational programs, voted to create a General Education Committee, mandated each local to appoint an education committee, and allocated funds to pay for educational programs in the locals and for a part-time education director for the international. Although these moves were intended by the male leadership of the union to restrain Local 25's militance and autonomy, they also committed the union as a whole to social and educational activities for members.[6] By the 1930s, these activities had become an integral part of the union, and when the strikes of 1932 and 1933 tripled the union's membership, the structure was already in place for meeting the social and welfare needs of the new recruits.

When David Dubinsky was appointed president of the union in 1932, he assumed the office with the strong belief that union members must be educated and their commitment to the union cultivated, and he took great pride in his union's pioneering efforts in the field of workers' education. Yet he also wanted to mark it with his own stamp. "Education without some salesmanship was not education. In my book, that meant showmanship," he later wrote. A mass pageant that he attended as part of an international Socialist congress in Vienna in 1931 was pivotal in developing his understanding of workers' programs:

> Thousands upon thousands of Austrian trade unionists took part. It was staged in a huge stadium, with at least a quarter million people watching. The whole thing was most impressive. I could not get it out of my mind—the mood it created of unity and hope, the friendship it built. . . . I kept wondering how we could do something like that pageant, for the ILG's great influx of new members, raw, green, inexperienced.[7]

This "influx of new members" was the problem that the ILG's Local 25 had faced in the 1910s and that Local 65 would face in a few years. The solution devised in each case was education broadly defined. What distinguished the ILG international's efforts from those of its Local 25 twenty years earlier and those of Local 65 a few years later was that David Dubinsky had at his disposal a history, an institutional structure, a significant budget, and numerous contacts in the world of workers' education. In 1934, he replaced Fannia Cohn, who had come out of Local 25 to head the union's educational programs in the 1920s, with Mark Starr, a veteran labor educator from Great Britain who had come to the United States to teach at Brookwood Labor College. Dubinsky asked Starr to hire Louis Schaffer, labor reporter for the *Jewish Daily Forward,* to head the recreational division, and the union soon embarked on the course that would lead to the musical revue *Pins and Needles,* which opened in a Broadway theatre owned by the ILG in 1938.[8]

Accounts of the process whereby Dubinsky's epiphany in Vienna was transformed into a hit on Broadway vary, but they leave no doubt that the project emanated from and reflected the objectives and priorities of a powerful leader.[9] As he presided over a growing union, Dubinsky, a man who would eventually play a central role in New York City politics, never lost track of the necessity of forging and sustaining members' loyalty to the institution.[10] He was also acutely aware of the importance of the union's public image. For David Dubinsky, *Pins and Needles* would address both sets of concerns.[11]

While Dubinsky was consolidating his control over the personnel and direction of his union's Education Department, Local 65 was establishing its existence as a union representing workers employed by New York City's numerous wholesalers. The union itself was born in September 1933 in the living room of Arthur Osman, who had invited several co-workers from the Lower East Side's wholesale and warehouse district to discuss the possibility of organizing a union. The United Wholesale and Warehouse Employees first affiliated with the United Hebrew Trades and in 1935 secured a charter as a federal local of the American Federation of Labor, the federation's mechanism for incorporating workers organized on an industry-wide basis rather than along craft lines. Existence within the craft-oriented AF of L was uncomfortable at best for the new local, which rapidly began establishing contact with other locals in comparable economic sectors. In 1937, the Wholesale Dry Goods Employees Federal Union left the AF of L, having absorbed a group of skilled wholesale workers earlier organized by the CP's Trade Union Unity League, AF of L shoe warehouse locals, and locals organized by the CIO's Textile Workers' Organizing Committee; it affiliated with the CIO as Local 65, United Retail and Wholesale Employees of America, with complete jurisdiction over all warehouse employees in New York City.[12]

Arthur Osman, who had been drafted into full-time service to the union in 1936, was elected president of the new union local. With the assistance of an activist membership and effective rank-and-file organizers, he expanded the union from a few hundred members to more than three thousand 1938. In a 1968 interview, Osman recalled, "From the day we became affiliated with the CIO, we started and were constantly involved in an organizing campaign. We were organizing actually the people that no one else wanted."[13]

Local 65 organized in shops that were quite similar to those organized by the ILG. Most employed fewer than thirty workers, though some had around one hundred. The nature of the work in these wholesale shops required very different union strategies from those of the ILG, however. A strike in a small wholesale shop would not have the same impact as a strike in a manufacturing concern: a wholesaler and his managers, who often had begun as unskilled workers in such shops, could, if pressed, take and fill orders, receive deliveries, prepare shipments, and keep accounts current. "Because of this lack of capacity to cripple our employer," recalled Osman, "we had to devise methods of involving not only our total membership, but all sorts of other people including the community. . . . In those early days, we discovered [that] for us to win with our limited power, we had to involve the whole community and many communities."[14] Strike strategy therefore included applying pressure to the employer through the sources and outlets for his merchandise and through his neighbors and church or synagogue.[15] Such tactics required that members be actively involved beyond routine picket duty, posing special challenges to the union.

Local 65 leaders, like ILG officials, wanted to make their union the center of members' social and recreational life. Local 65 activists would clearly have agreed with the ILG Education Department publication asserting that "union loyalty is strengthened when members have a good time within their union."[16] Where the ILG was satisfied with member "loyalty," however, Local 65 believed that organizing was every member's responsibility, and therefore programs for members were to develop in them not only loyalty to the union but the knowledge, confidence, and commitment necessary to organize other workers. Where the ILG had the resources to pay organizers and business agents, Local 65, in its early years, relied on rank-and-filers to organize and recruit new members and continued to do so even when it was able to pay organizers.

On March 14, 1938, Arthur Osman delivered his annual message to the General Executive Board of Local 65. The text of the address—intended to acquaint board members "with the situation in our local, in our International Union, in the labor movement generally, and to point out the forces of progress and reaction which influence and are influenced by the activities of our organization"—was reproduced in the pamphlet *Organizing Wholesale,* which was widely distributed among the membership. Reviewing Local 65's accomplishments and the challenges ahead, Osman articulated the union's vision of itself and its membership. Three interrelated themes emerge: the responsibility of each member to "be a good neighbor—organize the shop next door"; the need for leadership to come from the rank and file; and the imperative that all union educational and recreational activities in some way prepare members to be organizers and leaders.

Osman, the revered and well-liked president of his union until 1950, believed that "good leadership is rank and file leadership."[17] Such a statement was certainly not intended to invite challenges to his presidency or to the stands he took; nevertheless, he wanted to see rank-and-file members involved in every phase of the union's work. Indeed, Local 65 policies cultivated leadership skills among members by encouraging them to lead organizing efforts, by decentralizing responsibility for addressing grievances, and by promoting educational and cultural activities for members. "We can't separate the question of organization from the question of education," Osman wrote in *Organizing Wholesale*.[18] Education, in one form or another, must be part of every activity of the union, and the union must develop new ways of reaching members.

Education for activism was important for a young union in a previously "unorganized" industry. Not only were workers not in unions, but employers themselves had few trade associations. Until the post-war years, when, in response to encouragement from Local 65, wholesalers organized employers' associations with which Local 65 would bargain, contracts were won on an arduous, shop-by-shop basis, often involving strikes.[19] By the 1930s, the ILG and the garment industry, in contrast, had long abandoned this mode of labor relations. In an autobiographical account written after forty-four years as president of the ILG, David Dubinsky noted: "At the start, we were a union of strikes. It was rare that we didn't have at least one strike every six months." By the end of the 1920s, however, "we were sick and tired of these perpetual strikes, so we gradually moved to long-term agreements."[20] He and officials of the union's joint boards met with manufacturers and their associations to iron out working conditions for union members and signed contracts that lasted as long as five years.[21]

Industry-wide negotiations strengthened the hand of Dubinsky and his top officials; yet such negotiations also responded to the nature of garment manufacturing, a volatile industry marked by high levels of subcontracting, cut-throat competition, and runaway shops.[22] The ILG sought to build this idiosyncrasy of its industry into a source of power by encouraging cooperation among employers and between employers and the union. Beginning with the Protocol of Peace, which ended the cloakmakers' general strike of 1910 by setting up a system of arbitration and regulation administered jointly by employers and the ILG, the union pursued collective bargaining that privileged negotiations between upper-level union officials and representatives of manufacturers' organizations over rank-and-file action.[23]

The ILG's brand of union leadership and pattern of contract negotiations brought a stability to the garment industry that was salutary for both workers and employers.[24] Yet this approach to labor relations also left a deep mark on the union's internal functioning, which became increasingly bureaucratic and centralized during the 1930s. Indeed, as more decisions were made by the international office and by the organizers and staff members who answered directly to Dubinsky, militant local members were systematically excluded from organizing campaigns and contract negotiations. As a result, members often became disaffected, and in some cases, the ILG lost shops to other unions.[25]

As a large, established union with locals across the country, the ILG sponsored cultural and educational activities that inevitably took a different shape than in a younger and more localized union such as Local 65. David Dubinsky needed to cultivate the sympathies of manufacturers and wanted to present the public with an image of unions as orderly, rule-abiding institutions that ultimately had the same goals as those with whom they negotiated. According to one of his close associates, under Dubinsky, in all union programs for members "the emphasis [was] on sound public relations within the union and with the outside world."[26]

Dubinsky was well aware of the risks of his approach to collective bargaining. Like Osman, he knew that bureaucratic unionism led to restless, discontented, and alienated members. The remedies he preferred, however, focused on fostering members' goodwill toward the union rather than altering his way of doing business. The ILG's cultural and educational programs thus became a diversified public relations campaign designed to maintain the sympathy of the general public as well as members.

Local 65, in contrast, required more than goodwill from its members; for logistical reasons, it needed a commitment to struggle. Because it organized in small shops and in a wide range of occupations and businesses, such slogans as "Every Member an Organizer" and "Organize the Shop Next Door" had to be more than rhetoric if the union was to grow and maintain itself. Although rank-and-file activists remained a minority in the union, union activities had a different tone from the one set by a union president who believed that workers' education was in large part "showmanship."

When Louis Schaffer joined the staff of the ILG, he quickly expanded the union's recreational programs, giving special attention to dramatic activities. He called on friends and contacts in the theatre world to direct and write for union theatrical productions. Within a year of starting this job, Schaffer, a man described as having a sharp "sense of publicity," proposed to Dubinsky a theatrical venture to be supported by the labor movement as a whole. William Green, president of the American Federation of Labor, endorsed Labor Stage, Inc., as "the expression of labor's social aspirations and a channel of self-expression for the organized labor masses."[27] Support from other unions and from the fracturing AF of L, whose ranks were divided over the issue of industry-wide organizing, never materialized, however, and Labor Stage became exclusively an ILG enterprise and was absorbed into the union's Education Department. By that time, Schaffer had located a suitable theatre, signed an eight-year lease, and set its renovation plans into motion.[28]

The first full-scale play the ILG put on at Labor Stage was successful with audiences but left its producer dissatisfied. *Steel*, by John

Wexley, which dramatized union organizing efforts among steel-workers, coincided with and drew attention to a Steel Workers Organizing Committee campaign in western Pennsylvania. Nonetheless, Schaffer believed that what the public really wanted was "amusement and not class consciousness."[29] Labor Stage's next production would combine large amounts of the former with smaller amounts of the latter in a show that brought to the ILG the spectacle and publicity lying at the heart of David Dubinsky's and Louis Schaffer's vision of union cultural activities.[30]

Pins and Needles was in preparation and rehearsal for more than a year, but when it opened, the production bore the unmistakable mark of the union's leadership. *Pins and Needles* became the ILG's vehicle for promoting itself not only to the general public and the labor movement but also to sympathetic public officials and the business representatives with whom the ILG negotiated. The first official performance was open "only to those invited by President Dubinsky": officials and executive board members of the ILG's New York locals and joint boards.[31] After several performances for rank-and-file union members, Dubinsky, at Schaffer's urging, planned a gala evening for "the carriage trade, leaders in the association with which our union bargains collectively, the professionals and the professional knockers." Invitations were extended to New York mayor Fiorello La Guardia and the entire City Council as well as state supreme court judges and various commissioners. Among other invited guests were officials of the Amalgamated Clothing Workers of America (ACWA), the regional director of the CIO, and several labor journalists, but Dubinsky also invited members of the National Coat and Suit Industry Recovery Board (the body created jointly by the ILG and the manufacturers' association when the NIRA was judged unconstitutional and its recovery boards disbanded) and officials of the Affiliated Dress Manufacturers' Association, the American Cloak and Suit Manufacturers' Association, the Industrial Association of Juvenile Apparel Manufacturers, and similar bodies.[32]

Through *Pins and Needles* performances at Labor Stage and on its nationwide tours, the ILG marketed itself to audiences from all ranks of society and all points on the political spectrum. Indeed, participants in the production have observed that the show attracted significant numbers from among the so-called carriage trade and others who would not have been expected to show support for a labor union or workers' theatre. According to one cast member, the Dupont family reserved an entire row of seats for a show in Wilmington, Delaware. They arrived in full formal attire but left at intermission.[33]

Despite such rebuffs, Louis Schaffer and David Dubinsky must have been pleased with their efforts. *Pins and Needles* created a nationwide audience for unionism and gave the ILG a distinctive identity with a general public that remained skeptical, at best, about unions. The ILG scored its greatest public relations coup, however, when it received an invitation for a command performance at the White House on March 3, 1938.[34] With the presidential seal of approval, the union could be ensured of the sympathies of the wide swath of the American public that made Roosevelt one of the best-loved U.S. presidents.

The revue's success can be attributed to two factors: it was a musical in a decade when such productions were immensely popular with a depression-weary public; it also made shrewd use of a combination of professional theatre personnel behind the scenes and ordinary garment workers behind the footlights. When Schaffer decided to launch a production that would provide "amusement and not class consciousness," he hired an aspiring composer-lyricist, Harold J. Rome, as well as choreographers, writers, designers, and directors to give the appropriate Broadway flavor to the lives of garment workers and to contemporary issues. Like the Theatre Union, Labor Stage produced professional-quality theatre that was based on the lives of working people. Unlike the Theatre Union, however, which employed professional actors to play industrial workers, Schaffer hired the professionals necessary for transforming garment workers into actors playing garment workers. Schaffer and Dubinsky wanted a revue that had both the appeal and novelty of featuring members of the union and the production values of a Broadway show.

In the skits and plays produced by members of Local 65, in contrast, union members participated not only as performers but as writers, designers, and directors. Despite the fact that many of the 65ers who took part were aspiring performers, professionalism of the sort that characterized *Pins and Needles* seems to have been of little concern to them. From script to stage, Local 65 Dram Group shows were in-house productions, and audiences consisted mostly of union members and their friends. Like the ILG, Local 65 chose and shaped audiences that best met its current needs, but these audiences were vastly different from those cultivated by the ILG.

The choice of performance venues for these theatrical productions reflects each union's goals for its shows. The ILG invested in the small house in the Broadway theatre district—albeit on its periphery—and when the Princess Theatre could no longer accommodate the crowds wanting to see *Pins and Needles,* the union moved the show to a larger Broadway theatre with a bigger marquee. Judging by a photograph taken for the union, the men and women who gathered under the marquee before and after the show could have been attending any other Broadway production (see photograph).

When members of Local 65 took to the stage, however, the scene was unmistakably political. Some of the performances took place in auditoriums such as Webster Hall, where numerous left-wing lectures, meetings, and performances were held, including some by the Workers' Laboratory Theatre. More frequently, however, 65ers performed in their union building, which was central to the union's identity and its programs for members. The two buildings the union occupied over the course of its lifetime were located close to the center of the warehouse and dry goods district in lower Manhattan, and each had a spacious auditorium.[35] Within its own space Local 65 produced shows that spoke directly to members and their friends and reflected 65's militant unionism. The performers remained physically close to their audience, and their shows were set against the backdrop of union slogans and murals depicting Local 65 struggles (see photographs).

One slogan urged members, "Make The Union Your Second Home," and Arthur Osman later recalled, "Our union [engaged] in

The audience gathers for a performance of *Pins and Needles* at the Windsor Theatre on Broadway. *Labor-Management Documentation Center, Cornell University (© UNITE, ILGWU Collection).*

Members of Local 65 entertain friends and coworkers at the union hall. *Robert F. Wagner Labor Archives, New York University, District 65/UAW Collection, negatives 00612 and 01272.*

activities which made the union hall the center of social activity."[36]
As the Local 65 play *Sing While You Fight* illustrates, members came
there to work on the newspaper, to take classes, to participate in
meetings, and in general, to while away a few hours with other young
people.[37] On Saturday nights, the auditorium became a nightclub
where members danced to music performed by 65ers and enjoyed
the plays and skits of the Dram Group. Refreshments were served by
waiters paid union wages.[38]

Saturday Night Socials were a vital part of the union's organizing strategy, aimed equally at current and prospective members.
Here members and their friends developed political networks, friendships, and a positive feeling for their union. Organizers frequently
invited employees in shops being organized, introducing these workers to the benefits of joining the union and, at the same time, giving
a role to performers at the socials' plays and skits.

Henry Corden was an active member of the Dram Group from the
time his shop was organized into the union in the mid-1930s until
World War II, when he took a better-paying, defense-related job. He
subsequently went on to a long career in Hollywood. Corden credits
the union for giving him his first opportunities in show business, but
what was most important to him was that he was part of the union's organizing efforts. "The wonderful thing about being involved with Local 65," he later recalled, "is that we knew we mattered, that we were
directly as well as indirectly involved in getting new members, new
shops to join the union. . . . [When] they were trying to organize particular shops, they would have the people come down and socialize on
a Saturday night, and we would be there doing sketches."[39] Union
leadership reinforced the sense that performances were part and par-
cel of the organizing process. In 1940, after a long and expensive campaign, the union's newspaper *New Voices* printed the following headline: "Sears Workers See *Mikado* and Join Local 65."[40] The newspaper's
editor was no doubt enjoying some tongue-in-cheek humor, but he
was also applauding the work of union members in *Wholesale Mikado*,
one of 65's most successful productions.

The union also affirmed the value of Dram Group performances by incorporating them into its institutional rituals and celebrations. *Sing While You Fight,* for example, had its premiere at the 1941 installation meeting for new officers, attended by forty-five hundred members. Two years earlier, members at the installation meeting were treated to a dramatization of *Organizing Wholesale,* which highlighted the union's "past activities and experiences, its struggles and successes." At the end of the union's "7 in 7" membership drive (to bring seven thousand new members into the union in seven months), the new members were inducted at Madison Square Garden on January 13, 1942, in a program that featured a pageant depicting the union's history and accomplishments, performed by members of 65.[41] At these mass events, the union used theatrical productions by members to promote a certain vision of itself and of the role of rank-and-file members in its strength and effectiveness.

The ILG encouraged its members to attend *Pins and Needles* and even scheduled five o'clock performances for after work. When it sought a wider audience, however, it appealed to manufacturers, politicians, and the general public, groups it believed would support its approach to labor relations. When Local 65 looked beyond its own membership, it also sought audiences sympathetic to its model of unionism. Members of other "red unions" often attended Local 65 Saturday Night Socials, as did left-wing members of the ILG. Nettie Harary Shrog, a cast member of *Pins and Needles* who was also active in an opposition group within her ILG local, recalls mixing with 65ers and dancing at their socials.[42] Local 65's Dram Group also competed each year in the Trade Union Theatre Tournament sponsored by the CP-affiliated New Theatre League. Local 65's perennial competitor for top awards was another red union, the International Fur and Leather Workers Union.[43] The Dram Group played to a broader audience when it performed in 1940, along with other union groups, at the New York World Fair as part of the fair's recognition of organized labor.[44] Still, after such moments of fame and glamour, the Dram Group returned to its union hall and its performances for members, potential members, and friends, reinforcing a strong attachment to the union and its brand of militant unionism.

Copy

The theatrical productions of the International Ladies Garment Workers Union and of Local 65 reflected the institutional priorities and political outlooks of their respective unions. The ILG, intent on making a big splash among the diverse groups whose sympathies it courted, developed a professional revue that it produced in its own Broadway theatre. Local 65, dependent on the activism of its rank-and-filers and organizing on a shop-by-shop basis, brought workers in wholesale and shipping establishments to its building for entertainment put on by union members themselves. Nevertheless, the accounts of participants in *Pins and Needles* and in the productions of Local 65 are in many ways remarkably similar.

Participants from both groups felt great pride in representing unions and unionism and enjoyed performing for receptive audiences. They believed that through theatre, they had a particularly effective way of conveying the message of unionism. Participation in these theatrical ventures was a politicizing and even empowering experience.

Like many of the young people in workers' theatre, the ILG and Local 65 members who became involved in their union's theatrical productions had already developed an interest in theatre and performance. Jack Sorian of the ILG and 65's Pete Stein had taken part in plays produced at settlement houses, and the ILG's Nettie Harary Shrog performed regularly at events sponsored by and benefiting various left-wing causes. Milt Reverby of Local 65 was active in the Theatre Collective, an offshoot of the Workers' Laboratory Theatre, and Rose Morrison, also of Local 65, had worked with the New Theatre League.[45]

Other performers in the two unions were simply looking for a good time. Eugene Goldstein, for instance, was indifferent to theatre but was attracted to the perks of performing in *Pins and Needles*, especially a vacation at Unity House, the union's resort, where the cast rehearsed and first performed the show. Several members of the Dram Group and of the cast of *Pins and Needles* were already taking part in some other union activity and were looking to fill another evening. Irving Baldinger was working as a volunteer on Local 65's newspaper *New Voices* when he joined the group putting together the show *Wholesale Mikado,* and Olive Pearman Ashford had played on her local's basketball team before looking into Labor Stage.[46]

Whether or not these young people had prior theatrical interests or larger theatrical ambitions, what they found in being part of these productions was the camaraderie of peers engaged in a shared project. Like Lucy Kaye, who spent many hours commuting between her parents' home in Brooklyn and the Workers' Laboratory Theatre apartment in Manhattan, members of the ILG and of Local 65 were willing to dedicate themselves to long hours of rehearsals and meetings because of the opportunity to have a great time without spending too much money and to socialize with others like themselves. For these women and men, the union indeed became a second home and their closest friends were the people with whom they rehearsed and performed. "For the first time in my life I felt safe," says Henry Corden of his days with the Dram Group and Local 65. "It was a place I could go and it was just lovely. We all thought alike, we all smelled alike, we all dressed alike."[47]

In addition to creative outlets and camaraderie, members found in their union's theatrical productions a personal meaning for unionism. Dram Group productions and *Pins and Needles,* at the very least, raised members' awareness about the work of the union and their willingness to contribute to it, which was not a trivial accomplishment. Jack Sorian joined the union because he worked for a closed shop, but after he read about plans for Labor Stage in the union's newspaper, he went to the theatre as soon as it opened: "The paint wasn't even dry yet," he recalled fifty years later. He ended up performing in *Pins and Needles* for two years. He saw Labor Stage and *Pins and Needles* as "a cultural outlet for members, completely separate from union business," but his involvement in the show led to participation in other union activities, such as joining picket lines and attending rallies.

For other union members who were equally disinclined toward political activism, taking part in theatrical productions created opportunities to be active in the union in a way that felt appropriate and rewarding. Like Sorian, Local 65 member Larry Shepherd joined the union because his shop signed a union contract. He had little interest in or knowledge about the functioning of the union, but he liked to draw and soon began producing a comic strip for *New Voices* about the trials and tribulations of a hapless warehouse worker in an unorganized shop. This led to his working with members of the Dram Group to create the play *Curly,* based on his cartoons. Having a longstanding interest in theatre, he stayed in the group, realizing that theatre was also part of the union's work and that it gave him an opportunity to partake in organizing efforts: "I did my organizing through theatre," Shepherd matter-of-factly stated many years later.[48]

In addition to the long hours of rehearsal, these young people spent many hours together over soft drinks at nearby luncheonettes. In the highly charged atmosphere of New York City in the 1930s, discussions inevitably turned to politics. Several members of Local 65's Dram Group were in the Young Communist League, for instance, and invited others to join, though they did not ostracize those who turned them down.[49] Not surprisingly, given the overall tone of the ILG, the politics and activism of *Pins and Needles* cast members were more moderate; with exceptions such as Nettie Shrog, a rank-and-file activist in the dressmakers' local, and Al Schmidt, a rank-and-file organizer, most would not have identified themselves as politically active, though they certainly considered themselves "politically aware." As Eugene Goldstein said, "Everybody was politically aware. I don't think there was anybody who was nonpartisan."[50]

When *Pins and Needles* went on tour, the closeness among cast members and the working and living conditions they encountered around the country were politicizing, causing some to reexamine their relationship with the union leadership. Members had the opportunity to be active on behalf of groups outside the ILG, joining local picket lines and giving special performances for various political groups and causes, including a fundraiser for the Spanish loyalists sponsored by the American League against War and Fascism. "I don't think the union was too happy about that," noted Eugene Goldstein.[51] What the union was not happy about was the fact that its members were performing for an organization affiliated with the

Communist Party. For their part, Goldstein and others were angered by the union's efforts to control their activities outside the performances.

This confrontation was resolved by a mutually acceptable compromise: cast members had to state clearly that they were not performing as representatives of the ILG. But this incident proved to be only the opening skirmish in a series of clashes between the cast and union officials. Emotions soon rose on both sides with regard to the issue of racial segregation. When the cast arrived in Chicago, Olive Pearman and Dorothy Tucker, the two African American members, were sent to stay in a distant neighborhood. "I was mad as hell," said Al Schmidt, fifty years later, and he and others protested, but to no avail. In Denver, cast members were more successful: they staged an early sit-in a restaurant and insisted that everyone be served. They were eventually all seated, but in a back room.[52]

Many of the new recruits to the ILG in the 1930s were African Americans, and the union made special efforts to welcome them. But challenging racial discrimination was not part of the agenda for the *Pins and Needles* tour.[53] In Los Angeles, when several members of the cast wanted to go to the hotel manager to protest their segregated accommodations, the tour manager threatened to send home anyone who did such a thing. "They told us we were not out to change the world," says Goldstein.[54] The issue never disrupted the production, but it generated dissatisfaction with union leadership. "If a labor group isn't going to [challenge racism], who's going to do it?" asked Shrog.[55] The extent of the ILG's capitulation to dominant racist norms is evident in the extant publicity photographs of *Pins and Needles*. The two African American cast members do not appear in any of the union's photographs of the show. Olive Pearman Ashford has fond memories of the White House command performance but is absent from all existing photographs of the event. (see photograph).[56]

The final issue of contention between the cast and the producers of *Pins and Needles,* and the most acrimonious one, was the replacement of members of the union with "ringers." Although the show boasted performers who were, in the words of the opening

ILGWU president David Dubinsky (left) and President Franklin Delano Roosevelt (*right*) pose with selected members of the *Pins and Needles* cast following the command performance at the White House. *Labor-Management Documentation Center, Cornell University (© UNITE, ILGWU Collection).*

number, "everyday men and women who work hard for a living—we're from the shops," when Schaffer formed the second and third companies, and in the remaining two years of the show's run, he began to hire professional actors who joined the union or borrowed a union card in order to audition. For many ILG cast members, this confirmed suspicions that they had held all along: "We realized that the spontaneity and amateurishness of the show could only last so long. Sooner or later they would be putting in the better-looking and better-qualified people. It was inevitable," recalled Hy Gardiner.[57] Several members of the cast sued the union, and many more became disillusioned with an institution that they had believed in and that had given them unique opportunities.

Schaffer's high-handedness in casting professionals, the union's countenancing of racism directed at its own members, and the distance it put between itself and its cast members' political sympathies all tested the limits of David Dubinsky's conception of workers' cultural programs and workers' education as "showmanship." In his effort to cement the loyalty of ILG members as well as the goodwill of the general public, Dubinsky was willing to sacrifice the commitment and expectations of members who performed in *Pins and Needles*.

The fact that a project designed to cultivate sympathy and loyalty among members alienated some and reinforced the views of dissenters demonstrates the politically charged nature of cultural and recreational activities organized by a union for its members. The activities acquired different meanings for those organizing them and those participating in them, reflecting the gulf between the experiences and outlooks of union leaders on one hand and those of members on the other. Shrog no doubt spoke for many cast members when she said of the tour, fifty years later, "We felt like the ambassadors of unionism."[58] Nonetheless, these union members' view of unionism was at odds with that of their official leaders.

In Local 65, in contrast, the views of union leaders and of Dram Group members were far more compatible. Indeed, several key figures in the Dram Group also were or became key figures on the union staff: Rose Morrison, whose energy and spirit animated the Dram Group, was a receptionist for the union and later developed records and reports on its organizing campaigns; Milt Reverby and Sol Molovsky became paid organizers in the late 1930s; Irving Baldinger also became a paid organizer and later the managing editor of *New Voices;* and Pete Stein, originally assigned by the Works Progress Administration to work with Local 65 recreation programs, stayed on as an organizer and a staff member in the union's Recreation Department.[59]

These men (Rose Morrison left the union in the early 1940s) would all have long associations with Local 65. As young men in the union, they were active both as rank-and-filers and as part of an inner core of union leaders. We might speculate that the Dram Group was the recreational wing of the union's leadership, but the participation of these individuals in rank-and-file activities can also be seen as evidence of the union's youth: in age and in experience, leaders remained close to the membership at large. And theatre provided one avenue for maintaining close relations between rank-and-filers and union officers and staff.

The experiences of union members in *Pins and Needles* and in the theatrical productions of Local 65 demonstrate the influence of the institutional context and the enduring power of theatrical productions. Where *Pins and Needles* cast members ended up feeling betrayed by their union, Dram Group members grew more identified with their union. Both in both unions participation in theatrical productions seems to have made the members more militant and more activist. Although this tendency was congruous with Local 65's goals in sponsoring such activities, it clearly went against the grain of ILG policy and preferences.

*   *   *

The workers' theatre movement acted on the belief that theatre could transform the consciousness of audiences. At least one segment of this movement, theatre groups within unions, had its greatest impact on the performers rather than the audiences. Theatre produced in unions such as the ILG and Local 65 shared the didacticism and pro-labor politics of such groups as the Workers' Laboratory Theatre, and they provided for participants the same camaraderie and sense of shared purpose. Such experiences were a happy consequence of the activities of the Workers' Lab, but they were integral to the raison d'être of the Dram Group and *Pins and Needles*. It is undeniable that the outcome for participants was very similar, yet theatrical production and the sense of community among participants that it generated in union-sponsored groups cannot be separated from the inner dynamics of the unions sponsoring them.

If the workers' theatre movement gave unions a new tool for public relations, it also gave members new avenues into the life of the union. Through its theatrical productions, a union could cultivate the loyalty of its members while projecting a favorable image of itself to the public. These activities also put the union on display for its members, allowing them to observe and evaluate its functioning.

During the 1930s, the contest over the direction and meaning of union activities such as theatre remained undecided. Rank-and-file voices compelled the attention of union officials and drew strength from union-sponsored activities. The balance of power thtat existed in this decade would prove to be fragile and as these activities acquired more resources they sufferd a loss in autonomy and rank-and-file perspective.

6. INTERLUDE

Leisure and Popular Entertainment in Labor Plays

In the number "Social Significance," cast members of *Pins and Needles* urged:

> Sing me a song of social significance
> All other things are taboo.
> We want a ditty with heat in it,
> Appealing with feeling and meat in it.[1]

With this song, *Pins and Needles* articulated two related principles of workers' theatre: working-class people want amusement in their lives, but they want it to be relevant to their experiences and to the important issues of the day.

Workers' theatre served the needs of the labor movement by educating audiences about labor issues, applauding their militance, and promoting their loyalty to their unions. The skits and songs of the movement also developed a critique of popular entertainment expressed not only in lines and lyrics—"We're tired of moon songs / Of star and of June songs," sang the garment workers in *Pins and Needles*—but in the very genres that workers' theatre used to convey its various messages.[2]

Setting aside models of political theatre developed in the Soviet Union and Weimar Germany, workers' theatre artists in the United

States deliberately used the idioms and imagery of vaudeville, radio, Tin Pan Alley, and melodramatic morality play in productions that wove together union politics and mainstream entertainment.[3] Yet workers' theatre's relationship to popular entertainment was not an unambivalent one: workers' theatre wanted to position itself within the mainstream of American culture at the same time as it wanted to critique that mainstream.

"Americanism" was a vital concept on the left in the 1930s, as labor unions and the Communist Party—as well as their constituents, most of whom were sons and daughters of immigrants—sought to identify themselves as all-American.[4] Workers' theatre took great pains to forge for itself an American identity, but it used that identity to question and challenge the labor movement as well. Workers' theatre associated being American with enjoying popular entertainments and amusements. In doing so, it suggested that the labor movement needed to take seriously its constituents' desires for leisure and entertainment.

Using conventional genres of popular entertainment served several purposes in workers' theatre. It allowed political theatre to place itself within the mainstream of American popular entertainment, and it provided a language and body of images with which to put forward its own agenda for the labor movement. The use of well-known forms of performance also functioned like the representations of gender, ethnicity, and race in workers' plays: it created an appeal based on what was familiar to its audiences. Yet using dominant gender, ethnic, and racial ideologies ultimately limited the depth of workers' theatre's critique of social relations. Could workers' theatre stay radical in its cultural critique while using dominant cultural forms?

*   *   *

The women and men involved in workers' theatre were very much aware of the political theatre that had developed in the Soviet Union and Germany, and many drew their inspiration from that source, though they learned that American audiences expected other kinds of entertainment.[5] The Workers' Laboratory Theatre began in the early 1930s, for instance, by performing translations of pieces produced by the German-language theatre group Proletbuehne, and Workers' Lab productions such as *Tempo, Tempo* and *The Belt* borrowed techniques from German and Soviet political theatre.[6] After a few years, however, the group abandoned European styles and turned to what one of its key members called "native forms of entertainment."[7] The resounding failure of one of the most ambitious of the experiments with European political theatre, the Theatre Union's production of Bertold Brecht's *Mother,* clarifies the relationship between politics and culture as workers' theatre in the United States understood it.

Different participants in the production of *Mother* offered their own explanations for the show's dismal failure with audiences and critics alike. Brecht accused the Theatre Union of bastardizing his concept of Epic Theatre, which was to revolutionize theatre by appealing to audiences' reason rather than their emotions; the Theatre Union argued that the production's genre was unintelligible to the American public.[8] What neither saw clearly was that workers' theatre in the United States was far less concerned with creating new genres than with making existing genres accountable to the interests of their audiences. Where Brecht sought to reshape theatre as well as class politics, the American workers' theatre movement accepted the major premises and conventions of popular performance and used them to address issues of working-class power and politics.

The failure of this expensive experiment signaled to workers' theatre companies that they should remain close to the known and tested in popular entertainment rather than attempt to educate audiences in a new theatrical language. For the Theatre Union, whose plays were performed by numerous groups across the country with varying degrees of professionalism and skill, the genre of choice (from which *Mother* proved to be the only exception) was the melodrama. Melodrama derived its popularity from the use of common symbols of good and evil and its efforts to move spectators to share the pain, and therefore the determination, of characters on the stage. Moreover, by selecting melodrama, the Theatre Union placed itself within a long tradition of politically motivated popular theatre.

In the nineteenth century, reformers frequently delivered their message of conversion and enlightenment through melodramas that dramatized the impact of slavery or intemperance on the innocent and the vulnerable. Strike plays updated the technique to address the evils of capitalism and racism. With their clearly identifiable good guys (workers and their allies) and bad guys (bosses, sheriffs, and bankers), these plays rallied spectators to the struggle for higher wages and better working conditions.[9]

In *Stevedore*, for instance, the black dockworkers and the white organizer are unmistakably heroes, and the members of the existing all-white dockworkers' union are unmistakably villains. In *Marching Song*, Inspector Hamilton Feiler, "chief of the red squad," is described as "a big lumbering man. He chews an unlighted cigar." Warren Winkle, owner of the building that used to house a factory and now houses unemployed workers and families, is also clearly villainous: "His face shows dissipation, good nature, lack of guile; but his eyes are shrewd. His paunchy body is well massaged and in the pink of condition."[10] Adding to the industrialist's aura of evil is the fact that he is accompanied by his secretary, with whom he exchanges a long kiss when he thinks no one is watching.

If the enemies of the working class are portrayed as self-satisfied, threatening, and corrupt, working-class leaders are characterized by their commitment to their community, their integrity, and a certain dose of vulnerability. Bill Anderson, the union organizer in *Marching Song*, is "a middle-aged worker, awkward, small of stature. His movements are those of a man whose body has been concentrated for many years on a single arduous mechanical operation. . . . He is both embarrassed and transfigured by this new intensity of purpose."[11] Anderson is tortured to death by Feiler and his henchmen and becomes a martyr to the cause. His energy in life and his memory in death spur the workers of Brimmerton to solidarity, militance, and a general strike.

Waiting for Lefty, one of the most performed strike plays of the 1930s, also includes a melodramatic cast of characters: Harry Fatt, the cigar-chewing "labor fakir" who opposes the strike; Agate, the committed militant; and, of course, Lefty Costello, who never appears on stage because, while the committee is debating whether or not to strike, he is found murdered, presumably by opponents of the strike. The vignettes, which constitute most of the play and explain how individual committee members became taxi drivers and militant unionists, also present good men faced with moral dilemmas and, true to melodramatic form, risking their livelihood to choose good over evil.

Ironically, when Clifford Odets himself discussed the play, he compared it to a minstrel show.[12] Scholars have interpreted *Waiting for Lefty* as the last gasp of Soviet-inspired "agit-prop" and the first flicker of Socialist realism, but Odets himself was much closer to the pulse of workers' theatre: his play conveyed its messages in a genre that was a staple of American popular entertainment.[13] Despite the elements of melodrama, agit-prop, and Socialist realism in *Waiting for Lefty,* its minstrel-show structure—"chorus, end men, specialty men, interlocutor," as Odets described it[14]—made it much more similar to other short forms, such as the variety show, that had a long tradition in American entertainment.

The variety show, in which specialty acts and short sketches follow each other in rapid succession, was far more widespread in workers' theatre than the melodrama. However popular with their vociferously enthusiastic audiences the Theatre Union's strike melodramas were, they required more resources than workers' theatre groups, whether independent or associated with schools or unions, usually had at their disposal. As John Gassner—dubbed by the right-wing *New York Herald Tribune* "the best left-wing dramatic critic in America"—noted, "it was more economical" to produce short pieces than a full-length play, especially in a young movement.[15]

Making a virtue out of necessity, workers' theatre sought forms of performance that could be adapted with limited time and resources for sets, costumes, and rehearsals. Like the minstrel show

Odets had in mind while writing *Waiting for Lefty,* the variety show and the musical revue could easily be mounted as series of acts. Once it realized that the abstract agit-prop pieces adopted from the Proletbuehne were not reaching the audiences it sought, the Workers' Laboratory Theatre began producing programs composed of selections of songs, skits, and puppet shows.[16]

Producers of workers' theatre were highly self-conscious of borrowing from mainstream culture: when Brookwood Labor College began sending out troupes to perform in mining towns, mill villages, and urban workers' communities in the early 1930s, it called its productions the Labor Chautauqua. The chautauqua movement, which began in the early twentieth century, was a largely middle-class reformist effort to educate and uplift the public. By taking the name "chautauqua" and modifying it with "labor," Brookwood critiqued conventional chautauqua programs, at the same time using the name to attract audiences. Conventional chautauquas, Brookwood implied, were remiss for not addressing the needs and interests of working people; the name "chautauqua," however, drew audiences aware of the educational and recreational value of such shows.

Brookwood's Labor Chautauqua program was usually made up of a series of "acts" alternating with songs. One 1934 chautauqua opened with three songs from the songbook that was sold to audience members, followed by an introduction to the school and the troupe, a short play about relief programs, more songs, a mass recitation, songs, a ventriloquist, a performance by an a capella quartet, another play, more songs, a third play, and a closing song.[17] Chautauqua programs also included puppet shows and other variety acts. This format of ten to twelve fast-moving numbers allowed performers to make changes in response to specific requests or feedback on their programs, just as other traveling shows did.[18]

Labor-oriented theatre continually prodded mainstream culture, taking it to task for not dealing with the concerns of working-class Americans. The tone of Brookwood's traveling performances was quite tame, however, in comparison with that of others in the workers' theatre movement. Where Brookwood accepted the chautauqua largely on its own terms of providing educational entertainment and entertaining education, workers' theatre frequently went much further in its critique of mainstream entertainment and subjected popular culture to merciless parody. Ironically, though, at the same time as it expressed its most stinging indictment of popular amusements, workers' theatre also placed itself squarely within an established tradition of American popular entertainment.

Parody and self-parody lay at the heart of popular performance genres in the late nineteenth and early twentieth centuries. Nineteenth-century burlesque played on and inverted gender conventions of theatre as well as of society more generally; vaudeville skits simultaneously mocked and sympathized with the immigrants that appeared in stereotypes in its shows; and Tin Pan Alley songs tried to outdo each other in wittiness while drawing attention to their own preciousness.[19] Within this context, workers' theatre easily maintained a love-hate relationship with popular entertainment. On one hand, the workers' theatre movement blamed American popular entertainment for a variety of ills, the greatest of which was distraction of working people from their own interests.[20] On the other hand, leaders of the movement called on its writers and directors to use popular genres in developing shows for working-class audiences.

The Workers' Laboratory Theatre production *World Fair* epitomizes this dialectical relationship between politics and popular entertainment. The WLT's most elaborate mobile production, *World Fair* was developed in the summer of 1933, the year of the Chicago World Fair. It transformed this carnival of American boosterism into a stinging critique of New Deal politicians and skewered such fairs and circuses for preying on the public's gullibility. At the same time, however, *World Fair* based its own appeal on the popularity of circuses and tent shows themselves.[21]

The inaugural performance of *World Fair* took place at a picnic for the Communist Party's *Daily Worker* at Pleasant Bay Park in the Bronx on July 30. As the picnickers entered the park, they were greeted by the boom of a big brass band. When they followed the direction of the noise, the first thing they saw was a large tent, a clown, "a freakishly dressed person in a college cap, and general barkers, all ballyhooing for the show inside, 'Only ten cents, the Greatest Show on Earth.'" Once inside, spectators were treated to a "Rogues' Gallery" of New Dealers; the "House of Culture," against a backdrop depicting Rockefeller Center; the "House of Morgan," featuring "the speculators, bulls, bears and jackasses buying, selling and shouting"; and finally, the "House of Agriculture," represented by "The Song of the Landowners and the Bankers" (to the tune of "Old MacDonald had a Farm"). Powerful leaders in business and politics were, the show intimated, no different from the cheap entertainers at fairs and amusement parks.

As a piece of political entertainment, the WLT's *World Fair* operated at three levels. First, the form itself announced to audiences that they would find the same kind of amusement here as at the Chicago World Fair. Second, the genre provided familiar images to convey the WLT's views of various political leaders. Finally, and most important, in presenting its own World Fair, the WLT attacked the Chicago exposition for obscuring the important issues of the day. Where the fair in Chicago was billed as celebrating "A Century of Progress," the WLT's announced a "Capitalist Century of Progress."

In contrast with the Labor Chautauqua's largely implicit critique of its mainstream counterpart, *World Fair* took explicit aim at the Chicago World Fair: the show was a direct response to the injustices the Workers' Lab saw embodied in the Chicago exposition. Yet the WLT's *World Fair* functioned like Brookwood's Labor Chautauqua. Just as the Labor Chautauqua highlighted the absence of labor from conventional chautauquas, the WLT's *World Fair* drew attention to the absence of workers and their perspectives from the Chicago World Fair. Albeit more pointedly than the Labor Chautauqua, the WLT's *World Fair* demanded redress not only in political and economic realms but in the realm of amusement as well.

The need for entertainment oriented toward working-class Americans was a central concern of workers' theatre, regardless of the other political agendas it promoted; and workers' theatre consistently expressed this need by placing itself within the main currents of American culture. Using popular culture to advance a cultural critique was a risky proposition, however, even when the critique was as moderate as that of the ILG. *Pins and Needles* represents both the greatest accomplishments of the variety show and theatrical parody adapted to the politics of labor-oriented theatre and the pitfalls of working too closely within accepted modes of popular entertainment. The effort to use entertainment idioms with which audiences were familiar opened the possibility that workers' theatre would be caught within the conventions of those genres, unable to differentiate itself from the culture that it was critiquing and thus unable to make its critique heard. In *Pins and Needles*, we see most clearly how workers' theatre could lampoon the upper class and ridicule the state in clever parodies of popular genres without causing the least discomfort to the targets of its barbs.

The show elaborated on both the performances of earlier workers' theatre troupes and the mainstream revue format, which, like WLT productions and the Labor Chautauqua, combined parodies of popular shows and current events with song-and-dance numbers.[22] *Pins and Needles* highlighted the lives and loves of garment workers, using contemporary popular culture to comment on current social and political developments. The number "Mussolini Handicap" mocked the Italian dictator's domestic policies by comparing them to games of chance. In a reference to the popular Irish Sweepstakes of the 1930s, the song introduces the winners of "the greatest contest of its kind in the history of the world—the All-Italy Maternity Sweepstakes": "Winner of the Sardinian Marathon Endurance . . . In sixteen years, nineteen bouncing bambinoes!"[23]

Another number, "We'd Rather Be Right," borrowed its title from the Rodgers and Hart revue *I'd Rather Be Right* and its music from the dance tunes of the 1920s and 1930s. The piece features three 100 percent Americans discussing ways to carry out their campaign to "make America bigoted and better." Their theme song begins with the lines: "If you find you can't reply to your / Opponents, why don't [you] try to / Call them Un-American."[24]

The revue *I'd Rather Be Right* belongs to a musical genre that was a mainstay of the musical theatre and vaudeville in the early twentieth century. Writing for the current season rather than for posterity, songwriters filled their works with references to politics, fashion, inventions, sports figures, social scandals, newspaper headlines, and the latest fads.[25] The musical revue was thus ideally suited to workers' theatre, which was entertainment with an explicit political message.

Satire and social commentary were so deeply ingrained in popular entertainment, however, that labor-oriented theatre ran the risk that their audiences would be inured to the combination of entertainment and political critique. Political theatre has frequently been accused of sacrificing audiences' amusement to their "indoctrination" or to "propaganda," but *Pins and Needles* ended up losing much of its political bite in its efforts to entertain. Indeed, as journalist Heywood Broun commented in his review of the show, "while stout ladies in ermine must realize that they are being kidded, few if any have rushed screaming into the night."[26] Although *Pins and Needles* sparred with contemporary culture, then, politics ended up bowing to entertainment: in gaining the ability to amuse many while offending few, *Pins and Needles* lost the ability to deliver a clear and sharp critique. Indeed, the revue highlights the difficulties faced by workers' theatre when it tried to identify itself simultaneously as inside and outside mainstream American culture.

To a large extent, though, the nonthreatening nature of *Pins and Needles* reflected the ILG's own centrist politics. The more militant Local 65 produced shows that mirrored its left-wing politics, demonstrating that it was possible to preserve an activist edge while donning the comfortable garb of popular entertainment. Local 65's preferred genre was the musical comedy, a form of popular culture that could provide clear models for working-class action.

The musical comedy, developed in the 1880s and perfected in the first three decades of this century by George M. Cohan and Jerome Kern, told a story about ordinary Americans using vernacular music and dance. The musical revue, in contrast, derived its entertainment value from elaborate production numbers and satirical sketches with no story line.[27] When the musical comedy moved onto the silver screen in the late 1920s, it adopted the extravagant productions of the musical revue but followed the lives of distinct characters, often young working women whose livelihood depended on the success of their show.[28]

Local 65's *Wholesale Mikado* and *Sing While You Fight* could not offer lavish production numbers, but they told stories in song of earnest young people whose financial security hinged on their ability to secure a union contract. In *Curly,* the shy, pushed-around office clerk is accompanied in his transformation to militant unionist by a chorus of workers promising, "Anything your heart desires will come to you" when you join the union. Like Hollywood, Local 65 offered escape from grim reality and visions of hope for those with little in their pockets. For 65ers, however, happiness came not from making a hit show or marrying a millionaire but from joining the union: "Join up Local 65, your dreams will come true," pledged one of the songs from *Curly.* And while the Golddiggers of 1933 sang, "We're in the money," leaving audiences to imagine its source, for members of 65, riches came from union membership:

> The skies will be sunny,
> We'll make more money
> In the drive of '65.[29]

The benefits of unionism were not exclusively monetary, however. Curly makes a whole new set of friends, and in *Sing While You Fight,* the two main characters find meaningful recreational activities and, ultimately, love. Jean and Bill, who meet at the union hall, are each involved in different union activities—Jean in the union's newspaper, Bill on athletic teams—but they find each other again at a Saturday Night Social where Bill sings "I Met My Love at the Social Hall." In joining the union, working people could thus find gratifying leisure activities and, in the process, romantic bliss.

Sing While You Fight makes explicit some of the strategic assumptions of workers' theatre and the labor movement of the 1930s, as well as the reality of working-class identity in those years. The labor movement was composed of young people who had grown up with commercial entertainment and its promises of sensual gratification and amusement.[30] They did not check these aspirations at the door when they entered the union hall. The women and men who produced workers' theatre shaped a labor movement that provided space where young working people like themselves could find fulfillment of their personal, emotional needs along with gratification of their material needs for adequate wages and safe working conditions.

*   *   *

Like any political movement, the workers' theatre movement was faced from the outset with strategic choices regarding its appeal to its intended audiences. Very early on, it rejected the experimentalism of European political theatre in favor of more "home-grown" genres. Was this an effective political choice? Did the use of conventional genres of popular entertainment in workers' theatre open more possibilities than it closed? Certainly such a strategy made it easier to place leisure and entertainment on the agenda of the labor movement. A romantic musical revue such as *Sing While You Fight* makes it clear that recreational activity in a union context supports young people's involvement. Similarly, stock characters and nursery songs in *World Fair* made accessible to audiences the WLT's global critique of American culture and politics. In contrast, *Pins and Needles* succeeded far beyond Dubinsky's most grandiose vision because audience members who should have felt targeted by the revue's numbers seem not to have felt in the least bit offended: after all, it was good-natured entertainment in a long-standing American tradition.

On balance it would appear, then, to be a toss-up: in some cases American popular entertainment styles, images, and motifs allowed workers' theatre to communicate a social and political critique, and in other cases the strategy dulled the critique. Yet a look at the organizations that produced *Sing While You Fight, World Fair,* and *Pins and Needles,* respectively, suggests that the impact of the genre on the political message of a theatrical production is not random. Nor can one conclude, in the end, that adopting certain performance idioms significantly shaped the politics of the critique: the Workers' Lab and Local 65 were grass-roots, self-consciously left-wing, CP-identified organizations that used American popular culture to support their politics; the ILG studiously avoided any radical associations and used the musical revue to prove its mainstream commitments. In adopting the guise of American popular entertainment, the workers' theatre movement made a compelling case for the proposition that it is possible, and indeed crucial, to sing while you fight. What you fight for, however, remains distinct from how you sing about it.

7. ACT III

Workers' Theatre Becomes
Union Recreation

Nineteen thirty-seven witnessed stunning events in the history of the labor movement in the United States: the sit-down strike in the General Motors plants in Flint, Michigan, resulted in a dramatic victory for the year-old United Auto Workers Union, and "Big Steel," the largest steel producers, signed contracts with the Steel Workers' Organizing Committee. Yet in the same year, the recalcitrant "Little Steel" manufacturers locked striking steelworkers out of their plants, leaving them victims to the brutality of an openly pro-business police force, an event remembered as the Memorial Day Massacre. Organized labor won decisive victories, but unionized workers continued to face obstinate and powerful opponents.[1]

The year was equally noteworthy for developments in the workers' theatre movement: the Theatre Union produced one of its most successful melodramas, *Marching Song,* but ongoing financial difficulties forced the group to disband. Brookwood Labor College entered into negotiations with the rapidly growing UAW to cosponsor a workers' educational institution in Detroit, but before long, Brookwood also had to face financial facts: it could no longer afford to stay open, despite all the efforts of teachers, students, and administrators. Finally, the magazine *New Theatre,* the official organ of the workers' theatre movement, launched a new, more technically oriented periodical, *Theatre Workshop,* but had to cease regular publication.

In that same year, however, a new player in the theatre scene was mounting what would be one of its most daring and successful productions: the New York City unit of the Federal Theatre Project premiered its Living Newspaper, *One Third of a Nation,* in August at Vassar College. When the production later opened for an extended run on Broadway, working people in large numbers went with their union locals to see this dramatic exposé of the dangerous and disease-ridden housing that New York City's poor and working classes had endured for more than one hundred years.

The New Deal's Federal Theatre Project was a curious extension of the workers' theatre movement. Contemporary observers and later scholars view the FTP as belonging to the same movement as the Workers' Laboratory Theatre, the Theatre Union, and the ILG of *Pins and Needles* but, at the same time, as moving workers' theatre in the direction of more professional, better-funded productions. The Federal Theatre Project also transformed the workers' theatre movement almost beyond recognition: the FTP's greater resources made the existence of smaller, independent groups even more difficult and hastened the demise of many, at least in New York City; by providing material assistance to dramatic programs sponsored by unions, the FTP also accelerated the institutionalization of workers' theatre within the structures of individual labor unions.

By the late 1940s, workers' theatre was no longer the terrain of activists who promoted unionism and challenged unions to be more inclusive and responsive to the needs of their members. It had become part of the institutional apparatus through which unions provided services to members—including recreation—while officials and staff conducted all the business of the union. Workers' theatre thus continued to exist, but its earlier militance and critical edge were now blunted by its bureaucratic patrons. The Federal Theatre Project played a pivotal role in this mutation: it kept alive interest in theatre among union members, but it also cleared the field of smaller, independent players and reinforced the identification of workers' theatre as an activity of union education and recreation rather than a vehicle for politicizing and motivating audiences.

*   *   *

At the founding convention of the United Automobile Workers of America, two men who had studied at Brookwood Labor College, Merlin Bishop and Roy Reuther, persuaded leaders of the new union to propose a resolution to fund education at both the international and local levels. The convention voted to require that a fixed amount of each member's dues be allocated to educational activities. Bishop, who was appointed the union's first education director, went right to work organizing classes, distributing relevant literature to locals, forming sports teams and musical groups, and encouraging the development of dramatic activities, because, as he put it, "labor dramatics are a fundamental part of any workers' education program." He arranged for the Detroit Contemporary Players to perform a series of skits for sit-down strikers in Flint and used his Brookwood contacts to ensure that the college's Labor Players, in what was to be their last annual tour, would perform in cities that had UAW locals.[2]

Brookwood Labor College played a key role in the early work of Bishop with the UAW. Not only had Brookwood provided him with the training necessary for serving as education director of a new union poised for dramatic growth, but the school had offered to assist the UAW's educational work by paying half his salary. In exchange, the school would have a voice in hiring the director and would receive assistance from the UAW, which funded scholarships for its members to attend Brookwood.[3] This arrangement was short-lived, however, and although the union offered scholarships for a summer session at Brookwood in 1937, such assistance was not enough to sustain the school. By the mid-1930s, the network of progressive labor activists that had supported Brookwood had dissolved, its members pursuing their goals through left-wing political parties and the newly formed CIO. The latter also began developing its own educational and recreational programs and cut back its financial assistance to the school.[4] Thus some of the new unions started taking over the functions performed by Brookwood Labor College, including the production of workers' theatre.

This phenomenon occurred in revitalized existing unions as well as in newly formed ones. In 1940, for instance, the Department of Cultural Activities of the Amalgamated Clothing Workers of America published a glossy booklet, *Amalgamated Cultural Activities 1940,* publicizing its programs for members. Among the activities it highlighted were "theatricals," noting that "dramatics in the Amalgamated go all the way from simple one-acts to three act plays and operettas."[5]

Cultural activities were not new to the Amalgamated in the late 1930s. Born in the same ethnic and occupational milieu as the ILG, the ACWA had a long-standing commitment to its members' education. In 1920, six years after its founding, the union established an Education Department that sponsored classes and organized lectures. These activities flagged in the second half of the 1920s but picked up again with the surge in union membership after 1934. Union locals and joint boards organized their own programs throughout the period, but in 1938, the ACWA international office created the Department of Cultural Affairs, which, in addition to holding conferences on workers' education and cultural activities, provided resources and coordinated educational and cultural activities for the union as a whole.[6] Following the pattern of the ILG, when organizing successes swelled the ranks of Amalgamated members and the union's coffers, union leaders committed new resources to educating members about unionism and promoting their loyalty to the union.

Beginning in the mid-1930s, workers' theatre became increasingly identified with unions. These institutions now had the resources and the constituencies to support it, and they were also backed by various federal programs: through the New Deal's Works Progress Administration (WPA), the federal government strived to find work for unemployed artists and educators as well as laborers and technicians; many were put to work in unions.[7] The Federal Theatre Project in particular reconfigured the workers' theatre movement. It created new avenues of professional development for the women and men who had struggled for years with groups such as the

Workers' Laboratory Theatre and the Theatre Union, and it provided resources for unions wanting to produce theatre by and for their members.

The FTP, like its parent agency, the Works Progress Administration, was intended first and foremost to put Americans back to work. Accordingly, the Federal Theatre created employment for the legions of theatre people put out of work by the Great Depression: writers, directors, designers, choreographers, and performers of all sorts. In the vision of its dynamic director, Hallie Flanagan, however, the FTP would not only create jobs for those artists but revitalize live performance and bring theatre to new audiences around the country. "Was it not our function to extend the boundaries of theatre-going, to create a vigorous new audience, to make the theatre of value to more people?" asked Flanagan in *Arena,* her memoir of the years she spent as national director of the FTP.[8] To achieve these ambitious goals, the Federal Theatre Project cultivated a wide variety of theatre and performance genres: it produced Shakespeare and the Greek classics as well as vaudeville and puppet and circus shows, and promoted the work of new playwrights and experimentation in theatrical production. Through its National Service Bureau and its Community Drama Units, it worked as well to integrate theatrical production into the life of communities and their institutions.

Participants in workers' theatre groups of the early 1930s point to the FTP as responsible, in part, for the decline of their movement. "To put it sharply," stated Michael Blankfort in an interview in 1977, "the Federal Theatre killed the Theatre Union because we couldn't compete. The Federal Theatre was federally subsidized. We had to go out and raise money for every production."[9] Members of the Theatre Union, Blankfort among them, had been devoting themselves for four years to a project that was never far from financial collapse. The end, suggests Blankfort, came as a relief, especially since many members found employment in the FTP.

For members of the Workers' Laboratory Theatre, the appeal of the new government relief agency was irresistible. After years of a hand-to-mouth existence performing on picket lines and at political rallies, the actors jumped at the opportunity to earn a regular pay-check, and the troupe was absorbed wholesale into the Federal Theatre Project as the One-Act Experimental Play Unit.[10] The One-Act Unit disbanded after one program, but, according to Jay Williams—himself a WLT member under his given name, Harold Jacobson, and later an actor in FTP productions—Workers' Lab members "dispersed through the New York Federal Theatre Project, their names turning up frequently in connection with various productions" as actors, stage managers, directors, and one costume designer.[11]

As Blankfort's and Williams's comments indicate, the workers' theatre movement provided the Federal Theatre with an experienced pool of theatrical personnel eligible for FTP jobs.[12] Groups such as the WLT and the Theatre Union also provided Hallie Flanagan with much of the vision that guided her work in the Federal Theatre. In 1931, Flanagan herself had brought workers' theatre to the attention of the mainstream theatre world through the *Theatre Arts Monthly* article, "A Theatre Is Born," where she praised groups such as the Workers' Lab for their ambition, vitality, and inventiveness.[13] Their work inspired her, as director of the Vassar Experimental Theatre, to produce at least one play each year that focused "on some aspect of the present." In 1932, the play was *Can You Hear Their Voices?* which she wrote with her student, Ellen Clifford, and which was well received on the left as well as among mainstream audiences.[14] This dramatization of the plight of tenant farmers (based on a story in *New Masses* by Whittaker Chambers) was subsequently performed by numerous workers' theatre groups.

While FTP director, Flanagan frequently reminded critics and supporters alike of the value of creating theatre that addressed the central concerns of audiences' lives and made contemporary society and politics intelligible. In a talk to the staff of the Living Newspaper *One Third of a Nation,* Flanagan emphasized the potency of theatre and of the FTP in particular: "By a stroke unprecedented in dramatic history, we have been given a chance to help change America at a time when twenty million unemployed Americans proved it needed changing. And the theatre, when it is any good, can change things."[15]

The FTP undoubtedly presented stiff competition to small, local workers' theatre groups, but it also continued the work begun by groups such as the Workers' Laboratory Theatre and the Theatre Union. As Jay Williams put it,

> The Federal Theatre contained all the areas of the experimental and social theatre, and managed to solve nearly all the problems connected with them which had stymied all the independent groups that preceded it. About all that was left out was straightforward agit-prop, which had been abandoned by most of the workers' theaters anyway.[16]

Indeed, many plays produced by the Federal Theatre Project had first been performed by workers' theatre groups such as the Theatre Union or were written by playwrights who had honed their skills in writing for the workers' theatre movement. The Theatre Union's *Stevedore,* for instance, was performed by the Seattle unit of the FTP, and *Let Freedom Ring,* which had toured through textile towns in the Northeast after its Theatre Union run, was produced by the FTP in Detroit. Michael Gold and Michael Blankfort's defense of John Brown and indictment of racism, *Battle Hymn,* was presented to audiences in New York and San Francisco.[17]

The Federal Theatre Project thus benefited significantly from the accomplishments of the workers' theatre movement, but it also contributed to the movement by sustaining unions' interest in theatre. The FTP courted organized labor for the audiences it could deliver, for in truth, the Federal Theatre needed the audiences of workers' theatre as much as it needed its scripts and artists. According to Ethel Aaron Hauser, who worked in the New York unit's promotion staff, "we had to go out and get our audiences because, first of all, [WPA administrators] were checking on how many people were coming into the theatre."[18] The FTP's public relations strategy ensured that large numbers of those people were members of unions.

The FTP, as a federally funded works program, could justify its existence on the basis of the numbers of Americans it took off relief rolls, but with critics questioning the use of federal funds to support theatre, the project had to be certain both that it produced what audiences wanted to see and that it filled the seats. The FTP therefore hired unemployed publicists and press agents to market the project's productions to different segments of the public.[19] Among the specific groups recruited to attend performances were members of labor unions, who were targeted through reduced ticket prices for theatre parties and an information campaign.

In New York, the Federal Theatre assigned special staff to attract union members, and the New York unit's Promotion Department included a staff member "in charge of all contacts and sales in the labor union field."[20] The New York unit's Information Department also had a staff member, Irvin Curtis, specifically assigned to the Labor and Fraternal Division. Curtis worked assiduously to place ads in the labor press, to encourage those publications to review FTP shows, and otherwise to give exposure to the Federal Theatre. In 1939, he was in contact with approximately one hundred twenty-five papers, with a combined circulation of more than one million, including the *Transport Bulletin, Fraternal Outlook* (organ of the International Workers' Order), the *New Leader* (organ of the League for Industrial Democracy), the *UOPWA News* (of the United Office and Professional Workers), the *Building Trades Press,* and the *Trade Union Courier.*[21]

Curtis and his colleagues were quite successful in bringing groups of union members to Federal Theatre productions. From July 1, 1936, to June 30, 1937, the FTP in New York sold eighty-one theatre parties to unions, for a total of almost sixty thousand tickets. The project sold another thirty-three parties to unions for *One Third of a Nation,* which ran in New York City from January through October 1938. As a result, members of unions such as the ILG, the United Electrical Workers, and several teachers' union locals had the opportunity to attend a play that vividly brought attention to their living conditions.[22] In cities where the Federal Theatre Project did not employ a permanent staff, it developed other strategies for attracting audiences of union members. In Detroit, for instance, the FTP cosponsored the production of *Let Freedom Ring* with the UAW, which provided its members free tickets to the show.[23]

FTP's outreach to unions helped fill seats in order to convince lawmakers and the public that there was a demand for its productions, and it also addressed Hallie Flanagan's desire to "extend the boundaries of theatre-going." When UAW members saw *Let Freedom Ring* in Detroit, theatregoing became a union activity, an outing that identified unionism with theatre. Going to an FTP play could also pique union members' interest in theatre production, especially when the show highlighted issues close to their experiences.

Members of the United Office and Professional Workers of America (UOPWA), for instance, were among the numerous trade unionists who attended *One Third of a Nation* in 1938. The union also had an active theatre group sponsored by its New York Joint Council. In March 1939, the UOPWA Players produced its own skit about recruiting union members, and later that year, the group announced that it was available to "liven up your meetings with short skits." "Tell us your problems," they urged in the union's Joint Council's newsletter, "so that we can dramatize them."[24] *One Third of a Nation* seems to have confirmed for members of the UOPWA that their experiences and problems could be put on the stage. Largely because of this model, their union provided resources for their own theatrical productions, and performance and playwriting became ongoing components of the union's educational programs for members.[25]

As a source of inspiration, FTP productions such as *One Third of a Nation* replaced the strike plays after the demise of the Theatre Union. Where union members in previous years had attended *Stevedore* or *Marching Song*, they now attended FTP productions and came back to their unions energized to put on their own shows about their specific struggles. The FTP promoted theatrical activity in unions by other means as well. In New York City, the FTP's Community Drama Unit sent theatre professionals to work with union locals on their productions, and unions across the country could turn to the play lists produced and distributed by the FTP's National Service Bureau.

The FTP's Community Drama Unit was established to provide "expert guidance to social centers and other community organizations in the development of dramatic interests." The drama directors dispatched by the FTP were instructed to promote this goal by various

means—including organizing theatre parties to Federal Theatre productions—but their main job was to direct shows produced by the organizations in which they were working.[26] Community drama directors worked with churches, synagogues, settlement houses, and
schools, in addition to the ILG's Labor Stage and many other unions,
including Local 65, the Transport Workers' Union, the Bookkeepers
and Stenographers' Union, the National Maritime Union, and the International Fur and Leather Workers Union.

By the time the FTP was sending out community drama directors, the Workers' Laboratory Theatre and its successor, the Theatre
of Action, were long gone, and members of the Theatre Union were
concluding that they could no longer shoulder the financial burdens
of producing theatre. Although a director paid by the FTP could
have alleviated some of those burdens and extended the life of the
Theatre Union by reducing production costs, independent theatre
groups do not appear to have received any assistance from the FTP.
By its choice of beneficiaries, the federal agency indicated the desire
to draw clear lines between professional and nonprofessional theatre: professional theatre artists with appropriate credentials and experience were to perform under the auspices of the FTP, while ordinary men and women could indulge their interest in theatre
through productions sponsored by a variety of community institutions with the assistance of the FTP. Such community productions
would, in turn, generate new audiences for the Federal Theatre's
own productions. Professional but noncommercial theatre groups,
and performing groups that did not abide by the conventions of professional production, were left to fend for themselves, competing
against the FTP on one hand and commercial theatre on the other.
Thus theatre groups in unions, which presumably had no professional aspirations and presented no competition to the FTP's own
productions, benefited handsomely while the Theatre Union had to
cease functioning.[27]

When Milton Luban of the FTP's Community Drama Unit first
started working with the furriers in the summer of 1938, they already
had an existing theatre group, and Luban found "considerable tal-

ent among them." A "red union," the Furriers' Union had been active in the New Theatre League, and "several well-known playwrights interested in trade union theatre [were] writing special scripts for the organization," among them Albert Maltz of the Theatre Union. Their first production under Luban's direction, however, was *Waiting for Lefty,* produced in June. That fall, the furriers produced a one-act play about the Spanish Civil War, which received "several curtain calls." Earle Farnsworth, the Community Drama Unit supervisor, reported much improvement in the performers. He noted in his weekly report of October 1 that Luban "has been drilling each member individually to bring about good diction and to correct for accents. Also he has used pantomime and improvisation to develop some imagination and technique."[28]

Such professional assistance no doubt helped aspiring actors in the Furriers' Union, who continued to produce their own shows long after Luban's departure. In 1941, the union was still active in theatre, competing in the New Theatre League's Trade Union Theatre Tournament.[29] Although the furriers had not waited for the FTP in order to embark on theatrical ventures, the services provided by the agency undoubtedly strengthened their commitment to theatrical production and made it one more program the union could offer members.

New York City unions no doubt benefited disproportionately from the FTP, since the New York unit was the project's largest, and the FTP does not seem to have operated any Community Drama Units elsewhere. Outside New York City, the project's support for theatrical production in unions was more indirect and operated largely through its National Service Bureau (NSB). In addition to keeping records on FTP productions and coordinating various resources, this division catalogued hundreds of plays, listing for each one the number of parts, a summary of the action, specific property requirements, and a brief note on the level of skill and resources needed for a successful production. The NSB published, among others, lists of antiwar plays, new plays, ethnic plays, and labor plays, including full-length works such as *Stevedore* and *Let Freedom Ring* and skits such as Fannia Cohn's *All for One.*[30] When Julia Bristol of the United Auto Workers' Ford Organizing Committee contacted the National Service Bureau about producing a play for a UAW organizing campaign, for example, the bureau sent her its list of labor plays. Later it sent her the script for the play the committee had selected, Howard Koch's *The Lonely Man,* in which Abraham Lincoln is reincarnated as a law professor defending the rights of union organizers in a Kentucky mining town.[31] The services of the Federal Theatre Project cultivated interest in theatre among union members and strengthened unions by expanding their capacity for providing educational, cultural, and recreational programs for their members. The FTP thus helped make workers' theatre part of institutional unionism in a period when new recruits were expanding union membership rolls, and it provided as well the cultural resources for growing union bureaucracies.

Other divisions of the Works Progress Administration assisted the FTP, most notably the Professional and Service Project and the Workers' Education Service, both of which employed teachers to work in labor unions.[32] In its efforts to put Americans back to work, the WPA looked to the various institutions around which people constructed their lives and pursued education and recreation. Because WPA programs were prohibited from competing with established institutions—in this case public education and commercial entertainment, among others—the numerous voluntary organizations that shape the American social landscape became sources of WPA employment. As a result, unions and other community organizations were able to expand their activities and diversify their programs.

In Philadelphia, for instance, WPA programs played a pivotal role in the life of the Joint Board of the ACWA. The Philadelphia Education and Recreation Division of the WPA paid instructors for union-sponsored courses in public speaking, English, and citizenship (for immigrants seeking naturalization) and a discussion group on current events. When the Joint Board opened its building's new wing, the entertainment at the celebration included a musical comedy, the debuts of the Amalgamated Chorus and the Amalgamated Band, and a performance by "adorable children tap dancers," all sons and daughters of ACWA members. The WPA had provided the drama coach, the chorus director, and the "Dancing Instructress." In addition, ACWA members, officials, and friends were treated to a performance of the "Federal Theatre's eight-act vaudeville."[33] Although the Amalgamated committed some of its own resources to its members' leisure-time pursuits in Philadelphia, Nora Piore, the education director hired by the ACWA Joint Board in 1937, could not have developed as extensive a program without the assistance of education and cultural staff paid by an outside agency.

Government funding for union members' activities proved to be short-lived, however. Congressional support for federally funded jobs had never been unanimous, and the election of more Republicans to Congress in 1938 made many of President Franklin Roosevelt's relief programs even more vulnerable than before. The Federal Theatre Project was especially irksome to right-wing critics because of the "socially significant" plays it produced, the perceived large number of left-wing artists on its rolls, and its work with unions, settlement houses, and other political groups.[34] The vote on June 30, 1939, to terminate the Federal Theatre Project, a bald expression of growing anti-red sentiment, sent a clear message about reordered priorities in federal spending. Other WPA programs were allowed to survive into the early 1940s, but they faced consecutive rounds of budget cuts. By this time, however, the approach of war had begun to transform unions' concerns and, consequently, the programs they sought for their members.

In December 1942, Harry Minturn, former director of the Chicago unit of the FTP, suddenly became very popular among UAW local education directors in the Detroit area. Minturn was just finishing a stint working with soldiers at Camp Custer under the auspices of the WPA War Services Division, which had absorbed what remained of the drastically diminished Workers' Education Service.[35] UAW education staff requested that Minturn be assigned to their union locals to develop a musical revue on war-related issues for members of the United Auto Workers employed at the bomber plants and Ford plants producing war material. As Frank Marquart, education director for Local 600, told the WPA, a musical show "centered in war work themes and shown at mass meetings would greatly bolster morale of over 100,000 Ford workers in this locality."[36] According to WPA correspondence, Minturn was indeed assigned to work with UAW locals in the Detroit area for about a week and a half.

Autoworkers' morale certainly needed bolstering in 1942, as overtime work, crowded housing, and racial tensions added to the general uncertainty about the war. Wartime conditions exacerbated tensions among autoworkers as well as conflict between members and leaders. White autoworkers, squeezed like all autoworkers by rising inflation and unfair corporate labor practices, frequently reacted with violence against black workers taking advantage of new job opportunities in war plants and moving into their neighborhoods and housing complexes.[37] At the same time, UAW members who felt that, as workers, they bore a disproportionate burden of wartime exigencies challenged the union's no-strike pledge and other policies with wildcat strikes.[38] Such actions would grow into a forceful wave of rank-and-file defiance of the policies of an increasingly distant and bureaucratic leadership.

It is therefore not surprising that UAW education directors, charged with promoting members' understanding of unionism and commitment to their union, would seek upbeat entertainment for their members. Whereas musicals organized by rank-and-filers in Local 65 highlighted militance and activism, UAW staff more likely envisaged a show that would defuse members' criticism of union officials along with dissatisfaction with working and living conditions. In seeking to bring Harry Minturn to Detroit, union staff were concerned about the well-being not just of union members but of the union, which was ill-equipped and ill-disposed to respond positively to rank-and-file challenges.

Like the UAW, unions across the country were reorienting member activities toward the war effort and away from potentially more controversial issues. When the ILGWU announced that further performances of *Pins and Needles* would be postponed indefinitely, the headline in the union's newspaper read, "No Time for Songs of Social Change." The article explained that the show was closing be-

cause "social significance is just a little out of date right now."[39] Of
more pressing concern was the war in Europe: "It's up to us to assist
those who fight Hitlerism," urged another article a few weeks later.
One of the ILG's efforts for the troops was a canteen for servicemen
operated by the union's Women's Service Brigade in the Labor Stage
building, which had formerly housed performances of *Pins and Needles* with its "songs of social significance."[40]

A couple of months later, Local 65 opened its own "65" Canteen
for Servicemen, where soldiers enjoyed entertainment provided by
members, along with refreshments, Ping-Pong, and pool.[41] The canteen was only one piece of a much broader program of educational
and recreational activities oriented toward the war: the union opened
its Saturday Night Socials to soldiers, and like ILG members, 65ers
took classes related to civilian defense, raised funds for the war effort, and generally worked to maintain the morale of union members
and their families.[42]

The Dram Group continued to perform skits and short plays, but
these now turned audiences' attention to struggles against Hitler
rather than struggles against employers. In June 1942, the "Drammers" adopted the slogan "20 Grand Slams Against Hitler" to publicize their plan "to write TWENTY new victory skits and sketches, with no
group having less than TWENTY people. . . . Each of the three groups
will appear before TWENTY THOUSAND people, members of the Union
and other organizations. Everyone in these audiences will be enlisted
in the drive to smash Hitler and the Axis." Among the pieces produced
were *What's Your Price?* a skit publicizing the drive for twenty thousand
pints of donated blood, and *This Aryan Spirit,* an anti-Nazi satire.[43]

Without trivializing the deep concern that unionists felt for their
union brothers fighting overseas and for the victims of Nazism, it is
important to note that the shift away from a focus on the union itself
facilitated the shift in union cultural and social activities away from
union politics and toward more conventional entertainment. Once
the Canteen for Servicemen unhooked the union's cultural and dramatic activities from explicit questions about activism and organizing,
the culture of the union, it would appear, was largely depoliticized.

When Local 65 moved into its new building in 1944, it inaugurated its Club 65 in the building's tenth-floor lounge; facilities included a Ping-Pong table, a juke box, and a bar serving alcoholic
beverages, sodas, sandwiches, and snacks. Club 65, which was in operation every night of the week, became the new site for the union's
Saturday Night Socials.[44] Local 65 continued valiantly to host these
affairs into the 1950s, encouraging members to participate as entertainers and as revelers. But they were no longer the politicized, energetic events of earlier years. They offered members amusement
and diversion in what was becoming an increasingly hostile cold war
environment.

The decline and eventual disappearance of theatrical activity at
Local 65 paralleled the general decline of workers' theatre in the
1940s. The spring of 1942 was the first in four years that the Dram
Group did not compete in a New Theatre League tournament. The
New Theatre League had rapidly felt the effects of the FTP's competition but had continued to send directors into the field and to
sponsor trade union theatre tournaments. The league sporadically
published a journal, now called *New Theatre and Film,* but by 1940, it
was reduced to a mimeographed newsletter that appeared only a few
more times. By 1941, the organization was in the hands of a few
committed followers who were rapidly losing steam. When the New
Theatre School closed in 1942, the organization went out of existence altogether.[45] A few independent troupes continued to use theatre skits to explore social issues and to summon audiences to action,
and several labor schools remained open, offering dramatics as part
of their curriculum. But these were now largely isolated occurrences,
with little bringing them together: no national organization, no publication, and only a few of the personal ties that had formed the warp
and weft of the workers' theatre movement.

After 1940, what remained of the workers' theatre movement
had become one of the many activities sponsored by unions for their
members. The independent groups that had produced theatre with
the explicit purpose of building a militant labor movement had dis-
integrated under pressures from many directions. The stresses of col-

laborative work with the chronic problem of insufficient funds took their cumulative toll at the same time as an improved economy and federal programs such as the FTP held the promise of more adequately remunerated work. Meanwhile, pro-union New Deal federal legislation and well-coordinated industrywide labor organizing campaigns were bearing fruit in the new and expanded unions that took over some of the functions of independent workers' theatre groups.

The disintegration of the workers' theatre movement was also part of the larger decline of left-wing cultural activity at the end of the 1930s. The red-baiting that shut down the Federal Theatre Project also weakened left-wing organizations and activists, and the antiwar position that the Communist Party adopted after Hitler and Stalin signed the Non-Aggression Pact in 1939 alienated many artists and intellectuals from the party.[46] Finally, the demands of the war itself left little time or personnel for planning, organizing, and producing the concerts, expositions, performances, and sports events that had made up the cultural life of the left in the 1930s: many joined the armed forces, and others were employed full-time and overtime in war-production plants.[47]

Opportunities for audiences of working people to see their experiences validated and their militance affirmed on the stage all but disappeared. Though one might argue that, for a while at least, real-life labor victories replaced staged ones, working people and labor activists continued to need positive representations of themselves and their struggles, especially when union officials, bound by a wartime no-strike pledge, severely rebuked rank-and-filers' wildcat strikes, and public support for unions, which had never been strong, began eroding during and immediately after the war.[48] With the end of a diverse and wide-ranging workers' theatre movement and of federally sponsored labor plays, images that reflected and affirmed the experiences of working people were now available almost exclusively to those fortunate enough to belong to unions that supported members' efforts to create their own views of themselves.[49]

In the postwar years, the creation of such images on the stage, even within unions, became rare. After the closing of Labor Stage, the

ILG's Cultural Department was folded back into the Education Department, which showed little interest in dramatic production. Like other union education departments, the ILG's focused largely on "tool" courses—training in union procedures for union officials—and its Recreation Department concentrated almost entirely on sports. In the UAW, educational programs became platforms for promoting union policy rather than arenas for exploring social issues.[50]

For a brief moment in 1947, the UAW had the opportunity to restore workers' theatre to its programs for members, but this new venture into labor theatre made little long-term impact on the union. Union Theatre, a project of the University of Michigan Labor Extension Service, sought to reignite interest in workers' theatre in the UAW and other unions by producing plays for union locals and encouraging members to mount their own productions. When the Labor Extension Service was shut down—a victim of red-baiting and of a major General Motors Corporation initiative against it—the Detroit Union Theatre was supported by the UAW Recreation and Education Department and several other Detroit unions and continued to exist for at least two years.[51] Although this lifespan is noteworthy for a workers' theatre group in the late 1940s, the Detroit Union Theatre left few traces of its existence.

Throughout the 1940s and 1950s, Local 65 (renamed District 65 in 1950) worked assiduously to continue activities for members, including theatre, all the while fending off threats from both right and left. As the cold war attacks on labor intensified, Local 65, with its legacy of Communist leadership, was particularly vulnerable. The late 1940s and early 1950s witnessed internal dissent over whether or not to sign the non-Communist affidavits mandated by the Taft-Hartley Act, as well as efforts to create effective structures for working with other left-wing unions. In 1950, Local 65 merged with the left-led locals that had seceded from the parent union, Retail, Wholesale and Department Store Union, to form the Distributive Workers' Union, which later that year merged with two other left-wing unions to form the Distributive, Processing and Office Workers of America. Local 65, now District 65, remained in the leadership of the new union. In the same period, key leaders faced grand jury investigations on charges of subversion under the Smith Act and, in 1953, were questioned in hearings before the House Committee on Un-American Activities.[52]

Nevertheless, Club 65 continued to thrive. For members, it offered opportunities for inexpensive socializing among friends and co-workers, and for union officials, such activity held out the hope that a unified and satisfied rank and file could see the union through the most difficult of times. Union members even returned to the stage when an off-Broadway theatre company, the Greenwich Mews, helped them prepare performances for union meetings and trained them in theatrical production techniques. But this collaboration ended when the union claimed that it needed the space the theatre group had been using for its rehearsals.[53]

The Detroit Union Theatre and District 65's collaboration with the Greenwich Mews were among the handful of projects seeking to sustain a left-wing, labor-oriented culture in the 1950s. Nettie Shrog, who had been in the cast of *Pins and Needles,* and Arthur Vogel, who had performed with the Workers' Laboratory Theatre and co-authored the one full-length play it had produced, worked with a group called Stage for Action, which served as a clearinghouse for left-wing performers and organizers seeking politically oriented entertainment.[54] Given the fiercely anti-radical climate of those years, it is hardly surprising such a venture soon faded away.

More successful than left-wing theatrical endeavors was the folk-song movement of the 1940s and 1950s, which maintained itself through the efforts of an active core of singers and songwriters associated with People's Song, Inc., an equivalent of the New Theatre League. Earl Robinson, a key player in the Workers' Laboratory Theatre who had originally come to New York to study music at Juilliard, transferred the energy and inspiration he had given the Workers' Lab to the folk-song movement and worked to keep alive a left-wing culture during the bleakest of years.[55]

But efforts such as Stage for Action and People's Song were isolated incidents, no longer anchored to the kind of movement that had flourished in the 1930s, inspiring workers' theatre ventures within unions and linking them to a broader context of labor-oriented theatrical and cultural activity. Without such links to a broader subculture or to the audiences nurtured in that subculture, those men and women interested in pursuing workers' theatre had little support. When leaders of District 65 stated that they could no longer provide room for the Greenwich Mews, workers' theatre at Local 65 came to an end.

*   *   *

The history of workers' theatre in the 1940s is the history of a movement that became institutionalized. Having blossomed largely in local, grassroots enterprises, workers' theatre was adopted by unions to serve their own purposes, with the assistance of a nationwide federal agency, the Federal Theatre Project. In the process, workers' theatre became tamed, especially as World War II shifted union leaders' attention away from domestic and internal union politics toward events abroad. No longer a megaphone for militant activists, workers' theatre—what remained of it—became part of the portfolio of "services" that union bureaucrats offered members in exchange for their dues. And eventually theatre would disappear from the agenda of union cultural and educational directors altogether.

For a few years, unions supported workers' theatre after independent groups ran out of steam and were supplanted by the Federal Theatre Project. But this shelter had no commitment to workers' theatre beyond what it offered as a program for members. When unions no longer felt the need for the kind of activity represented by theatre, they discontinued it, putting an end to a rich and lively chapter in the history of labor-oriented theatre in the United States. The next chapter in this history would open only when new social movements created a political and cultural environment in which such theatre could once again find a role and a voice.

8. EPILOGUE

Can Workers' Theatre Survive the Decline of the Labor Movement?

"What is the legacy?" asked Perry Bruskin of the workers' theatre movement of the 1930s, six decades later.[1] In the early 1990s, Bruskin, a veteran of the Workers' Laboratory Theatre, began a documentary film to preserve the work and spirit of a theatre group that had profoundly shaped both his life and the varied and dispersed efforts to make theatre a weapon in the political struggles of the depression decade. For Bruskin, who has had a successful career as a theatre producer, the answer to the question of legacy lies in the professional mainstream theatre, where the social commentary of such plays as *Waiting for Lefty* and *Stevedore* lives on in recent Broadway productions such as the *Kentucky Cycle* and Tony Kushner's *Angels in America*. But for the labor historian interested in unions and organizing campaigns, the search for the legacy of workers' theatre must also encompass the "alternative theatre" movement of the 1960s and 1970s and the resurgence since then of theatre produced by and for working people and union members. Ironically, the search for a legacy leads back to the 1930s themselves, as women and men producing labor-oriented theatre in the last twenty years have turned to that decade for answers to their own questions.

Most immediately, the workers' theatre movement of the 1930s lived on in the dwindling dramatic productions of unions in the 1940s and 1950s and, more generally, in their cultural and educational programs. Workers' theatre as an insurgent movement, challenging participants to new understandings of their lives and of collective action, and as a means of political education within the labor movement, however, lives on in the theatre projects that emerged inside and outside unions beginning in the mid-1970s. Forty and fifty years after Perry Bruskin and his friends lived the belief in theatre as a weapon, a new generation of labor activists and activist theatre artists discovered theatre as a means of working toward their political goals. Here the legacy of the workers' theatre movement of the 1930s is clear, not only in the thematic and stylistic continuity that exists between the 1930s and the 1980s but in the self-consciousness of contemporary labor-oriented theatre artists vis-à-vis their models in the 1930s. For while they are addressing today's audiences and today's issues—including racism, sexism, and imperialism— they are looking over their shoulders to the golden age of workers' theatre: the 1930s.

*   *   *

When workers' theatre grew into a movement of its own in the 1930s, it was part of the period's distinctive political culture of the left. Forty years later, when theatre once again became visible in the labor movement, it was also part of a distinctive political culture, one based on the cultural activism of the social movements of the 1960s and 1970s. As many have observed, the political and youth movements of the 1960s were remarkably "theatrical," as activists consciously "staged" rallies and demonstrations for greatest visual and dramatic impact.[2] This theatricality was literal as well as figurative: in cities across the country, street theatre groups became part of actions calling for an end to the war in Vietnam and satirizing government repression of the New Left.[3] In this fertile political and cultural environment, troupes such as the San Francisco Mime Troupe (SFMT) and El Teatro Campesino combined performance and activism, on the belief that theatre had the power to educate and mobilize audiences for action. These troupes would serve as models and inspiration of a new generation of political theatre and, eventually, labor-oriented theatre.

The Mime Troupe (pronounced "Meem Troupe" by those in the know), the oldest and longest-lived of the political theatre troupes to blossom in the 1960s, began in 1959 with highly improvisational pieces performed in parks and on street corners. In such venues, the Mime Troupe lampooned U.S. involvement in Vietnam, conventional gender roles, the CIA, and local politics.[4]

R. G. Davis, the founder and guiding spirit of the SFMT in its early years, came to political theatre from a background of dance, mime, and theatre. In his account of the origins of the mime troupe, he noted that the greatest influence on his artistic development was the French mime Etienne Decroux, with whom he studied in Paris for six months in 1957.[5] Nevertheless, the Mime Troupe's understanding of culture and politics echoes much of the 1930s workers' theatre critique of mainstream theatre: "Our commitment is to change, not art; we have tried to cut through the aristocratic, lifeless and commercial notion of what culture is and make theatre in content and style a fresh, entertaining and radical force of change in America today."[6]

In the anti-statist, anti-imperialist politics of the New Left, the Mime Troupe's work struck a powerful chord, inspiring numerous other theatrical ventures, among them El Teatro Campesino, which was originally organized around labor issues. The troupe's founder, Luis Valdez, had performed with the SFMT and in the mid-1960s became involved with the grape-pickers' strike and the fledgling United Farm Workers of America (UFW). Valdez recruited strikers to develop sketches that were performed on picket lines and at rallies and union meetings, and the young Teatro Campesino became the cultural arm of the UFW, carrying into Chicano communities the tradition of workers' theatre. Despite its origins in a union movement, El Teatro Campesino rapidly became oriented more specifically toward Chicano culture and concerns, drawing on traditional Chicano performance genres and idioms.[7]

Neither of these troupes focused significantly on labor-related issues or identified themselves directly with union campaigns. Nonetheless, in numerous indirect ways they paved the way for the eventual rebirth of labor-oriented theatre in the 1970s by maintaining a visibility for political theatre and serving as models for emerging groups around the country. Although the political climate has dramatically changed in the three decades since the two groups were founded, both continue to perform in the 1990s around the United States and Europe, reminding audiences of theatre's power to express often-silenced political viewpoints and reinvigorating their proponents.

The work of long-lived troupes such as these two and of the more ephemeral ones that emerged beginning in the 1960s became known to participants and scholars alike as "people's theatre," or, in the words of one practitioner, "theatre for the 98 percent"—since, according to Maxine Klein, only 2 percent of all Americans attend "establishment theatre."[8] Not only did such theatre consciously align itself with grassroots political movements and actions, but, like the workers' theatre of the 1930s, it rejected what it saw as the shallowness, commercialism, and high cost of mainstream theatre.

With political and cultural sensibilities rooted in the rallies, demonstrations, and ideals of the antiwar and student movements of the 1960s, "people's theatres" addressed issues of class, race, gender, sexual preference, militarism, and violence. According to Klein, artistic director of Little Flags Theatre Collective, these groups shared "a common positive-action-thrust, a non-authoritarian working dynamic and a utilitarian goal. It is not commerce or corporate power but people's views that speak most persuasively to and through them."[9] Characteristic of people's theatre were the several dozen groups that convened at The Gathering, in St. Peter, Minnesota, in the summer of 1981. For one week, more than six hundred "people's culture workers" performed their work for one another and discussed their movement. There were clowns, mimes, and melodrama; feminist theatres, Chicano theatres, and the Travelling Jewish Theatre; theatres for inner-city youth and a theatre by and for the disabled.[10]

Douglas Paterson, founder of the Dakota Theatre Caravan in

South Dakota and of the graduate program in people's theatre at the University of Nebraska-Omaha, tried to define the movement that this gathering represented. For all their variety in style and thematic and ethnic focus, these groups, he noted, shared a consciousness about their theatrical work as part of larger social, political, and cultural struggles, and "a desire to align with the audience, not attack, insult, accuse, or condescend to them, or profit off them."[11]

The concept of theatre produced for "the people" rather than the elite goes back to late-nineteenth-century France and Germany, and many practitioners and observers of 1930s workers' theatre saw in it the beginnings of a similar people's theatre in the United States.[12] The characteristics defining people's theatre groups in the 1970s largely describe workers' theatre groups of the 1930s as well, but the theatre represented by The Gathering reflected and grew out of the social movements and counterculture of the 1960s. In the two and a half decades since the turbulent spring of 1968, many artists and activists have continued to emphasize the political nature of their work and the importance of creating a culture that reflects the lives and experiences not only of the privileged but of the marginalized and disenfranchised as well.[13]

"Arts activism" has engaged artists and their audiences in anti-nuclear campaigns, anti-intervention actions, anti-apartheid demonstrations, and organizing efforts across local issues in cities across the country. Yet interest in the arts among "progressive" artists and activists goes beyond their usefulness in advancing particular political goals. Art and culture have themselves been identified as terrains of contention in the struggle for "cultural democracy," in which "each voice contributes to building culture, and each of us takes a role in cultural debate and decision making."[14]

In 1976, cultural activists sharing such views formed the Neighborhood Art Program's National Organizing Committee (NAP-NOC), later renamed Alliance for Cultural Democracy (ACD) to establish the networks necessary to expand and promote their work. Reflecting the emphasis that black nationalist and Chicano movements, among others, placed on highlighting the distinctive values, histories, and traditions of nondominant cultural groups in American society, the ACD affirms that "culture is an inalienable right, and that political and economic democracy cannot exist without cultural democracy—the right of all peoples to create and preserve their own culture."[15]

Unlike much of the New Left activism of the 1960s, which was tied to college campuses, NAPNOC (and later ACD) worked closely with community-based organizations. According to Daniel Friedman, a scholar of the workers' theatre movement of the 1930s and performer in political theatre groups in the 1970s, this shift from college campuses to communities opened up people's theatre to workplace issues, unionism, and questions of class. In a survey of theaters "perform[ing] for or striv[ing] to perform for an audience made up primarily of workers," Friedman found that, with three major exceptions—the San Francisco Mime Troupe, El Teatro Campesino, and New York Street Theatre Caravan—theatre groups addressing working-class issues were established after 1970.[16]

Maxine Klein's own Little Flags Theatre, established in the early 1970s, illustrates the movement of political theatre toward labor issues. Klein was active in antiwar protests while teaching at the University of Minnesota and at Boston University and directed and produced plays with political content. Little Flags Theatre, which took its name from a poem by Ho Chi Minh, was formed following the successful production of *Fanshen,* a play Klein wrote about the Chinese revolution. Next came *Tanya,* also by Klein, about the Cuban revolution. Although these productions met with acclaim both from the left and from mainstream theatre critics, it was during the production of her *Furies of Mother Jones* that Klein experienced her greatest rewards as a playwright and director.

The Furies of Mother Jones, first produced in 1975, moves back and forth in time between turn-of-the-century Appalachia and the late 1960s, when Jock Yablonski was challenging the entrenched, corrupt machine of United Mine Workers' president Tony Boyle. During the run of the show, in a theatre in a working-class section of Boston, several miners on tour to raise funds for strikers in Kentucky attended a performance and stayed afterward to meet with Klein and the cast. For Klein, "It was the high point of my life. . . . I had never seen in the theatre such pleasure. . . . I had never known the power theatre could have when you really tell people's stories. . . . This was reaching the heart; they were so proud of how I depicted the lives of the miners and their wives."[17] *The Furies of Mother Jones* set Little Flags in the direction of producing plays about American working people for audiences that included many union members. After its run in Boston, the play went on a tour of coal-mining areas, where it was warmly received. Little Flags began performing regularly for union benefits, conventions, and other labor-related events.[18]

Among Little Flags's most successful subsequent productions was *Boston Remembers,* a celebration of the Boston strikes of 1886 and 1919, a work compared by one critic to *Waiting for Lefty,* which, he noted, had been banned in Boston.[19] The focus of Klein and the Little Flags Theatre on domestic labor and class relations placed their work within the lineage of the workers' theatre movement of the 1930s; at the same time, they contributed to the renaissance of labor-oriented theatre across the United States. A performance of Little Flags around 1980 in Ann Arbor, Michigan, helped plant the seeds for the creation of another long-lived labor-oriented theatre troupe, Workers' Lives, Workers' Stories.[20]

Workers' Lives, Workers' Stories also embodies the transition from New Left political theatre and people's theatre to labor theatre. Elise Bryant, the founder of the group, had come to Ann Arbor from Detroit in 1969 to attend the University of Michigan, where she was active in student organizing and in the Black Action Movement strike. She left school after two years and joined a group that would soon become the Common Ground Theatre. As Bryant later described it, Common Ground "was doing political theatre of the Julian Beck school of theatre—using sound and motion to communicate ideas with more of a leftist, liberal orientation, not radical, but more political than any other theatre."[21] In 1981, Bryant and Common Ground Theatre traveled to St. Peter to take part in The Gathering.

Bryant began focusing on working people's lives and experiences in her theatre work when, as a staff member at the University of Michigan's Labor Studies Center, she was asked to develop a piece for an upcoming conference on workers' culture. For Bryant, the daughter of an autoworker, this turned into an opportunity to explore her own background and to integrate her experience in political theatre with her commitment to labor issues. Working with two other organizers for the conference, Bryant developed plans for Workers' Lives, Workers' Stories, "because that was what we were really talking about: theatre in which the performers would tell their own stories."[22] She recruited participants by sending flyers to local unions in the area. The troupe of six that eventually formed included an autoworker, a secretary, an unemployed worker, a building painter, and a computer programmer. In the 1990s, Workers' Lives, Workers' Stories continues to perform for unions and other sympathetic organizations, representing the stories of the performers and other working people.[23]

According to Bryant, Common Ground provided a model for Workers' Lives, Workers' Stories. The most powerful Common Ground productions were those that began with members of the troupe talking about their own experiences with growing up, sexuality, family. From their discussions of their own lives, the texts of their performances emerged.[24] Whereas Common Ground, a feminist theatre, affirms the lives and experiences—the "stories"— of women, Workers' Lives, Workers' Stories presents positive, affirming images of working people. Workers' Lives, Workers' Stories continued Common Ground's use of personal experience, drawing on the oral histories collected by the Labor Studies Center as well as material from the lives of its members.[25]

Like other people's theatre groups, Common Ground saw itself as part of the larger progressive project of reclaiming power for marginalized groups: lesbians and gay men, white women and women of color, men of color. For Workers' Lives, Workers' Stories, Bryant refocused this conception of theatre on the lives of working people, thus creating a workers' theatre troupe for the 1980s and 1990s. Like the workers' theatre troupes of the 1930s, Workers' Lives, Workers' Stories performers include union activists and theatre artists committed to using their art for social change, and they perform for union meetings and other labor-related events. In 1993, Bryant wrote and produced *Working for a Living*, a full-length musical about the day-to-day struggles of working-class Americans and the internal politics of unions. The play was performed for numerous union occasions, including the Labor Heritage Foundation's annual Great Labor Arts Exchange in Washington, D.C., and the Union Labor Industry Show in Detroit.[26]

Workers' Lives, Workers' Stories has inspired similar projects in UAW locals in the Detroit area. In 1985, director Cheryl Robinson helped organize a theatre group in the United Auto Workers' Local 735 at the suggestion of local president Ron Murray. Actors, musicians, writers, and technical staff for Local 735's Workers' Concept Theatre, all members of the local, produced shows for the union's special events and for the UAW's Family Education Center at Black Lake, Michigan. Meanwhile, members of Local 1200 formed the Labor Players of Local 1200 and frequently shared the stage with Workers' Concept Theatre.[27]

The Detroit area was not the only site for such experiments. In New York City The Labor Theatre was founded in 1973 to "bring relevant theater to working people whose lives we portray." For almost a dozen years, it produced plays about working people, their history and their unions.[28] In 1979, Jehane Dyllan created Union Sister Productions, which developed a one-woman show about atomic worker and activist Karen Silkwood and other plays about labor issues commissioned by unions. Dyllan performed *Silkwood* for women's organizations, antinuclear groups, and unions and was commissioned by the Communications Workers of America to write a play about union organizing and working people's lives.[29] One of the unions that sponsored a performance of *Silkwood* was District 1199, National Union of Hospital and Health Care Employees. One year later, the union put on its own show, *Take Care,* a musical revue based on discussions with union members. Over a six-week period, the professional cast of *Take*

Care performed the show at hospitals over the lunch hour, at union meetings and rallies, and in high school auditoriums and community centers for approximately fifteen thousand New Yorkers.[30]

Take Care was the theatrical centerpiece of the large-scale, multi-faceted Bread and Roses Cultural Project of District 1199, which included conferences, concerts, art exhibits, and street festivals.[31] Like *Pins and Needles* in the 1930s, *Take Care* and the Bread and Roses Cultural Project were hardly representative of contemporary labor-oriented theatre: the revue was performed with an Equity cast and was part of a generously funded national labor arts project. Moreover, Moe Foner, mastermind of the Bread and Roses Project, had grown up in the labor movement of the 1930s and 1940s rather than in the youth movements of the 1960s and 1970s. Nevertheless, Bread and Roses set a standard for labor arts projects and offered a distinctive model for using the arts to publicize and promote the cause of labor, at a time when labor activists were feeling a strong need for new approaches to unionism.

Beginning in the 1970s, changes in U.S. and global economies weakened the status of working-class Americans, and throughout the 1980s, corporations exacted contract concessions from unions and exported manufacturing jobs overseas, while state and federal governments supported employers' efforts to break unions. In response, labor activists in the 1980s devised new tactics, including sophisticated "corporate campaigns," creative shopfloor organizing, and effective coalition-building with community organizations.[32] Militant organizing campaigns in the 1970s and 1980s also included music, theatre, and other forms of artistic expression. "Unions see their role in the work-force diminishing, and they need to come up with innovative ways not only to educate their membership but to organize workers, and they're willing to be more innovative. They are willing to look at things that they wouldn't look at otherwise, in other times," notes Laurel Blaydes, who writes and performs labor songs.[33]

Blaydes is well positioned to assess unions' interest in cultural programs for members. As codirector of the Labor Heritage Foundation (LHF), she responds to requests from unions for workshop leaders, programs, and performances for various union events. One indicator, according to Blaydes, of unions' greater interest in labor-related entertainment is their selection of performers for their national conventions: before the mid-1980s, she points out, "you never would have seen any of this labor-type music at national conventions. . . . You would have seen a Las Vegas comedian or something. Now just about every national [union] convention uses the LHF or uses people that they have heard of through the Labor Heritage Foundation . . . to drive home the union message in a cultural way at their conventions."[34]

The Labor Heritage Foundation began in 1979 when a handful of individuals from the Washington, D.C., area offered a workshop on labor songs. In 1983, the group incorporated as Labor Heritage Foundation, an organization "dedicated to raising awareness of workers' culture within the labor movement and among the general public."[35] The original workshop has evolved into the annual Great Labor Arts Exchange, a three-day event that brings together musicians, storytellers, theatre artists, poets, muralists, cartoonists, and others to share songs, techniques, and support for creating art by and for working people, art that can enrich union meetings and organizing drives and can involve rank-and-file union members in the labor movement.[36]

In addition to organizing these gatherings, LHF works with unions seeking singers, songwriters, and other artists; produces videos, concerts and television and stage shows focusing on labor arts; trains union members to use music and other art forms; and prepares and distributes collections of labor songs, phonograph records, and audio and audiovisual cassettes. LHF also works with union activists during strikes and organizing campaigns. Like the New Theatre League in the 1930s, LHF lies at the hub of a network of labor artists, providing them with resources and facilitating unionists' access to their work.[37]

Music remains an important focus of LHF—probably because two of the founders and most active members, Joe Uehlein and Joe Glazer, are musicians themselves—but theatre is also very visible in LHF activities. Elise Bryant is a regular participant in the annual Arts Exchanges, and among LHF's most frequently requested workshop is one conducted by Service Employees International Union member Julie McCall entitled "Say It with a Song or a Skit."[38]

In contrast to Workers' Lives, Workers' Stories, in which performers tour with their productions, McCall seeks to cultivate rank-and-filers' skills in writing their own pieces for themselves. Her favorite technique is the translation of popular songs into labor songs. At the 1990 Great Labor Arts Exchange, she led several participants in writing a song for a Teamsters' Union local protesting takebacks and speedups by Coca-Cola in Atlanta. The song, "Coke Is It," referred to the drink's ad slogan and used the tune for "She'll Be Comin' 'Round the Mountain":

> Who's the class union buster? Coke is it (fight back!)
> Who's the class union buster? Coke is it (fight back!)
> Their secret formulation is the workers' exploitation
> Who's the greedy corporation? Coke is it.

Though McCall conducts workshops every year at the Arts Exchange, she says she will not do more than two workshops for any union local, because after that, she believes, members should be able to carry on without her—or she hasn't done a very good job.[39]

LHF organizers and supporters are acutely aware of the importance of using contemporary idioms—Joe Uehlein has a rock band that sings labor lyrics, and labor rap singers have appeared at recent Arts Exchanges—but they also recognize that their work has roots going back several decades. Each year, LHF presents a Joe Hill Award "for lifetime contributions to the advancement of workers' culture." In making these presentations, LHF honors individuals whose work precedes and informs the current generation of labor artists; at the same time, LHF pays homage to the history of its own work and identifies itself with the music and arts of earlier labor activists.

Joe Glazer, founder and long-time chair of the Labor Heritage Foundation, is one of a handful of labor artists and educators whose work links current projects and the workers' culture of the 1930s. Others in this position include Joyce L. Kornbluh, Emanuel Fried, and Moe Foner. Kornbluh, who coauthored a play about working women with Bette Craig of The Labor Theatre, performed with the New Theatre of Philadelphia as a child in the late 1930s. After college, she went to work for the Amalgamated Clothing Workers of America and remained in the field of labor education; since retiring from a long and productive career at the Labor Studies Center at the University of Michigan, Kornbluh has continued to teach a course on workers' culture for Antioch University's program in labor studies. A regular and revered participant in LHF Arts Exchanges, she was awarded the organization's Joe Hill Award in 1993.[40]

Two years earlier, LHF had presented the award to Emanuel Fried, who, under the name Eddie Mann, had performed in Theatre Union productions and in the Workers' Lab's *The Young Go First*, the Lab's first and only full-length production.[41] Subsequently, Fried worked as a union organizer for the UAW, the United Electrical, Radio and Machine Workers of America, and the International Association of Machinists. Blacklisted in the 1950s, he became an insurance salesman and completed undergraduate and graduate degrees at the State University of New York College at Buffalo in the early 1970s. He returned to theatre and playwrighting in the 1960s; his play *The Dodo Bird*, which poignantly dramatizes the impact of technological change on steelworkers, was produced by The Labor Theatre in 1975.[42]

Moe Foner, creator of the Bread and Roses Cultural Project, grew up in a family of left-wing activists and became involved in the student movement at Brooklyn College in the mid-1930s. He followed the work of the Theatre Union and other workers' theatre groups with his brothers (one of whom would be a long-time union leader, and two of whom would be fired from teaching positions at City College because of their left-wing politics) and had a band that performed at union and political functions. Foner became education director of Local 1250, Retail, Wholesale, Department Store Union, and later went to work for Local 65 when Local 1250 merged into it. He remained at 65 until 1954, when he became activities director and newspaper editor of Local 1199, then a small union of pharmacists.[43]

Throughout the 1940s and 1950s, Foner applied the lessons he learned in the 1930s about the importance of entertainment and cultural activities in political organizing. In 1947, he produced *Thursdays Till Nine* with members of Local 1250; the musical played to packed houses in the fourteen-hundred-seat auditorium of the Fashion Trades High School.[44] While working for Local 65, Foner was one of the prime movers behind Club 65. At both unions he hired up-and-coming entertainers such as comedian Sam Levenson and singer Harry Belafonte. Ossie Davis and Ruby Dee became regulars at Local 1199 affairs, as did Sidney Poitier and Will Geer, who had begun his career in 1930s workers' theatre.[45] In 1979, when the opportunity arose to submit a proposal for funding to the then-flourishing National Endowment for the Arts and National Endowment for the Humanities, Foner had several decades of experience as impresario in labor-oriented arts production. The proposal was funded, and the Bread and Roses Project came into being.

Foner's approach to union entertainment stands in contrast to much of grass-roots workers' theatre in the 1930s and much of labor-oriented theatre in unions since the 1970s. Believing that union members wanted quality entertainment, the kind they could not afford in commercial venues, Foner always hired professionals. The Bread and Roses Project likewise employed professional theatre artists, musicians, and visual artists to create productions about working people. Although the project is based in a union, one could argue that its work more closely resembles that of theatre organizations such as the Theatre Union than the productions of Local 65, where Foner began his career.

Indeed, recent labor-oriented theatre includes the same range of groups that had characterized the workers' theatre movement of the 1930s. The Bread and Roses Project and The Labor Theatre, in working with theatre professionals, inherit the tradition of the Theatre Union, whereas the UAW Local 735's Workers' Concept Theatre and the Labor Players of Local 1200 continue the work of Local

65's Dram Group. Workers' Lives, Workers' Theatre and the Little Flags Theatre Collective, as union-oriented cultural activists, most closely resemble such groups as the Workers' Laboratory Theatre and the Minneapolis Theatre Union.

Though the workers' theatre movement disappeared rapidly after the close of the 1930s, and workers' theatre became highly circumscribed and institutionalized, the women and men who had taken part in the cultural life of the labor movement of the 1930s and early 1940s were deeply marked by those experiences. Some, such as Glazer, Kornbluh, Foner, and Fried, were able to sustain their dedication to labor arts until activists once again turned to performance as part of their efforts to build an effective movement that was responsive to the needs of its constituencies.

These individuals are all keenly aware that they cannot re-create the 1930s, and such is not their goal. In fact, it is their younger colleagues in labor arts who seem most attentive to the 1930s. Consciousness about the workers' theatre movement of the 1930s pervades contemporary labor-oriented theatre. One of the first plays The Labor Theatre produced was *Waiting for Lefty*. The Labor Theatre also referred back to the 1930s through new plays it developed and produced: *Singly None: An Evening with John L. Lewis* traces the life of the labor leader from childhood but focuses on his years at the helm of the CIO; *Working Our Way Down,* subtitled "A Musical Documentary of the Depression Years," follows Ed and Marie Gunter as they leave their rented farm in Tennessee in 1929 and move to the auto plants of Detroit and finally the shipyards of California during World War II.[46] Across the country, in 1980, the Portland Players II developed a show based on interviews conducted with participants in the 1934 longshoremen's strike along the West Coast.[47] In 1986, members of several union locals in southeastern Michigan performed the play *Sit-Down '36*—based on recollections of participants in a 1936 strike in South Bend, Indiana—under the auspices of the UAW's Education Department.[48]

The work of Shaun Nethercott reflects the different ways contemporary labor theatre uses and positions itself vis-à-vis the 1930s.

Nethercott first came to the Detroit area in 1986 to work on a project that would mark theatrically the fiftieth anniversary of the Flint sit-down strikes of 1937. The resulting production, *'37–'87* was an exploration of the experiences of the sit-down strike and of current conditions in Flint, where General Motors was still the largest employer but was threatening to close down completely its already vastly reduced operations. Though not a workers' theatre production in that it was produced by students and faculty at the University of Michigan-Flint, *'37–'87* attracted autoworkers and examined problems that lie at the heart of workers' theatre: working conditions, bosses, and strikes (see photographs and figure).[49]

Nethercott next worked with Cheryl Robinson and Workers' Concept Theatre. Robinson developed a show of 1930s workers' theatre skits that toured through union locals in the Detroit area. To make these pieces available to other groups, Nethercott published the scripts in a booklet, *Agitprop Workers' Theatre, 1931–1939.*[50] Workers' Concept also planned to put on a revival of *Pins and Needles,* but funding fell through.

In *'37–'87,* workers sit at the bar and complain about working conditions. Note the mix of modern and historical elements. *Courtesy of Shaun Nethercott.*

Workers end the day at their rooming house, in '37–87. *Courtesy of Shaun Nethercott.*

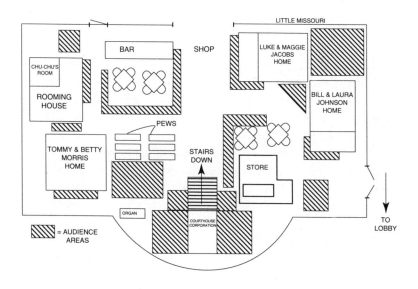

Figure 1. Floor plan for '37–'87. *Courtesy of Shaun Nethercott.*

At one level, the fascination of contemporary labor artists and activists with the 1930s is not difficult to fathom. The 1930s witnessed a flourishing of workers' theatre in many genres and venues. For union activists in the last two decades, the workers' theatre of the 1930s is the most recent and most prominent model of dramatic productions for audiences of workers. Yet we must also note that workers' theatre in the 1930s was produced in a context of optimism: the federal government appeared to be giving its blessing to collective bargaining, and new unions were making impressive gains in previously unorganized industries and corporations.

In those years, theatre was used to agitate, educate, and organize, to encourage people to join unions and go out on strike, and to sustain the morale of those who made such commitments. When audience members at the first performance of *Waiting for Lefty* poured into the street after the actors shouted the last words of the play, "STRIKE! STRIKE! STRIKE!" they were rehearsing an action that working people all over the country were taking part in with noteworthy success.[51] Forty years later, when The Labor Theatre performed the play, no such reaction was reported. Massive walkouts were no longer the useful strategy they had once been, and the wildcat strikes of the early 1970s had made little impact on the effectiveness of organized labor or the responsiveness of specific unions to their members.[52]

A play such as *Waiting for Lefty* would hold different meanings for audiences in the 1970s than it did for audiences in the 1930s. Moreover, in the 1970s, *Waiting for Lefty* would hold different meanings as well for the play's producers, whose belief in union militance was dramatically at odds with the reality of contemporary unions, which had become ossified institutions riven with internal dissension, overburdened with administrators, and incapable of stemming the flow of jobs to lower-wage regions of the nation and the globe.

The Labor Theatre was not trying to re-create the atmosphere of that first electrifying performance of Odets's play, any more than the Portland Labor Players II were trying to re-create the dockworkers' strike with their production of *1934: Blood and Roses*. Yet the numerous labor-oriented productions focusing on the 1930s reflect an attraction to the historical past seldom found in the workers' theatre of the 1930s, in which historical productions did not occupy the central position they do in contemporary workers' theatre. Although dramatic portrayals of the depths of the Great Depression might remind audiences that others' experiences were equally if not more distressing, a union member worried about whether the plant where she works will be closing, or whether her employer will demand concessions at contract talks in exchange for weak promises not to close up shop, might well see dramatizations of successful strikes and union actions as a mockery of contemporary conditions. Nevertheless, audiences seem to enjoy greatly productions harking back to the 1930s. The Portland Labor Players II had originally planned only a few performances, but when word of the show spread, they ended up performing throughout the summer of 1980 in several cities in Oregon and Washington and even at the Oregon State Fair—though only after a battle with fair organizers, who wanted to withdraw their invitation on the grounds that the show was "one-sided."[53] In Flint, '37–'87 ran to full houses, and The Labor Theatre's *Working Our Way Down*—subtitled "An Upbeat Look at the Great Depression Based on Documentary Sources Featuring the Obscure Men and Women Who Were Part of Our Struggle for a Better Life"—was enthusiastically received.[54]

Where workers' theatre productions in the 1930s were frequently lessons in union organizing and strategizing, in the 1980s, they often became lessons in labor history and community history. In the cases of '37–'87 and *1934: Blood and Roses,* the productions grew out of efforts to recuperate the history of working people in a particular community. *1934* was the outcome of a six-month project sponsored by the Pacific Northwest Labor College, "a labor-owned and governed institution," and funded by the Oregon Humanities Commission. The college's humanities coordinator conceived of the project as "a way of delivering labor history to working-class audiences and uniting socially conscious art (and artists) with a politically receptive constituency."[55] The production '37–'87 originated with the Labor History Project of the University of Michigan at Flint, which was formed to assist "those whose history was left out of the history books to recapture the past."[56] Participants in the project, university faculty members, specifically wanted to reacquaint the people of Flint with their history and with the accomplishments of the Flint working class.

Such history projects were hardly unique in the 1970s and 1980s. These years witnessed a renewed interest in "people's history" nurtured by a generation of historians whose political and intellectual commitments bore the imprint of the civil rights, antiwar, and feminist movements of the 1960s and 1970s. For practitioners of this approach to the past, people's history "generally refers to efforts to encourage a progressive, accessible and frequently oppositional historical vision in a variety of community and organizational contexts."[57] Projects such as the Brass Workers' History Project and the Baltimore Neighborhood Heritage Project and documentary films such as *Union Maids* and *With Babies and Banners* represent efforts to make history, especially the history of marginalized groups, more accessible to those groups and to involve them in rediscovering and reinterpreting that history.[58]

Several of these efforts have focused on unions and union members documenting their own histories, frequently in collaboration with academic historians. In the 1970s, with a grant from the National Endowment for the Humanities, the Amalgamated Clothing and Textile Workers' Union embarked on a nationwide project to collect oral histories of retirees and develop traveling exhibits on the history of the union and of textile and clothing workers.[59] Around the same time, the Iowa Federation of Labor undertook a documentation of the history of labor in Iowa through interviews with about one thousand union members in various occupations and communities. Beginning in 1975, unions affiliated with the federation paid a one-cent per capita tax to fund the Iowa Labor History Oral Project, and larger unions made substantial contributions as well. As part of the project, Shelton Stromquist, a historian at the University of Iowa, published an oral history of Iowa's labor intended for scholars of history as well as the women and men who made that history.[60]

For organizers and directors of people's history projects, such endeavors had the power to move audiences to political action. The Baltimore Neighborhood Project, for instance, began in 1977 with a group of academics and neighborhood activists who wanted to "democratize the historical record" and make the history of Baltimore's ethnic working-class neighborhoods part of contemporary Baltimoreans' sense of identity and place. Some of the members also saw the project as an opportunity to politicize the residents of these neighborhoods. According to Linda Shopes, one of the key organizers and interviewers, "Some of us believed that if community residents began to connect their personal histories with broader social processes, they not only would be personally enriched but might feel that their communities were 'worth something' and so be moved to take a more activist, critical stance with respect to their social and economic circumstances."[61]

For Shopes and her colleagues, activism among community residents would grow out of a sense of pride in their neighborhoods and heritage. For Jeremy Brecher and other organizers in the Brass Workers' History Project, involving brass workers themselves in recovering their past would lead to an appreciation of not only their community but also their own worth. "The attempt to understand the conditions of one's life and the forces that have shaped them is a fundamental aspect of human dignity," they wrote in the introduction to *Brass Valley*, a book combining photographs and oral history produced by the project.[62] Nurturing self-respect and pride in one's experiences seems to have been central to the goals of people's history endeavors, an emphasis that links these projects and contemporary labor-oriented theatre.

Stimulating "pride in themselves and their union," promoting "positive representations of workers' lives," "enhanc[ing] the dignity of working people": these are the goals of people working in labor theatre and labor arts today.[63] Many of them, especially those in unions, want to use performances to entertain but also "to inform, to agitate, to get people involved in their union and in the political world," in the words of the UAW's Workers' Concept Theatre.[64] Before disaffected

union members and unorganized working people can become activists, however, they must overcome the debilitating psychological effects of a labor movement in decline and images of unions in the popular media as corrupt institutions representing greedy, overpaid
workers.

Labor artists thus see their primary work as counteracting such
images, among both the general public and themselves. Using the
stories of contemporary working people's struggles and joys and the
accounts of the successes and accomplishments of earlier genera-
tions of unions, labor artists hope to raise working people's morale
and affirm their ability to make an impact. Raising audiences' self-
esteem will in turn lead to involvement in union activities and ultimately to political effectiveness. Underlying this vision, however, is
the same bedrock that has supported working people's movements
since the nineteenth century: the belief in workers' solidarity and the
ability to get things done by sticking together.

Theatre, music, and other arts are important tools for building
this solidarity. Elise Bryant talks about theatre as "a tool for empowerment, for affirmation" among working people.[65] The work of the
Labor Heritage Foundation is based on the premise that "music, visual art, drama, and other forms of cultural expression are fundamental tools in building a community-based consensus around social
issues, be it civil rights, environmental or labor issues."[66] As imple-
ments with which to build a movement, theatre and other arts are no
longer the "weapons" that they were in the 1930s when theatre was a
part of workers' arsenal in class warfare.

This linguistic shift perhaps reflects the legacy of the antiwar and
anti-intervention movements of past decades and a greater awareness
of the destructiveness of warfare and all violence. More important,
the shift to a metaphor implying construction rather than violence
suggests a distinctive outlook on the status of organized labor. In the
1930s, labor went on the offensive and was often met with uniforms
and firearms; "class warfare" was a literal description of relations between workers and employers rather than a metaphorical one. Since
the early 1970s, labor-management relations have been transformed

by a changing world economy and political climate. Under such circumstances, the strategies of earlier years are no longer as effective as before: the hiring of "permanent replacements" makes the strike an all-but-empty threat against employers. Labor must develop new approaches, new strategies, and, therefore, new metaphors. Theatre and other arts thus become "tools," instruments for rebuilding working people's pride, reconstructing crumbling unions, and restoring the vitality and effectiveness of the labor movement.

*   *   *

What, then, is the legacy of the workers' theatre movement of the 1930s? A belief in the power of live performance for touching audiences where they are most vulnerable, for creating images of themselves that can stand up to the insults of employers and the state, and, ultimately, for reminding them of the importance of resistance. Some see in the outcroppings of union militance and creative union strategies in the 1980s the groundwork for a full-scale renewal of organized labor.[67] The productions of such groups as The Labor Theatre, Workers' Concept Theatre, the Bread and Roses Cultural Project, and Workers' Lives, Workers' Stories are part of that groundwork, providing the vision and vigor for the next wave of union power.

Angels in America and the Study of Workers' Theatre

On July 16, 1995, I attended a performance of Tony Kushner's *Angels in America*, Part I, *The Millennium Approaches,* and Part II, *Perestroika,* in Minneapolis. The performance of this epic indictment of the politics of AIDS and homophobia took place in a 1920s theatre palace recently restored to its original glitter and grandeur. The audience was made up largely of lesbians and gay men and progressive political activists. Watching the crowd mill around during intermissions, I was struck by how much of the experience of seeing this play took place in the lobbies and around the beverage counters. Sometime during the extended intermission between Part I and Part II, I realized that the scene I was watching paralleled what I had been studying for a dozen years: just as I had envisioned the subjects of my research basking in theatrical productions that were about their lives, so I now watched friends embrace, co-conspirators renew acquaintance, and all savor the energy of a large-scale theatrical production that was about their lives. As a result, I realized as well that this political production (like many I had studied) understandably, if not intentionally, bifurcated the audience into those "in the know," who responded enthusiastically to jokes and allusions meant for them, and "outsiders," sympathetic allies who enjoyed the enthusiasm of the insiders. Like the workers' theatre productions of the 1930s, *Angels in America* was as much about context as about content.

The experience of *Angels in America* was both reaffirming and sobering to me as a scholar of political theatre and the labor movement. The production confirms that theatre that forcefully addresses contemporary social issues and that attacks mean-spirited and even deathly social policies and attitudes can find an audience. In many ways, *Angels in America* works toward the same goal as workers' theatre groups since the 1920s. From the Brookwood Labor Players and the New Playwrights Theatre, to Workers' Lives, Workers' Stories and Bread and Roses, all the labor arts and labor theatre projects discussed in this book, whatever the political or artistic differences among them, affirm both the struggles and the pains of their subjects and participants and their power to transform the conditions of their lives. Spectators of workers' theatre, particularly in the heyday of the movement in the 1930s, describe the same audience animation I witnessed at the performance of *Angels in America,* which results from this sort of theatre's honesty and belief in the potential for social change.

This contemporary play about the struggles of gay men in a period of right-wing repressiveness, a play that belongs in the same tradition as the workers' theatre movement and can be seen as part of its legacy, stands as a challenge to activists in the contemporary labor movement. Labor-oriented theatre since the 1970s has benefited greatly from the emergence of theatre connected to the antiwar, feminist, and other political movements. If this grandiose production about gay men and AIDS can win a Tony Award and gain enough success on Broadway to warrant a national commercial tour, one might well ask, Couldn't a play about plant closings, union busting, and workers' creative responses to employer initiatives receive the same treatment?

Without dismissing the differences that exist between the constituencies of the lesbian and gay pride movement and those of the labor movement, I would argue that *Angels in America* presents the labor movement with a model of what is possible for political theatre in the 1990s. There are audiences willing to pay commercial theatre ticket prices to attend performances that highlight their lives and experiences and that offer alternatives both to the vacuousness of mainstream commercial theatre and to the attitudes, values, and policies promoted by corporate capital and the religious right. In the 1930s, the workers' theatre movement, nurtured by unions, labor schools, and a vast network of political groups and organizations, helped create and sustain a climate favorable to labor activism and organizing. A single labor-oriented production comparable to Tony Kushner's gay extravaganza cannot create a new political climate; it could, however, provide cultural sustenance for labor-oriented theatre projects such as Workers' Lives, Workers' Stories and for the activists who carry on their work, paving the way for the victories that, we must believe, lie ahead, no matter how distant.

In reigniting enthusiasm for a political cause and renewing bonds of community among supporters of that cause, political theatre performances constitute rehearsals for more direct political action. In the context of a dynamic and successful labor movement, as in the 1930s, such rehearsals prepared participants for the events of the following day or week or month. In the context of the labor movement of the 1980s and 1990s, such rehearsals keep alive the hope and the energy necessary to counter the demoralization that pervades labor and the left; they ensure that when the political winds change, there will be actors ready to claim their roles in the drama of progressive political change.

NOTES

CHAPTER 1

1. Clifford Odets, *Waiting for Lefty,* in *Three Plays* (New York: Random House, 1935), 52.

2. "Shifting Scenes," *New Theatre,* May 1935, 28; Harold Clurman, *The Fervent Years: The Group Theatre and the Thirties* (1948; rpt. New York: Da Capo Press, 1985), 147–48 (quotation).

3. On the New Theatre Nights, see Jay Williams, *Stage Left* (New York: Charles Scribner's Sons, 1978), 137–39; Ben Blake, *The Awakening of the American Theatre* (New York: Tomorrow Publishers, 1935), 42–43; "Brookwood Players Appear in New York," *Brookwood Review,* April 1926, 4.

4. Raymond Williams, *Drama in a Dramatised Society: An Inaugural Lecture* (Cambridge; Cambridge University Press, 1975), 11.

5. Augusto Boal, *Theatre of the Oppressed,* translated by Charles A. McBride and Maria-Odilia Leal McBride (New York: Theatre Communications Group, 1985), ix.

6. Diana Taylor, *Theatre of Crisis: Drama and Politics in Latin America* (Lexington: University Press of Kentucky, 1991), 49.

7. Raymond Williams, *Drama in Performance* (New York: Basic Books, 1969), 179.

8. Marvin Carlson, "Theatre Audiences and the Reading of Performance," in *Interpreting the Theatrical Past: Essays in the Historiography of Performance,* ed. Thomas Postlewait and Bruce A. McConachie (Iowa City: University of Iowa Press, 1989), 82–97. The field of theatre semiotics offers important insight for understanding the role of audience and context in performance. See Keir Elam, *The Semiotics of Theatre and Drama* (New York: Methuen, 1980); and Lars Kleberg, *Theatre as Action: Soviet Avant-Garde Aesthetics,* translated from the Swedish by Charles Rougle (London: Macmillan, 1993), esp. chap. 5, 9.

9. Contrasts between such performances are discussed by Bonita Bray in her study of a Canadian production of the play: "Against All Odds: The Progressive Arts Club's Production of *Waiting for Lefty,*" *Journal of Canadian Studies* 25 (Fall 1990): 106–22.

10. Paul Thom, *For an Audience: A Philosophy of the Performing Arts* (Philadelphia: Temple University Press, 1993), 205.

11. *Theatre Survey* 6 (1965): 65–82.

12. Key works in this body of scholarship include Malcolm Goldstein, *The Political Stage: American Drama and Theatre of the Great Depression* (New York: Oxford University Press, 1974); Ira A. Levine, *Left-Wing Dramatic Theory in the American Theatre* (Ann Arbor: UMI Research Press, 1985); Gerald Rabkin, *Drama and Commitment* (Bloomington: Indiana University Press, 1964); and Sam Smiley, *The Drama of Attack: Didactic Plays of the American Depression* (Columbia: University of Missouri Press,

1972). Susan Duffy's bibliography, *The Political Left in the American Theatre of the 1930s* (Metuchen, N.J.: Scarecrow Press, 1992), provides an exhaustive compilation of scholarship on the workers' theatre movement of the 1930s and is evidence of the enduring interest in this topic.

13. Lizabeth Cohen, *Making a New Deal: Industrial Workers in Chicago, 1919–1939* (New York: Cambridge University Press, 1990); Elizabeth V. Faue, *Community of Suffering and Struggle: Women, Men, and the Labor Movement in Minneapolis, 1915–1945* (Chapel Hill: University of North Carolina Press, 1991); Gary Gerstle, *Working-Class Americanism: The Politics of Labor in a Textile City, 1914–1960* (New York: Cambridge University Press, 1989); Robin D. G. Kelley, *Hammer and Hoe: Alabama Communists during the Great Depression* (Chapel Hill: University of North Carolina Press, 1990); Peter Rachleff, *Hard-Pressed in the Heartland: The Hormel Strike and the Future of the Labor Movement* (Boston: South End Press, 1993).

CHAPTER 2

1. "Brookwood Players Appear in New York," *Brookwood Review,* April 1926, 4.

2. George A. Knox and Herbert M. Stahl, *Dos Passos and "The Revolting Playwrights"* (Uppsala, Sweden: American Institute, Uppsala University, 1964), 102.

3. Jay Williams, *Stage Left* (New York: Charles Scribner's Sons, 1974), 27–28; Ben Blake, *The Awakening of American Theatre* (New York: Tomorrow Publishers, 1935), 10–13; Malcolm Goldstein, *The Political Stage: American Drama and Theatre of the Great Depression* (New York: Oxford University Press, 1974), 11.

4. Karen J. Blair, "Pageantry for Women's Rights: The Career of Hazel Mackaye, 1913–1923," *Theatre Survey* 31 (May 1990): 23–46. On pageantry in the early twentieth century, see David Glassberg, *American Historical Pageantry: The Uses of Tradition in the Early Twentieth Century* (Chapel Hill: University of North Carolina Press, 1990).

5. Hazel Mackaye, "The Drama and the Labor Movement," attached to letter to A. J. Muste, July 10, 1925, Brookwood Labor College Papers, Archives for Urban and Labor Affairs, Walter Reuther Library, Wayne State University [hereafter BLC], Box 43, Folder 13; minutes, Brookwood faculty meeting, May 8, May 26, October 28, December 16, 1925, BLC, Box 7, Folder 1; "Students Write and Produce Labor Play," *Brookwood Review,* March 1926, 3.

6. Brookwood faculty meeting minutes, November 17, 1926, BLC, Box 7, Folder 12; "Deeter Heads Drama and Public Speaking," *Brookwood Review,* October–November 1926, 3; "Student Plays Produced," *Brookwood Review,* February–March 1928, 3.

7. On labor dramatics at Brookwood, see Richard J. Altenbaugh, *Education for Struggle: The American Labor Colleges of the 1920s and 1930s* (Philadelphia: Temple University Press, 1990), 102–16; Colette A. Hyman, "Culture as Strategy: Workers' Theatre and the American Labor Movement in the 1930s," Ph.D. dissertation, University of Minnesota, 1990, 66–74.

8. Irwin Marcus, "The Interaction between Political and Cultural Radicalism: The Greenwich Village Revolt, 1910–20," in *Cultural Politics: Radical Movements in*

Modern History, ed. Jerold M. Starr (New York: Praeger, 1985), 51–78; on the Paterson Strike Pageant, see Steve Golin, *The Fragile Bridge: Paterson Silk Strike, 1913* (Philadelphia: Temple University Press, 1988).

9. On the values and assumptions underlying the work of the Provincetown Players, see Robert Karoly Sarlos, *Jig Cook and the Provincetown Players: Theatre in Ferment* (Amherst University of Massachusetts Press, 1982). See also Helen Deutsch and Stella Hanau, *The Provincetown: A Story of the Theatre* (New York: Farrar and Rinehart, 1931).

10. For a biographical sketch of Gold, see Michael Folsom, "The Pariah of American Letters," in *Mike Gold: A Literary Anthology*, ed. Michael Folsom (New York: International Publishers, 1972), 7–19. On Gold and the Provincetown Players, see Sarlos, *Jig Cook*. Gold's place among left-wing writers is documented in what remains the standard work on radical writers in the United States until World War II, Daniel Aaron, *Writers on the Left: Episodes in American Literary Radicalism* (New York: Harcourt, Brace and World, 1961).

11. "Plan Workers' Theatre," *New York Times*, May 22, 1925, 15. Little documentation on the Workers' Drama League remains. The group is mentioned in Blake's *Awakening of American Theatre* (10–11) as among the precursors of the workers' theatre of the 1930s; Blake, the pen name of Bernard Reines, a member of the Workers' Laboratory Theatre, probably knew about the league firsthand. His account is cited in all secondary works that mention this theatre group, e.g., Goldstein, *Political Stage;* Gerald Rabkin, *Drama and Commitment* (Bloomington: Indiana University Press, 1964); Ira A. Levine, *Left-Wing Dramatic Theory in the American Theatre* (Ann Arbor: UMI Research Press, 1985).

12. "Workers to Stage 'Strike,'" *New York Times*, May 25, 1926, 25.

13. Michael Gold, quoted in Liliane Randrianarivony-Koziol, "Techniques of Commitment in the Thirties: A Study of the Selected Plays of John Howard Lawson," Ph.D. dissertation, Indiana University, 1982, 35.

14. On the influence of Soviet theatre on U.S. workers' theatre, see Hyman, "Culture as Strategy," 7–9; and John Fuegi, "Russian Theatre Experiments and the American Stage," *Minnesota Review*, n.s., 1 (Fall 1993): 102–12. Lynn Mally, *Culture of the Future: The Proletkult Movement in Revolutionary Russia* (Berkeley: University of California Press, 1990), studies the kind of theatre that most inspired Gold. See also Huntly Carter, *The New Spirit in the Russian Theatre, 1917–1928* (New York: Brentano's, 1929).

15. Levine, *Left-Wing Dramatic Theory*, 59.

16. Ibid., 123; Thomas Allen Greenfield, *Work and the Work Ethic in American Drama, 1920–1970* (Columbia: University of Missouri Press, 1982).

17. Paul Sifton, *The Belt* (New York: Macauley, 1927), 25–45. When critics attacked Sifton's caricature of Henry Ford, Sifton defended himself in the press: "I would like to go on record as disclaiming my intent to ridicule Henry Ford as an individual. Personally, he seems to me to be a rather likable country-bred genius. Like most geniuses, he has a lopsided mental development. He can make more and better cars cheaper than anyone else. . . . Mr. Ford becomes ridiculous when he ceases to be an individual and steps before the world as a symbol. . . . His name is the key

word in the new cabala of the new religion of Mass Production." Press release, Paul Sifton, "Henry Ford and 'The Belt,'" Sifton Papers, Manuscript Division, Library of Congress, Box 46, Writings File: The Belt.

18. Karel Capek, *R.U.R.*, in *Fifteen Famous European Plays*, ed. Bennett A. Cerf and Van H. Cartmell (New York: Random House, 1943), 645.

19. Ibid., 673.

20. John Dos Passos, *Airways, Inc.*, in John Dos Passos, *Three Plays* (New York: Harcourt, Brace, 1928), 81–159.

21. Harold Williamson, *Peggy*, in *Carolina Folk-Plays*, ed. Frederick H. Koch (New York: Henry Holt, 1922), 28–56.

22. New Playwrights press announcement, quoted in Randrianarivony-Koziol, "Techniques of Commitment," 36; on New Playwrights' audiences, see ibid., 39–40; and Levine, *Left-Wing Dramatic Theory*, 77–79.

23. Richard Pells, *Radical Visions and American Dreams: Culture and Social Thought in the Depression Years* (New York: Harper and Row, 1973), 19; Calverton quoted in ibid., 15.

24. Sifton, *The Belt*, 183.

25. "Workers' Art," *New Masses*, April 1931, 22.

26. On the Theatre Guild, see Roy S. Waldau, *1928–1939: Vintage Years of the Theatre Guild* (Cleveland: Case Western Reserve University, 1972).

27. Capek, *R.U.R.*, 684.

28. "Memorandum on Brookwood History and Policy," 2, BLC, Box 6, Folder 7.

29. On the summer schools for working women, see Rita Rubinstein Heller, "The Women of Summer: The Bryn Mawr Summer School for Women Workers, 1921–1938," Ph.D. dissertation, Rutgers University, 1986; and Mary Frederickson, "A Place to Speak Our Minds: The Southern Summer Schools for Women in Industry," Ph.D. dissertation, University of North Carolina, 1981.

30. On Commonwealth College, see Altenbaugh, *Education for Struggle*, esp. 81–91. For a recent study of Highlander, see John M. Glen, *Highlander: No Ordinary School, 1932–1962* (Lexington: University Press of Kentucky, 1988).

31. Jonathan D. Bloom traces the impact of such tensions on Brookwood in "Brookwood Labor College, 1921–1933: Training Ground for Union Organizers," M.A. thesis, Rutgers University, 1978.

32. Judah J. Shapiro, *The Friendly Society: A History of the Workmen's Circle* (New York: Media Judaica, 1970), 45–49.

33. On the founding of Brookwood, see Bloom, "Brookwood Labor College"; and Altenbaugh, *Education for Struggle*, 70–81. On education in the Jewish labor movement, see Steve Fraser, *Labor Will Rule: Sidney Hillman and the Rise of American Labor* (Ithaca: Cornell University Press, 1993), 221–26; Irving Howe, *The World of Our Fathers* (New York: Simon and Schuster, 1976), 244–49, 310–24.

34. John Dewey, quoted in Robert Westbrook, *John Dewey and American Democracy* (Ithaca: Cornell University Press, 1991), 105. See also Lawrence A. Cremin, *The Transformation of the School: Progressivism in American Education, 1876–1957* (New York: Alfred A. Knopf, 1961), 219–36; and Stanley Aronowitz and Henry Giroux, *Education under Siege: The Conservative, Liberal, and Radical Debate over Schooling* (South Hadley, Mass.: Bergin and Garvey, 1985), 8–10.

35. Altenbaugh, *Education for Struggle,* 184–86.

36. Jean Carter, "Experimenting in Workers' Education," Affiliated Schools for Workers, Publicity, 1930, American Labor Education Service Papers, State Historical Society of Wisconsin [hereafter ALES/SHSW], Box 52; Eleanor Coit, Report of the Education Department, Affiliated Schools for Workers, January 1, 1929–October 1933, Eleanor Coit Papers, Sophia Smith Collection, Smith College [hereafter Smith/Coit], Box 11, Folder 11; Eleanor G. Coit, "Workers' Education and the Community," *American Teacher* 17 (December 1932): 6–7. Coit was especially fond of the work of Progressive educational theorist John L. Childs, author of *Education and the Philosophy of Experimentalism* (New York: Century, 1931). On the Affiliated Schools see Marion W. Roydhouse, "Partners in Progress: The Affiliated Schools for Workers, 1928–1939," in *Sisterhood and Solidarity: Workers' Education for Women, 1914–1984,* ed. Joyce L. Kornbluh and Mary Frederickson (Philadelphia: Temple University Press, 1984), 189–94.

37. "Editorial," *Progressive Education,* Jan. 1931, 3 (quotation); Caroline Pratt, "Growing Up and Dramatics," same issue, 7–9. See also Victor Turner, "Dewey, Dilthey and Drama: An Essay on the Anthropology of Performance," in *The Anthropology of Experience,* ed. Victor W. Turner and Edward M. Bruner (Urbana: University of Illinois Press, 1986), 33–44.

38. On dramatics programs at workers' schools as embodying the principles of Progressive educational theory, see Anne W. Petty, "The Dramatic Activities of Workers' Education: Highlander Folk School, 1932–42," Ph.D. dissertation, Bowling Green University, 1979.

39. Bonchi Friedman, *Miners* (Brookwood Labor College, 1926), American Labor Education Service Papers, Labor-Management Documentation Center, New York State School for Industrial and Labor Relations, Cornell University [hereafter ALES/ILR], Box 41.

40. Bonchi Friedman and Stanley Francis Guest, *Shades of Passaic* (Brookwood Labor College, 1926), ALES/ILR, Box 41.

CHAPTER 3

1. John Dos Passos, "Did the New Playwrights Theatre Fail?" *New Masses,* August 1929, 13.

2. Lawrence Goodwyn, *The Populist Moment: A Short History of the Agrarian Revolt in America* (New York: Oxford University Press, 1978), xviii–xx.

3. Irving Bernstein, *Turbulent Years: A History of the American Worker, 1933–1941* (Boston: Houghton Mifflin, 1970), 31–125; Steven Fraser, *Labor Will Rule: Sidney Hillman and the Rise of American Labor* (Ithaca: Cornell University Press, 1993), 289–307; Lizabeth Cohen, *Making a New Deal: Industrial Workers in Chicago, 1919–1939* (New York: Cambridge University Press, 1990), 292–94. Activists and scholars have also seen the NIRA and the 1937 National Labor Relations Act as imposing constraints on labor unions. For a critique of New Deal labor legislation, see Christopher Tomlins, *The State and the Unions: Labor Relations, Law, and the Organized Labor Movement* (New York: Cambridge University Press, 1985).

4. Harvey Klehr, *The Heyday of American Communism: The Depression Decade* (New

York: Basic Books, 1984), 28–48. Roy Rosenzweig, "Organizing the Unemployed: The Early Years of the Great Depression, 1929–1933," *Radical America* 10 (July–August 1976): 37–60.

5. Jay Williams, *Stage Left* (New York: Charles Scribner's Sons, 1974), 37–42. Under his given name, Harold Jacobson, Williams was a member of the Workers' Laboratory Theatre. On the Proletbuehne, see Daniel J. Friedman, "The Proletbuehne: America's First Agit-Prop Theatre," Ph.D. dissertation, University of Wisconsin, 1979.

6. Mordecai Gorelik, "Theatre Is a Weapon," *Theatre Arts Monthly* 18 (1934): 432–33.

7. David Lifson, *The Yiddish Theatre in America* (New York: Thomas Yoseloff, 1965), 432–83. See also Nahma Sandrow, *Vagabond Stars: A World History of Yiddish Theatre* (New York: Harper and Row, 1977).

8. The most useful surveys of 1930s workers' theatre are Williams, *Stage Left;* Malcolm Goldstein, *The Political Stage: American Drama and Theatre of the Great Depression* (New York: Oxford University Press, 1974); and Ira A. Levine, *Left-Wing Dramatic Theory in the American Theatre* (Ann Arbor: UMI Research Press, 1985). For a contemporary account by a participant, see Ben Blake, *The Awakening of the American Theatre* (New York: Tomorrow Publishers, 1935).

9. "Workers' Art," *New Masses*, October 19, 1929, 29.

10. "Workers' Art," *New Masses,* July 1930, 21; February 1931, 22; November 23, 1930, 22.

11. "The Artef Theatre and Its Accomplishments," *New Theatre*, February 1934, 14–15; Irving Howe, *The World of Our Fathers* (New York: Simon and Schuster, 1976), 489–90.

12. Paul Buhle, "Jews and Communism: The Cultural Question," *Radical History Review* 23 (December 1980): 9–36. On ethnicity in the left of the 1930s and in workers' theatre, see Chapter 4.

13. "Foreign Drama Clubs Will Compete Tonight," *Daily Worker*, February 24, 1934, 7.

14. Interview with Sam Pevsner, July 24, 1984; Williams, *Stage Left,* 46; "Shifting Scenes," *New Theatre*, April 1935, 30.

15. "New Theatre of Philadelphia," *New Masses,* January 8, 1935, 22.

16. Letter to the editor for A. B. Magil, *New Theatre,* June 1935, 21; Paul Sporn, "Working-Class Theatre on the Auto Picket Line," in *Theatre for Working-Class Audiences,* ed. Bruce McConachie and Daniel J. Friedman (Westport, Conn.: Greenwood Press, 1985), 155–70; Paul Sporn, *Against Itself: The Federal Theatre and Writers' Projects in the Midwest* (Detroit: Wayne State University Press, 1995).

17. Conversation with Tillie (Lerner) Olsen, Youngstown, Ohio, May 2, 1992. On Olsen's activities in the 1930s, see Deborah Rosenfelt, "From the 30s: Tillie Olsen and the Radical Tradition," *Feminist Studies* 7 (Fall 1981): 375–80; Linda Ray Pratt, "Tillie Olsen: Author, Organizer, Feminist," in *Perspectives on Women in Nebraska History,* ed. Susan Pierce (Lincoln: Nebraska Department of Education, 1984), 42–46.

18. Anne W. Petty, "Dramatic Activities and Workers' Education at High-

lander Folk School, 1932–1942," Ph.D. dissertation, Bowling Green University, 1979, 58–60, 84–88, 188; John M. Glen, *Highlander, No Ordinary School, 1932–1962* (Lexington: University Press of Kentucky, 1988), 36, 54–56.

19. Hollace Ransdell, "Report on Dramatic Extension Program of the Southern Summer School for Women," March 14–May 6, 1931, American Labor Education Service Papers, Labor-Management Documentation Center, New York State School for Industrial and Labor Relations, Cornell University [hereafter ALES/ILR], Box 111; Mary Frederickson, "Recognizing Regional Differences: The Southern Summer School for Women Workers," in *Sisterhood and Solidarity: Workers' Education for Women, 1914–1984,* ed. Joyce Kornbluh and Mary Frederickson (Philadelphia: Temple University Press, 1984), 156–57.

20. Mary Lee Hays to Louise Leonard McLaren, November 1932, October 1933, ALES/ILR, Box 112; December 11, 1933, April 1, 1934, McLaurin Study Questionnaires, ALES/ILR, Box 88.

21. On Commonwealth College, see William H. Cobb, "From Utopian Isolation to Radical Activism: Commonwealth College, 1925–1933," *Arkansas Historical Quarterly* 22 (Summer 1973): 132–47; Raymond Koch and Charlotte Koch, *Educational Commune: The Story of Commonwealth College* (New York: Schocken Books, 1972). On labor dramatics at Commonwealth and other labor colleges, see Richard J. Altenbaugh, *Education for Struggle: The American Labor Colleges of the 1920s and 1930s* (Philadelphia: Temple University Press, 1990), 102–16.

22. "Workers' Art," *New Masses,* August 1930 and April 1931; Williams, *Stage Left,* 127; Gorelik, "Theatre Is a Weapon," 420–33.

23. California Labor School Papers, State Historical Society of Wisconsin.

24. Michael Gold, "A Letter to Workers' Art Groups," *New Masses,* September 1929, 16.

25. Blake, *Awakening,* 21.

26. Ibid., 20–24; Williams, *Stage Left,* 45–47, 49.

27. Felicia N. Frank Liss, "The Magazines *Workers' Theatre, New Theatre,* and *New Theatre and Film* as Documents on the American Left-Wing Theatre Movement of the Thirties," Ph.D. dissertation, City University of New York, 1976, 478; Saul Maloff, "The New Theatre Movement in America," Ph.D. dissertation, University of Iowa, 1952, 55; Levine, *Left-Wing Dramatic Theatre,* 131.

28. Blake, *Awakening,* 26–27; Williams, *Stage Left,* esp. 78; Levine, *Left-Wing Dramatic Theory,* 131; "National Theatre Festival," *New Theatre,* March 1934, 12–13; Mark Marvin, "Theatre Marches," *New Masses,* May 8, 1934, 29; "Theatres Prepare National Drama Festival," *Daily Worker,* March 15, 1934, 7. The League of Workers' Theatres was not the first effort to organize workers' theatre groups, but it was the longest-lived, existing as the New Theatre League until the end of the decade. A fairly sizable organization, the Workers' Council, was formed in the late 1920s and claimed membership of close to one thousand, including twenty-one different groups. The only evidence of its existence, however, seems to be letters to *New Masses.* "Workers' Art," *New Masses,* March 1930, 20; December 1930, 20.

29. *Facts about the New Theatre League,* undated pamphlet, New Theatre League Papers, Billy Rose Theatre Collection, New York Public Library, Center for the

Performing Arts [hereafter NTL/NYPL]. On the role of *New Theatre* in the workers' theatre movement, see Liss, "The Magazine *Workers' Theatre*"; also John Howard Lawson, "Play on Dimitroff Is Feature in New Issue of the 'New Theatre,' " *Daily Worker,* July 23, 1934, 5; and Albert Maltz, "Current 'New Theatre' Provides Guides for Workers' Drama Groups," *Daily Worker,* September 17, 1934, 5. On the New Theatre School, see Douglas McDermott, "New Theatre Schools, 1932–42," *Speech Teacher* 14 (November 1965): 275–85. On the CP's shift to Popular Front ideology, see Klehr, *American Communism,* 167–85; and Fraser M. Ottanelli, *The Communist Party of the United States: From the Depression to World War II* (New Brunswick: Rutgers University Press, 1991).

30. Interview with Ben Irwin, April 19, 1988; Blake, *Awakening,* 57–61.

31. Interview with Ben Irwin.

32. Kurt Keller, "Report to the Trade Union Drama Directors Group," November 29, 1940, NTL/NYPL; Alice Evans, "According to Their Needs," *New Theatre News,* April 1940, 4; Brett Warren, "Theatres Where They Belong," *New Theatre News,* April 1941, 1–2; Alice Evans, "Trade Unions Compete," same issue, 3–4.

33. New Theatre School Catalogue no. 5, March 1936, NTL/NYPL, 7, 9; Petty, "Highlander Folk School," 99; Glen, *Highlander,* 36.

34. " '65' Dramatic Group Wins First Prize in New Theatre League Contest," *New Voices,* May 1, 1940, 8; "Two Prize Winners in the New Theatre League 1940 Trade Union Tournament Will Be Given at Assembly Hall, World's Fair, on June 30," *New York Times,* June 20, 1940 (from Clippings Collection, Billy Rose Theatre Collection, New York Public Library, Center for the Performing Arts [hereafter Clippings/NYPL]); "The Winner—'Sing While You Fight,' " *New Voices,* May 15, 1941, 6.

35. "Liston Oaks Speaks at Stanford Picnic," *Daily Worker,* September 5, 1933, 5; "Tonight Is 'Colonial Night' in New York," *Daily Worker,* March 6, 1931, 2; advertisement for Lenin Memorial Meeting, *Daily Worker,* January 11, 1930, 12. Interviews with Perry Bruskin, November 26 and December 19, 1985.

36. "Shifting Scenes," *New Theatre,* March 1936, 30, and September 1936, 24.

37. Minnesota's Farmer-Labor movement was one of the most successful third-party movements in the 1930s, and the Farmer-Labor Party was a dominant force in state politics in those years. In 1947, after a purge of leftists spearheaded by Hubert H. Humphrey, then mayor of Minneapolis, the Farmer-Labor Party merged with the Democratic Party to form the Democratic Farmer-Labor Party, which remains the name for the Democratic Party in Minnesota. See Millard Gieseke, *Minnesota Farmer-Laborism: The Third Party Alternative* (Minneapolis: University of Minnesota Press, 1979); John Earl Haynes, *Dubious Alliance: The Making of Minnesota's Farmer-Labor Party* (Minneapolis: University of Minnesota Press, 1984); Richard M. Vallely, *Radicalism in the States: The Minnesota Farmer-Labor Party and the American Political Economy* (Chicago: University of Chicago Press, 1989).

38. Ruth Shaw to Theatre Union, September 5, 1935, Theatre Union Scrapbooks, Theatre Union Papers, New York Public Library, Center for the Performing Arts [hereafter TU/NYPL]. On the Minneapolis Theatre Union, see Colette A. Hyman, "Culture as Strategy: Popular Front Politics and the Minneapolis Theatre Union, 1935–39," *Minnesota History* 52 (Winter 1991): 294–306.

39. Janet Ross to Margaret Larkin, November 15, 1935, Theatre Union Scrapbooks.

40. Interview with Ole Fagerhaugh and Doug Hanson, July 16, 1985.

41. Transcript of interview with Lucy Kaye, conducted by Jay Williams, n.d., in preparation for writing *Stage Left*, Jay Williams Papers, Mugar Memorial Library, Special Collections, Boston University. I am grateful to Mrs. Jay Williams for permission to use these transcripts.

42. On the collective living and working arrangements of the Workers' Lab, see Williams, *Stage Left*, 79–84; also interviews with Perry Bruskin and with Earl Robinson, December 11, 1985.

43. Warren I. Susman, "The Culture of the Thirties" and "Culture and Commitment," both in *Culture as History: The Transformation of American Society in the Twentieth Century* (New York: Pantheon, 1984), 171–75 and 200–204, respectively.

44. This was never an easy process and, in the Theatre Union especially, led to dissension and disaffection. See Mark W. Weisstuch, "The Theatre Union, 1933–1937: A History," Ph.D. dissertation, City University of New York, 1982, 205–15.

45. Harold Clurman, *Fervent Years: The Group Theatre and the Thirties* (New York: Da Capo Press, 1983), esp. 86–97. Also Wendy Smith, *Real Life Drama: The Group Theatre and America, 1931–1940* (New York: Alfred A. Knopf, 1990).

46. Interview with Frank Drucker and Ruth Drucker, April 18, 1988.

47. Clurman, *Fervent Years*, 172.

48. Williams interview with Lucy Kaye.

49. Interview with Earl Robinson; interview with Earl Robinson, Oscar Saul, Viola Kates Simpson, Eda Reiss Merin, Perry Bruskin, Sam Locke, November 3, 1981, conducted by Gwen Gunderson, transcript in Earl Robinson Collection, Southern California Library for Social Studies and Research.

50. Interview with Toby Cole, July 13, and July 31, 1994. On the John Reed Clubs, see Klehr, *American Communism*, esp. 72–76.

51. Interview with Ole Fagerhaugh and Doug Hanson.

52. Interview with Robinson et al. See also Williams, *Stage Left*, 152–54; Goldstein, *Political Stage*, 214, 274–75.

53. Interview with Perry Bruskin, November 26, 1985; Williams, *Stage Left*, 41.

54. Margaret Larkin to Kathryn Kennedy O'Connor, June 28, 1934, TU/ NYPL.

55. Interview with Victor Wolfson, October 30, 1987; interview with Samuel H. Friedman, October 31, 1987.

56. Theatre Union [Margaret Larkin] to Anna Severance, February 2, 1935, TU/NYPL.

57. Albert Maltz, "What Is Propaganda?" *New York Times*, April 28, 1935, sec. 10, 3.

58. Gorelik, "Theatre Is a Weapon," 422. In their preface to the dramatic selections in *Proletarian Literature in the United States: An Anthology* (New York: International Publishers, 1935), the editors—Granville Hicks, Michael Gold, Isidor Schneider, Joseph North, Paul Peters, and Alan Calmer—wrote, "Theatre will become what in its great days it always was: a school, a forum, a communal institution, a weapon in the hands of the masses for fashioning a sound society" (264).

59. Hyman Shapiro, "Training the Actor for the Proletarian Theatre," *Workers' Theatre*, July 1931, 2–3.

60. Margaret Larkin, "Building an Audience," *New Theatre*, October 1934, 26. Albert Prentis of the Workers' Lab expresses similar views in "Basic Principles," *Workers' Theatre*, May 1931, 1.

61. Charles R. Walker, "Theatre on the Left," *Nation*, June 24, 1939, 731; editorial, *New Theatre and Film*, April 1937, 17–18.

62. Erwin Piscator, "Objective Acting," in *Actors on Acting: The Theories, Techniques, and Practices of the Great Actors of All Times as Told in Their Own Words*, rev. ed., ed. Toby Cole and Helen Krich Chinoy (New York: Crown, 1976), 302.

63. Lawrence W. Levine, "William Shakespeare and the American People: A Study in Cultural Transformation," in *The Unpredictable Past: Explorations in American Cultural History* (New York: Oxford University Press, 1993), 164–66. On happenings, see Michael Kirby, ed., *Happenings* (New York: E.P. Dutton, 1965), 24–26; and Arnold Aronson, *The History and Theory of Environmental Scenography* (Ann Arbor: UMI Research Press, 1987), 153–64.

64. Maloff, "New Theatre Movement," 120.

65. Michael Blankfort, "Facing the New Audience: Sketches Toward an Aesthetic for the Revolutionary Theatre," part 1, *New Theatre*, June 1, 1934, 11.

66. John Howard Lawson, *The Theory and Technique of Playwriting* (New York: G.P. Putnam's Sons, 1936), 299. For a discussion of this work, see Levine, *Left-Wing Dramatic Theory*, 125, 128–29.

67. Lawson, *Playwriting*, 299–302.

68. Interview with Earl Robinson.

69. Interview with Ole Fagerhaugh, July 16, 1985.

70. Interview with Sylvia Regan Ellstein, November 15, 1985.

71. Margaret Larkin, "Building a Social Theatre: The History of the Theatre Union," typescript, n.d., TU/NYPL, 4; interview with Sylvia Regan Ellstein.

72. Publicity materials [1933–34], Albert Maltz Papers, State Historical Society of Wisconsin, Box 2, Folder 1; Larkin, "Building a Social Theatre," 5; "Announcement for Union Meetings" and "Ticket Distribution for *Peace on Earth*," TU/NYPL; "Shifting Scenes," *New Theatre*, April 1937, 38. See also Weisstuch, "Theatre Union," 137–47 and Blake, *Awakening*, 37–38.

73. "A Social Theatre," *Trend*, March–April 1935, Theatre Union Scrapbooks; see also Bruno Fisher, review of *Sailors of Cattarro*, *Arise*, n.d., n.p., Theatre Union Scrapbooks.

74. Blake, *Awakening*, 17.

75. Gary Gerstle, *Working-Class Americanism: The Politics of Labor in a Textile City, 1914–1960* (New York: Cambridge University Press, 1989), 158–203.

76. Weisstuch, "Theatre Union," 489–90.

77. Interview with Lawrence Spitz, March 6, 1991; Lawrence Spitz, "'Let Freedom Ring' on Tour," *New Theatre*, November 1936, 24–25.

78. Interview with Lawrence Spitz.

79. Chautauqua Report, March 30–April 26, 1933, Josephine Colby Papers, Tamiment Library, New York University, Box 1; "Labor Chautauqua Tour Meets with Fine Response," *Brookwood Review*, May 1933, 4.

80. Interview with Frank Winn, April 18, 1988; interview with Dominic Gianasi and Mildred Fingerhut Gianasi, April 19, 1986.

81. "Do You Want a Labor Chatauqua?" *Brookwood Review,* January 1935, 1; Altenbaugh, *Education for Struggle,* 112–13.

82. Brookwood Labor College, Tour Journals, 1936, BLC, Box 98, Folder 2.

83. Interview with Dominic Gianasi.

84. Interview with Paul Fagerhaugh and Doug Hanson, August 23, 1985.

85. Cecil Crawford to Salome Benowitz, April 28, 1936, BLC, Box 98, Folder 2.

86. Blake, *Awakening,* 39–40.

87. "Toward a Workers' Theatre," *New Republic,* December 27, 1933, Theatre Union Scrapbooks.

88. Clurman, *Fervent Years,* 71–72; Margaret Brenman-Gibson, *Clifford Odets, American: The Years from 1906 to 1940* (New York: Atheneum, 1981), 207.

89. Interview with Wilbur Broms and Dorothy Broms, July 25, 1985.

90. Interview with Ole Fagerhaugh, August 4, 1985.

91. Interview with Dominic Gianasi.

92. Interview with Freddie Paine, April 18, 1988.

93. Interview with Wilbur Broms and Dorothy Broms.

94. Interview with Edith Berkowitz Parker, October 14, 1985.

95. Interview with Sylvia Regan Ellstein; Goldstein, *Political Stage,* 66; Weisstuch, "Theatre Union," 221–25.

96. Richard Lockridge, review of *Stevedore, New York Sun,* April 19, 1934, Theatre Union Scrapbooks; Robert Garland, "'Stevedore' Exciting, Full of Violent Vitality," *New York Telegram,* April 24, 1934, Theatre Union Scrapbooks.

97. Gilbert W. Gabriel, review of *Stevedore, New York American,* April 19, 1934, Theatre Union Scrapbooks.

98. Percy Hammond, review of *Stevedore, New York Herald Tribune,* April 19, 1934, Theatre Union Scrapbooks.

99. Quoted in Weisstuch, "Theatre Union," 273.

100. Richard Pack and Mark Marvin, *Censored! The Censors See Red! The Record of the Present Wave of Terrorism and Censorship in the American Theatre* (New York: National Committee Against Censorship of the Theatre Arts, 1935). On discussion the production of the play in another city, see Tina Redd, "*Stevedore* in Seattle: A Case Study in the Politics of Presenting Race on Stage," *Journal of American Drama and Theatre* 7 (Spring 1995): 66–87.

101. Pack and Marvin, *Censored!*

102. Beth Cherne, "Rocking the Boat: Repression of Performance in the 1930s," paper presented at the annual meeting of the Association for Theatre in Higher Education, New York, August 1994 (in author's possession).

CHAPTER 4

1. Paul Peters and George Sklar, *Stevedore: A Play in Three Acts* (New York: Covici-Friede, 1934).

2. John Howard Lawson, *Marching Song* (New York: Drama Book Services, 1937).

3. On community-based organizing in the 1930s, see Gary Gerstle, *Working-Class Americanism: The Politics of Labor in a Textile City, 1914–1960* (New York: Cambridge University Press, 1989); Elizabeth Faue, *Community of Suffering and Struggle: Women, Men, and the Labor Movement in Minneapolis, 1915–1945* (Chapel Hill: University of North Carolina Press, 1991); Lizabeth Cohen, *Making a New Deal: Industrial Workers in Chicago, 1919–1939* (New York: Cambridge University Press, 1990), 340–49; Robin D. G. Kelley, *Hammer and Hoe: Alabama Communists during the Great Depression* (Chapel Hill: University of North Carolina Press, 1990); and Oliver Carsten, "Ethnic Particularism and Class Solidarity: The Experience of Two Connecticut Cities," *Theory and Society* 17 (1988): 431–50.

4. Fannia M. Cohn, *All for One: A Dramatic Skit* (New York: ILGWU Education Department, 1934); Irwin Swerdlow and Fannia M. Cohen, *In Union There Is Strength: A Play in One Act* (New York: ILGWU Education Department, n.d.), both in Fannia M. Cohen Papers, International Ladies Garment Workers Union Archives, Labor-Management Documentation Center, New York State School for Industrial and Labor Relations, Cornell University, Box 9, Folder 9.

5. Paula Rabinowitz, "Women and U.S. Literary Radicalism," in *Writing Red: An Anthology of Women Writers, 1930–1940,* ed. Paula Rabinowitz and Charlotte Nekola (New York: Feminist Press, 1987), 3–4; Daniel Aaron, *Writers on the Left: Episodes in American Literary Communism* (New York: Harcourt, Brace and World, 1961).

6. On CP gender ideology, see Van Gosse, "'To Organize in Every Neighborhood, in Every Home': The Gender Politics of American Communists between the Wars," *Radical History Review* 50 (Spring 1991): 117–19, 127–32.

7. A. Prentis, "The Miners Are Striking," *Workers' Theatre,* February 1932, 15–20.

8. "Tempo, Tempo!" *Workers' Theatre,* January 1932, 18–21.

9. Fred Wright and Sidney Jonas, *Shop Strife* (Brookwood Labor College, 1934), American Labor Education Service Collection, Labor-Management Documentation Center, Martin P. Catherwood Library, Cornell University [hereafter ALES/ILR], Box 41, Folder 5.

10. Hollace Ransdell, *Bank Run* (Southern Summer School for Women Workers in Industry, 1932), ALES/ILR, Box 41.

11. *Who Are the Workers?* (Bryn Mawr Summer School, 1937), ALES/ILR, Box 108. Although notes to the script indicate that this opening line is borrowed from a poem by Walt Whitman, it remains significant that the script relies so heavily on masculine worker imagery.

12. Hollace Ransdell, *On the Picket Line: A Workers' Play in One Act* (Southern Summer School for Women Workers in Industry, ca. 1932), ALES/ILR, Box 41.

13. Tom Tippett, *Mill Shadows: A Drama of Social Forces in One Act* (1932), Pamphlet Collection, Tamiment Library, New York University.

14. Albert Maltz, *Black Pit* (New York: G.P. Putnam's Sons, 1935).

15. Samuel Ornitz, "In New Kentucky," *New Masses,* April 3, 1934, 17–28.

16. Wendy Kozol, "Madonnas of the Fields: Photography, Gender, and 1930s Farm Relief," *Genders* 2 (Summer 1988): 1–23; Charles Shindo, "'A Woman Can

Change Better Than a Man': Ma Joad and Women's Work in *The Grapes of Wrath,*" paper delivered at the annual meeting of the Social Science History Association, Minneapolis, October 1990.

17. Ornitz, "In New Kentucky," 17.

18. On female consciousness and mass action, see Temma Kaplan, "Female Consciousness and Collective Action: The Barcelona Case, 1910–1918," *Signs* 7 (1982): 545–66. For an example of food riots in the United States, see Paula E. Hyman, "Immigrant Women and Consumer Protests: The New York City Kosher Meat Boycott of 1902," reprinted in *Women, Families, and Communities: Readings in American History,* vol. 2, ed. Nancy A. Hewitt (Glenview, Ill.: Scott, Foresman, 1990), 88–98. See also Ardis Cameron, "Bread and Roses Revisited: Women's Culture and Workingclass Activism in the Lawrence Strike of 1912," in *Women, Work, and Protest: A Century of U.S. Women's Labor History,* ed. Ruth Milkman (Boston: Routledge and Kegan Paul, 1985), 42–61.

19. Joe William Trotter, Jr., *Black Milwaukee: The Making of an Industrial Proletariat, 1915–1945* (Urbana: University of Illinois Press, 1985), 83–86.

20. Wright and Jonas, *Shop Style,* 5.

21. On the backgrounds of participants in the workers' theatre movement, see Colette A. Hyman, "Culture as Strategy: Workers' Theatre and the American Labor Movement in the 1930s," Ph.D. dissertation, University of Minnesota, 1990, 103–18.

22. Cohen, *Making a New Deal,* 120–47, 218–38; Ewa Morawska, *For Bread with Butter: The Life-Worlds of East Central European Immigrants in Johnstown, Pennsylvania, 1890–1940* (New York: Cambridge University Press, 1985), 266–97; and Thomas Gobel, "Becoming American: Ethnic Workers and the Rise of the CIO," *Labor History* 29 (Spring 1988): 173–98. Thomas Bell's *Out of This Furnace: A Novel of Immigrant Labor in America,* originally published in 1941 (rpt. Pittsburgh: University of Pittsburgh Press, 1987), presents a similar account of interethnic relations among second-generation immigrants; see part 4.

23. Maltz, *Black Pit,* 86–94.

24. On patterns of residential segregation in northern cities in these years, see Trotter, *Black Milwaukee,* also Kenneth Kusmer, *A Ghetto Takes Shape: Black Cleveland, 1870–1930* (Urbana: University of Illinois Press, 1976); Gilbert Osofsky, *Harlem: The Making of a Ghetto, 1890–1930* (New York: Harper and Row, 1966).

25. Cohen, *Making a New Deal,* discusses the use of black strikebreakers in the strikes of 1919. On race relations in the labor movement in the 1930s, see Horace Cayton and George Mitchell, *Black Workers and the New Unions* (Chapel Hill: University of North Carolina Press, 1939); August Meier and Elliot Rudwick, *Black Detroit and the Rise of the UAW* (New York: Oxford University Press, 1979); and Michael K. Honey, *Southern Labor and Black Civil Rights: Organizing Memphis Workers* (Urbana: University of Illinois Press, 1993). Even in a union described as "exemplary" with respect to issues of race, the Transport Workers' Union in New York, the rank and file resisted working with and competing with blacks, limiting leaders' willingness to challenge racially discriminatory hiring practices; see Joshua Freeman, *In Transit: The Transport Workers' Union in New York City, 1933–1966* (New York: Oxford University Press, 1989), 151–55.

26. Elizabeth England, *Take My Stand: A Play in One Act* (New York: New Theatre League, 1935), 25.

27. Albert Bein, *Let Freedom Ring: A Play in Three Acts* (New York: Samuel French, 1936), 145.

28. "Scottsboro! A Mass Recitation by the Proletbuehne," *Workers' Theatre*, April 1932, 17.

29. Langston Hughes, "Scottsboro, Limited," *New Masses*, November 1931, 18–21.

30. Ibid., 21.

31. Peters and Sklar, *Stevedore*, 97 103.

32. Gary Gerstle's description of the social life of the Independent Textile Union in *Working-Class Americanism* closely resembles Maltz's portrayal of interethnic cultural exchange in *Black Pit:* Greek, Portuguese, English, Polish, Irish, Italian, and Franco-Belgian all "participated in ITU festivities—organizing them, competing in races, dancing quadrilles [a French-Canadian style of square dancing] and singing French-Canadian folksongs; in the process, they partook of the French-Canadian festive spirit" (201). Such cultural sharing does not appear to have characterized racially mixed situations, even in unions that actively identified themselves as interracial. Both Lizabeth Cohen, in *Making a New Deal,* and Robin D. G. Kelley, in *Hammer and Hoe*, discuss the cultural life of successful interracial unions, but a distinctively black idiom does not seem to have been part of that shared union culture.

33. Lawson, *Marching Song,* 54.

34. Ibid., 152.

35. Maltz, *Black Pit,* 35.

CHAPTER 5

1. Lizabeth Cohen, *Making a New Deal: Industrial Workers in Chicago, 1919–1939* (New York: Cambridge University Press, 1990), 333–49.

2. McAlister Coleman, "The Rise of David Dubinsky," *The Nation,* May 14, 1938, 558–59; Benjamin Stolberg, *Tailor's Progress: The Story of a Famous Union and the Men Who Made It* (Garden City, N.Y.: Doubleday, 1944), 108–201; Paul Jacobs, *The State of the Unions* (New York: Atheneum, 1963), 112–36; Stanley Nadel, "Reds versus Pinks: A Civil War in the International Ladies Garment Workers' Union," *New York History* (January 1985): 49–72.

3. Local 65 has attracted little attention from historians; the two major studies of the union are dissertations: Robert Rogow, "Relationships among the Environment, Policies, and Government of a Labor Union: A Study of District 65, Retail, Wholesale, and Department Store Union, AFL-CIO," Ph.D. dissertation, New York University, 1965; and Jay Tabb, "A Study of White-Collar Unionism: Tactics and Policies Pursued in Building the Wholesale and Warehouse Workers' Union of New York," Ph.D. dissertation, University of Chicago, 1952. See also Alice H. Cook, *Union Democracy: Practice and Ideology, and Analysis of Four Large Local Unions* (Ithaca: Cornell University Press, 1963); chap. 3, which details the internal functioning of "Local 100," is widely known to be about Local 65.

4. On the backgrounds of Local 65 and ILG members who were involved in the unions' theatrical productions, see Colette A. Hyman, "Culture as Strategy: Workers' Theatre and the American Labor Movement in the 1930s," Ph.D. dissertation, University of Minnesota, 1990, 101–13.

5. Robert J. Schaefer, "Educational Activities of the Garment Unions, 1890–1948: A Study in Workers' Education in the International Ladies Garment Union and the Amalgamated Clothing Workers of America in New York City," Ph.D. dissertation, Columbia University, 1951, 46–55.

6. Annelise Orleck, "Common Sense and a Little Fire: Working-Class Women's Activism in the Twentieth-Century United States," Ph.D. dissertation, New York University, 1989, 385–96; Susan Stone Wong, "From Soul to Strawberries: The International Ladies Garment Workers Union and Workers' Education, 1917–1950," in *Sisterhood and Solidarity: Workers' Education for Women, 1914–1984,* ed. Joyce Kornbluh and Mary Frederickson (Philadelphia: Temple University Press, 1984) Nancy MacLean, "The Culture of Resistance: Female Institution Building in the International Ladies' Garment Workers Union, 1905–1925," *Michigan Occasional Papers in Women's Studies* 21 (1982).

7. David Dubinsky and A. H. Raskin, *David Dubinsky: A Life with Labor* (New York: Simon and Schuster, 1977), 189. See also David Dubinsky, "How *Pins and Needles* Was Born," pamphlet publication of radio interview with Alistair Cooke, n.d., David Dubinsky Papers, ILGWU Collection, Labor-Management Documentation Center, New York State School for Industrial and Labor Relations, Cornell University [hereafter Dubinsky Papers], Box 79, Folder 8.

8. Stolberg, *Tailor's Progress,* 294–95; Schaefer, "Educational Activities," 54; Orleck, "Common Sense," 426–27; Ricki Carole Myers Cohen, "Fannia Cohn and the International Ladies Garment Workers' Union," Ph.D. dissertation, University of Southern California, 1976, 237–38.

9. Dubinsky and Raskin, *David Dubinsky,* 189–92; Stolberg, *Tailor's Progress,* 293–98; Schaefer, "Educational Activities," 54–66.

10. J. M. Eisner, "Politics, Legislation, and the ILGWU," *American Journal of Economics and Society* 28 (1969): 301–14; A. H. Raskin, "Dubinsky: Herald of Change," *Labor History* 9 (1968), special issue on David Dubinsky, 21–24; Kenneth Waltzer, "The American Labor Party," Ph.D. dissertation, Harvard University, 1977.

11. The origins and development of *Pins and Needles* and ILG educational and cultural activities have been exhaustively detailed, from different perspectives, in the following dissertations: Harry Merton Goldman, "*Pins and Needles:* An Oral History," Ph.D. dissertation, New York University, 1977; Gary L. Smith, "The ILGWU's Labor Stage: A Propagandistic Venture," Ph.D. dissertation, Kent State University, 1975; and Schaefer, "Educational Activities."

12. Rogow, "Relationships," 8–12; Tabb, "White-Collar Unionism," 85–86; Jack Paley, foreword to *Organizing Wholesale: Annual Message by President Arthur Osman before the Opening Session of the General Executive Board, Monday, March 14, 1938,* by Arthur Osman (New York Local 65, 1938), 7–8. The author warmly thanks Irving Baldinger for his gift of his original copy of this pamphlet.

13. Oral history interview with Arthur Osman, conducted by Herbert Hill, July

12, 1968, Archive of Urban and Labor Affairs, Wayne State University, used with permission of Herbert Hill.

14. Interview with Arthur Osman. In contrast, retail establishments, which Local 65 also organized, were highly susceptible to strikes and risked losing their clientele permanently if shops were closed temporarily by a strike. See George G. Kirstein, *Stores and Unions: A Study of the Growth of Unionism in Dry Goods and Department Stores* (New York: Fairchild Publications, 1950), 121–23.

15. Tabb, "White-Collar Unionism," 169–70.

16. Ryllis Goslin and Omar Pancoast, *Growing Up: Twenty-One Years of Education in the ILG* (New York: Education Department, International Ladies Garment Workers Union, 1938), n.p.

17. Osman, *Organizing Wholesale*, 44.

18. Ibid., 36.

19. In 1960, when Local 65 had grown to thirty-two thousand members, it dealt with two-thousand employers, "only a small percentage of whom are organized in associations; thus much of its bargaining is carried on with individuals or at best with small groups" (Cook, *Union Democracy*, 40).

20. Dubinsky and Raskin, *David Dubinsky*, 118.

21. Dubinsky later recognized that five years was too long a period: "conditions change, and the workers get restless" and resort to unsanctioned work stoppages. He was later able to persuade manufacturers to accept three-year contracts (Dubinsky and Raskin, *David Dubinsky*, 118–19).

22. Joel Seidman, *The Needle Trades* (New York: Farrar and Rinehart, 1942); Roger Waldinger, "Another Look at the International Ladies' Garment Workers Union: Women, Industrial Structure, and Collective Action," in *Women, Work, and Protest: A Century of U.S. Women's Labor History*, ed. Ruth Milkman (London: Routledge and Kegan Paul, 1985), 86–109.

23. On the Protocol of Peace, see Stolberg, *Tailor's Progress*, 68–91; Melvin Dubofsky, *When Workers Organize: New York City in the Progressive Era* (Amherst: University of Massachusetts Press, 1968), 88–91.

24. Theresa Wolfson, "The Role of the ILGWU in Stabilizing the Women's Garment Industry," *Industrial and Labor Relations Review* (October 1950): 33–43.

25. Elizabeth Faue discusses this process in the context of labor organizing in Minneapolis in these years in *Community of Suffering and Struggle: Women, Men, and the Labor Movement in Minneapolis, 1915–1945* (Chapel Hill: University of North Carolina Press, 1991), 126–31.

26. Stolberg, *Tailor's Progress*, 184.

27. William Green, quoted in Smith, "ILGWU's Labor Stage," 61.

28. On the establishment of Labor Stage, see Smith, "ILGWU's Labor Stage," 54–66.

29. Stolberg, *Tailor's Progress*, 296–97; Smith, "ILGWU's Labor Stage," 74–78, 121–23.

30. On the origins of *Pins and Needles*, see Harry Merton Goldman, "*Pins and Needles*" and "When Social Significance Came to Broadway: *Pins and Needles* in Production," *Theatre Quarterly* 7 (Winter 1977–78): 25–26.

31. "*Pins and Needles*—November 6," *Justice,* November 1, 1937, 9; "ILGWU's Gift to B'way," *Justice,* November 15, 1937, 9 (quotation).

32. "*Pins and Needles* Clicks with Invitation Audience," *Justice,* December 1, 1937, 12; list of invitations to *Pins and Needles* opening, November 17, 1939, Dubinsky Papers, Box 79, Folder 7.

33. Harry M. Goldman and Theresa Goldman, "*Pins and Needles,*" *Performing Arts Journal* 7 (1977): 356–77; interview with Rose Newmark Rosenberg, conducted by Ethel Goldwasser, July 2, 1985, ILGWU Papers, Labor-Management Documentation Center, Martin P. Catherwood Library, New York State School for Industrial and Labor Relations, Cornell University; interview with Miriam Stein and Leon Stein, October 28, 1985.

34. The event is chronicled in Harry Merton Goldman, "*Pins and Needles:* A White House Command Performance," *Educational Theatre Journal* 30 (March 1978): 90–101.

35. In the early 1940s, the union purchased the building at 13 Astor Place, where its central offices remained, through the union's mutation into District 65 in the 1950s and District 65-UAW in the 1960s, until it closed its doors in 1994.

36. Sig Wenger, "Cultural Chats," *New Voices,* September 1938, 6; interview with Arthur Osman.

37. Songs from *Sing While You Fight* appear in *District 65 Songbook: Songs Reprinted from District 65's 1941 and 1952 Songbooks,* n.d., District 65 Papers, Wagner Labor Archives, Tamiment Library, New York University.

38. Interview with Irving Baldinger, September 10, 1987; interview with Sol Molovsky, June 28, 1991; "It's a Date Every Week—Saturday Socials Are Here," *New Voices,* September 15, 1940, 7.

39. Interview with Henry Corden, April 20, 1988.

40. *New Voices,* November 1, 1940. On the Sears campaign, see "Sears-Roebuck Drive Advances," *New Voices,* July 1, 1940, 1.

41. "*Organizing Wholesale* to Have Its Premiere at March 2 Meeting," *New Voices,* March 1939, 6; "*Sing While You Fight* Is Premiered; Union Audience Cheers Lively Revue," *New Voices,* February 1, 1941, 8; Tabb, "White-Collar Unionism," 95.

42. Interview with Nettie Harary Shrog, July 14, 1991.

43. "*Wholesale Mikado* Blazes Hit Year for Dram Group," *New Voices,* January 1, 1941, 8; Sol Molovsky, "Labor Takes the Stage: United Wholesale and Warehouse Employees, Local #65," *New Theatre News,* July–August 1940, 4; "The Winner—*Sing While You Fight,*" *New Voices,* May 15, 1941, 6.

44. "'65 Dramatic Group Wins First Prize in New Theatre League Contest," *New Voices,* May 1, 1940, 8; "100,000 Throng to Labor Festival; *Wholesale Mikado* Wins Acclaim," *New Voices,* July 1940, 4.

45. Interviews with Nettie Harary Shrog, December 18, 1985, and July 14, 1991; interview with Jack Sorian, December 18, 1985; interview with Pete Stein, December 12, 1987; interview with Milt Reverby, November 2, 1987; Rose Morrison Green, "Memoirs," typescript, n.d. I am grateful to Rose Green for sharing with me a portion of her memoirs.

46. Interview with Eugene Goldstein and Al Schmidt, November 13, 1985;

interview with Irving Baldinger, September 10, 1987; interview with Olive Pearman Ashford, December 20, 1985.

47. Interview with Henry Corden.

48. Interview with Larry Shepherd, March 7, 1988.

49. Anonymous interview.

50. Interview with Eugene Goldstein and Al Schmidt.

51. Ibid.

52. Ibid.; interview with Nettie Harary Shrog, conducted by Ethel Goldwasser, May 8 and June 28, 1985, ILGWU Collection.

53. Will Herberg, "Old-Timers and Newcomers: Ethnic Group Relations in a Needle Trades Union," *Jewish Frontier* (November 1953): 24–29. According to Herberg, 11.3 percent of the new members of Local 22, the dressmakers' local, were "negro." Ashford and Tucker both belonged to this local. Beginning in 1934, when each issue of the union's weekly newspaper, *Justice*, highlighted a member with a photograph and a biographical note on the front page, these members were frequently black or Puerto Rican women.

54. Interview with Eugene Goldstein and Al Schmidt.

55. Interview with Nettie Harary Shrog, conducted by Ethel Goldwasser.

56. This was brought to my attention by Olive Pearman Ashford, and a subsequent look at the photographs in the ILGWU's archival collection confirmed that neither she nor Tucker appears in any of them.

57. Hy Gardiner quoted in Goldman and Goldman, *"Pins and Needles,"* 370. This article has a complete account of the conflict. Hy Gardiner had been Hyman Goldstein until Schaffer persuaded him to Americanize his name.

58. Interview with Nettie Harary Shrog, conducted by Ethel Goldwasser.

59. Morrison left the union in 1942; Pete Stein remained on the staff well into the 1950s; Reverby remained in the union as executive secretary almost to the union's demise in 1994; Baldinger became director of the union's Welfare Plan and left 65 in the 1960s for a position managing union pension funds; Molovsky also remained close to 65 throughout his work life, in the United Storeworkers, a union that merged with Local 65 in the 1950s. In the late 1980s, Molovsky was president of Local 6 of that union and chairperson of the United Storeworkers' Council. Rose Morrison Green, "Memoirs" and "Meet the Members," *New Voices*, March 1, 1942, 6; interviews with Irving Baldinger, Sol Molovsky, Pete Stein, and Milt Reverby; Milton Reverby, "Review of My Life and Work Experiences," typescript, 1973, Wagner Labor Archives, Tamiment Library, New York University, 12–14.

CHAPTER 6

1. Program, *Pins and Needles*, n.p., 1938, Brown University Libraries.

2. Ibid.

3. Workers' theatre also drew on "folk" traditions, integrating songs and poems that would have been familiar to different groups of workers: Paul Peters and George Sklar incorporated African American hymns into the script of *Stevedore*, and Albert Bein wove into *Let Freedom Ring*, his textile workers' melodrama, a ballad that had been popular among textile workers since the turn of the century. (Paul Peters

and George Sklar, *Stevedore: A Play in Three Acts* [New York: Covici-Friede, 1934], 97–103; Archie Green, *Wobblies, Pile Butts, and Other Heroes: Laborlore Explorations* [Urbana: University of Illinois Press, 1993], 276–316.) Green, *Wobblies,* provides a useful discussion of the use of folklore in the Communist left and of the historiography of that phenomenon.

4. Gary Gerstle, *Working-Class Americanism* (New York: Cambridge University Press, 1989), 153–95; Fraser M. Ottanelli, *The Communist Party of the United States: From Depression to World War II* (New Brunswick: Rutgers University Press, 1991), 122–25.

5. On workers' theatre in Europe in the same period, see Frantisek Deak, "Blue Blouse," *Drama Review* 17 (1973): 35–46; David Bradby and John McCormick, *People's Theatre* (London: Rowman and Littlefield, 1978); Richard Stourac and Kathleen McCreery, *Theatre as a Weapon: Workers' Theatre in the Soviet Union, Germany, and Britain, 1917–1934* (London: Routledge and Kegan Paul, 1986). An awareness of European political theatre among individuals in U.S. workers' theatre is clear from articles appearing in the magazine *Workers' Theatre,* for example, Bernard Reines, "The Experience of the International Workers' Theatre," December 1931, 1–4; "How the 'Workers' Theatre' Works in Germany," May 1931, 6; and Mary Vaughn, "From the Report of the TRAM Theatres," Fall 1932, 13.

6. "Tempo, Tempo," *Workers' Theatre,* January 1932, 18–21; "The Belt," *Workers' Theatre,* March 1932, 6–8.

7. Al Saxe, "Take Theatre to the Workers," *New Theatre,* July 1934, 5.

8. Interviews with Victor Wolfson, October 31, 1987, and Sylvia Regan Ellstein, November 15, 1985. Berthold Brecht, "Criticism of the New York Production of *Die Mutter,*" in *Brecht on Theatre,* edited and translated by John Willett (New York: Hill and Wang, 1964), 81–84; telephone conversation with Ronnie Davis, March 8, 1989.

9. On nineteenth-century melodrama, see Frank Rahill, *The World of Melodrama* (University Park: Penn State University Press, 1967), 247–54; Robert C. Toll, *On with the Show: The First Century of Show Business in America* (New York: Oxford University Press, 1976), 151–55; and David Grimstead, *Melodrama Unveiled: American Theater and Culture, 1800–1850* (Berkeley: University of California Press, 1987), esp. chaps. 8 and 9. See also Bruce A. McConachie, *Melodramatic Formations: American Theatre and Society, 1820–1870* (Iowa City: University of Iowa Press, 1992). On melodrama in the plays of the Theatre Union, see Colette A. Hyman, "Culture as Strategy: Workers' Theatre and the American Labor Movement in the 1930s," Ph.D. dissertation, University of Minnesota, 1990, 279–81.

10. John Howard Lawson, *Marching Song* (New York: Drama Book Services, 1937), 58, 91.

11. Ibid., 55.

12. Clifford Odets, *"Waiting for Lefty," New Theatre,* February 1935, 20.

13. For interpretations of *Waiting for Lefty* as being on the cusp of agit-prop and Socialist realism, see Malcolm Goldstein, *The Political Stage: American Drama and Theatre of the Great Depression* (New York: Oxford University Press, 1974), 51–55; and Ira A. Levine, *Left-Wing Dramatic Theory in the American Theatre* (Ann Arbor: UMI Research Press, 1985), 105–6.

14. Odets, *"Waiting for Lefty,"* 20.

15. John W. Gassner, "The One-Act Play in the Revolutionary Theatre," in *The One-Act Play Today,* ed. William Kozlenko (New York: Harcourt, Brace, 1938), 246. The *Herald Tribune* is quoted on p. 244.

16. Harry Elion, "Two Workers' Theater Spartakiades," *Workers' Theatre,* May–June 1933, 2, 17; Nathaniel Buchwald, "A Theatre Advancing," *New Theatre,* January 1934, 19–20; Jay Williams *Stage Left* (New York: Charles Scribner's Sons, 1974), 138; Jean Friedman, "From the Workers' Laboratory Theatre to the Theatre of Action: The History of an Agit-Prop Theatre," M.A. thesis, University of California, Los Angeles, 1968, 71–77. I am indebted to the late Arthur Vogel for this citation.

17. Brookwood Chautauqua Program [1934], Brookwood Labor College Papers, Archives for Urban and Labor Affairs, Walter Reuther Library, Wayne State University [hereafter BLC], Box 96, Folder 24; Merlin Bishop to John Martindale, March 18, 1936, BLC, Box 96, Folder 26.

18. Brookwood Chautauqua Program, 1933, Josephine Colby Papers, Tamiment Library, New York University, Box 1; "Sacrifice Vacations to Chautauqua Trip," *Brookwood Review,* December 1933, 1; "Brookwood Players to Troupe in South," *Brookwood Review,* March 1936, 1.

19. Robert C. Allen, *Horrible Prettiness: Burlesque and American Culture* (Chapel Hill: University of North Carolina Press, 1991), esp. chap. 4; Robert W. Snyder, *The Voice of the City: Vaudeville and Popular Culture in New York* (New York: Oxford University Press, 1989), esp. 110–12; Philip Furia, *The Poets of Tin Pan Alley: A History of America's Great Lyricists* (New York: Oxford University Press, 1990), 6–8, 153–55.

20. Hyman, "Culture as Strategy," 268–76; Michael Blankfort, "Facing the Audience, Part II," *New Theatre,* July–August 1934, 14–15; and "Facing the Audience, Concluded," *New Theatre,* November 1934, 25–26.

21. "World Fair," *Workers' Theatre,* September–October 1933, 14–18. All further references to this production are from this article. The Chicago World Fair was a popular target of the left, as shown by the publication just a few weeks earlier of a lengthy article in *New Masses* denouncing the "rot beneath the glitter" and the "ballyhoo" of the fair. ("The Chicago Fair," *New Masses,* June 1933, 20–21.)

22. Toll, *On with the Show,* 305; Barbara Cohen-Stratyner, "Popular Music, 1900–1919," in *Popular Music, 1900–1919: An Annotated Guide to Popular Songs* ed. Barbara Cohen-Stratyner (Detroit: Gale Research, 1988), xvii–xx.

23. *Pins and Needles,* script, n.p., n.d., ILGWU Papers, Labor-Management Documentation Center, Martin P. Catherwood Library, New York State School for Industrial and Labor Relations, Cornell University.

24. Ibid.

25. Stratyner-Cohen, "Popular Music," xvii–xviii.

26. Heywood Broun, *"Pins and Needles," Pic Magazine,* August 9, 1938, reprinted in *Out of the Sweatshop: The Struggle for Industrial Democracy,* ed. Leon Stein (New York: Quadrangle/New York Times Books, 1977), 249–50.

27. Toll, *On with the Show,* 183–97.

28. Robert C. Toll, *The Entertainment Machine: American Show Business in the Twentieth Century* (New York: Oxford University Press, 1982), 137–41; Robert Sklar, *Movie-Made America: A Cultural History of American Movies* (New York: Vintage Books,

1979), 178; Andrew Bergman, *We're in the Money: Depression America and Its Films* (New York: Harper Torchbooks, 1971), 62–65.

29. *District 65 Songbook: Songs Reprinted from District 65 1941 and 1952 Songbooks,* n.d., n.p., District 65 Papers, Wagner Labor Archives, Tamiment Library, New York University. Other references to Local 65 lyrics are from this document. I would like to thank Sol Molovsky for providing me with a copy of the full script of *Curly.*

30. Robert S. Lynd and Helen Merrell Lynd, *Middletown: A Study in American Culture* (1929; rpt. New York: Harcourt, Brace and World, 1956), 263–71, and *Middletown in Transition: A Study in Cultural Conflicts* (New York: Harcourt, Brace and World, 1937), 260–65; Cohen, *Making a New Deal,* esp. chap. 3; Lary May, *Screening out the Past: The Birth of Mass Culture and the Motion Picture Industry* (Chicago: University of Chicago Press, 1983).

CHAPTER 7

1. See Sidney Fine, *Sit-Down: The General Motors Strike of 1936–37* (Ann Arbor: University of Michigan Press, 1970); Irving Bernstein, *Turbulent Years: A History of the American Worker, 1933–1941* (Boston: Houghton Mifflin, 1970), 432–98.

2. Report of the Education Department [UAW, 1937], Merlin Bishop Papers, Box 1, Folder 10, 42–43, Archives of Labor and Urban Affairs, Walter Reuther Library, Wayne State University [hereafter Bishop Papers]; "Address by Merlin Bishop before Conference on Workers' Education," May 27, 1937, Bishop Papers, Box 1, Folder 10. See also Thomas E. Linton, *An Historical Examination of the Purposes and Practices of the Education Program of the United Automobile Workers of America, 1936–1959* (Ann Arbor: University of Michigan School of Education, 1965), 35–37.

3. Merlin Bishop to Thomas Linton, June 10, 1957, Bishop Papers, Box 1, Folder 10; "Bishop Now Directing Auto Union Education," *Brookwood Review,* July 1936, clipping in Bishop Papers, Box 1, Folder 10; Linton, *Education Program,* 36.

4. "Education Program Is Planned for Summer," newspaper clipping, Bishop Papers, Box 1, Folder 10; Jonathan Bloom, "Brookwood Labor College and the Progressive Labor Network of the Inter-War United States," Ph.D. dissertation, New York University, 1992.

5. *Amalgamated Cultural Activities* (ACWA Department of Cultural Activities, 1940), 21, in Amalgamated Clothing Workers of America Records, Labor-Management Documentation Center, Martin P. Catherwood Library, New York State School for Labor and Industrial Relations, Cornell University, Box 291.

6. Robert J. Schaeffer, "Educational Activities of the Garment Unions, 1890–1948: A Study in Workers' Education in the ILGWU and the ACWA in New York City," Ph.D. dissertation, Columbia University, 1951, 97–105, 192–98; *Amalgamated Cultural Activities,* 6.

7. On the establishment of the WPA, see William E. Leuchtenberg, *Franklin Delano Roosevelt and the New Deal, 1932–1940* (New York: Harper and Row, 1962), 124–26; Irving Bernstein, *A Caring Society: The New Deal, the Worker, and the Great Depression* (Boston: Houghton Mifflin, 1985), 75–85.

8. Hallie Flanagan, *Arena: The Story of the Federal Theatre* (1940; rpt. New York: Limelight Editions, 1985).

9. Interview with Michael Blankfort, conducted by Lorraine Brown, July 22, 1977, Institute for the Federal Theatre Project and New Deal Culture, George Mason University [hereafter IFTP].

10. Interview with Perry Bruskin, conducted by John O'Connor, October 22, 1976, IFPT; interview with Ben Berenberg, conducted by Karen Wickre, August 16, 1977, IFTP. On the One-Act Unit, see Jay Williams, *Stage Left* (New York: Charles Scribner's Sons, 1974), 234; George Kazacoff, *Dangerous Theatre: The Federal Theatre Project as a Forum for New Plays* (New York: Peter Lang, 1989), 150–52.

11. Williams, *Stage Left*, 234–35.

12. The FTP was required to spend 95 percent of its allocation on wages; up to 10 percent of those hired, however, could be professionals, regardless of their eligibility status. The rest had to demonstrate both eligibility for relief and paid experience in theatre. See Jane DeHart Mathews, *The Federal Theatre Project, 1935–1939: Plays, Relief, and Politics* (New York: Octagon, 1980), 39–41; Willson Whitman, *Bread and Circuses: A Study of the Federal Theatre* (New York: Oxford University Press, 1937), 139–40.

13. Hallie Flanagan, "A Theatre Is Born," *Theatre Arts Monthly,* November 1931, 908–15.

14. "Writing on the Wall: Workers' Plays at Vassar College—A Letter from Hallie Flanagan," *Workers' Theatre,* June–July 1932, 4; "Can You Hear Their Voices?" *Workers' Theatre,* January 1932, 12; Malcolm Goldstein, *The Political Stage: American Drama and Theatre of the Great Depression* (New York: Oxford University Press, 1974), 43–44; Morgan Y. Himelstein, *Drama Was a Weapon: The Left-Wing Theatre in New York, 1929–1941* (New Brunswick: Rutgers University Press, 1963), 11.

15. Hallie Flanagan, "Talk to the Members of the Federal Summer Session," n.d., Hallie Flanagan Papers, vol. 2, 1937, Billy Rose Theatre Collection, New York Public Library, Center for the Performing Arts.

16. Williams, *Stage Left*, 231–32. For similar views in scholarly accounts, see Ira A. Levine, *Left-Wing Dramatic Theory in the American Theatre* (Ann Arbor: UMI Research Press, 1985) 151–55; Himelstein, *Drama Was a Weapon, 85–112;* Bernstein, *Caring Society,* 224–30.

17. Flanagan, *Arena.*

18. Interview with Ethel Aaron Hauser and Philip Barber, conducted by Lorraine Brown, February 20, 1976, IFTP.

19. Sue Ann Wilson, "Theatre Audiences," typescript, May 27, 1937, 3, Records of the Works Project Administration, National Records and Archives Administration, Record Group 69 [hereafter WPA Records], Box 457; Whitman, *Bread and Circuses,* 61–63; Tony Buttita and Barry Witham, *Uncle Sam Presents: A Memoir of the Federal Theatre, 1935–1939* (Philadelphia: University of Pennsylvania Press, 1982), 129–31.

20. Memo, Sue Ann Wilson to T. Mauntz, September 30, 1937, Library of Congress, Records of the Federal Theatre Project, at George Mason University [hereafter FTP/GMU]; "Filling the Seats: A Report on Audience Building," New York City WPA Federal Theatre Project, n.d., FTP/GMU, Box 16, Folder 1.3.50.

21. Irvin Curtis to D. Holway, November 22, 1938, FTP/GMU, Box 14, Folder 1.3.21; Curtis to Harry Davis, February 27, 1939, FTP/GMU, Box 963, Folder 4.1.43;

Curtis to D. Holway, January 11, 1939, FTP/GMU, Box 14, Folder 1.3.21; Curtis to Harry Davis, April 6, 1939, FTP/GMU, Box 963, Folder 4.1.43.

22. Ticket Sales, "One Third of a Nation," container 1051, FTP/GMU; "Analysis of Organized Audiences as Represented by Theatre Party Sales, July 1, 1936–June 30, 1937," New York City Department of Information, Box 450, WPA Records.

23. Report of the Education Department [UAW, 1937]; "Address by Merlin Bishop."

24. L. Janus and Kurt Keller, "Catch On???" March 4, 1939, United Office and Professional Workers of America, Archives Union Files, Labor-Management Documentation Center, New York State School for Industrial and Labor Relations, Cornell University [hereafter AUF/ILR], 282/12; "Dramatics Inc.!" *Joint Councillor*, September 1939, AUF/ILR, 282/12.

25. For the 1940 spring term, the union's educational and recreational activities included the UOPWA Players and a playwrights' group ("Educational Programs," spring term 1940, New York Joint Council, UOPWA, AUF/ILR, 282).

26. "Community Drama," Federal Theatre Project, Activity Reports, WPA Records, Box 519; Whitman, *Bread and Circuses*, 67–68.

27. Withholding support from groups such as the Theatre Union might not have been entirely the FTP's choice, as WPA projects were barred from competing with private enterprise. The result remains the same, however.

28. "WPA Coach Directs 'Waiting for Lefty,'" press release, July 7, 1938, Press Releases, WPA Records, Box 456; Weekly Reports, 1938, Manhattan I, WPA Records, Box 515.

29. "The Winner —'Sing While You Fight,'" *New Voices*, May 15, 1941, 6. The furriers' production of several scenes from the antiwar play *Bury the Dead* won third place in the 1941 tournament; the previous year, the union had won second place with a one-act play entitled *Renegade* ("'65' Dramatic Group Wins First Prize in New Theatre League Contest," *New Voices*, May 1, 1940, 8). The UOPWA entries won third place in 1940 and second place in 1941.

30. "Labor Plays," FTP/GMU, Box 945; on the National Service Bureau, see Flanagan, *Arena*, 261–67.

31. Correspondence between the NSB and various unions is found in Folder 2.1.26, "Labor Groups," Box 112, FTP/GMU.

32. On workers' education programs in the WPA, see Joyce L. Kornbluh, *A New Deal for Workers' Education: The Workers' Service Program, 1933–1942* (Urbana: University of Illinois Press, 1987).

33. "ACWA Opens New Bldg. Wing," *Pennsylvania Labor Record*, May 19, 1939, 2; Nora Piore to Dorothy Bellanca, October 14, 1935, ACWA Education Department, General Correspondence Out-Going, 1935–36, ACWA Papers, Box 47, Urban Archives Center, Temple University; "Knowledge and Fun," flyer, n.d., Barkas Papers, Box 36, Folder 136, Urban Archives Center, Temple University.

34. In reality, the "socially significant" plays produced by the FTP, like the number of Communists on the payroll, was quite small in the context of the Federal Theatre Project as a whole. Nevertheless, their concentration in New York City, where the project's central administrative offices were located, added to their

visibility and to their presumed impact on the FTP. Moreover, Flanagan herself believed that part of the mission of the FTP was to produce plays that advocated "for a certain cause in accord with general forward-looking tendencies," though, in her estimation, only 10 percent of FTP plays fell into this category (quoted in Goldstein, *Political Stage,* 288).

35. Kornbluh, *Workers' Education,* 112–13.

36. Frank Marquart to Florence Kerr, telegram, December 15, 1942. This and other correspondence regarding Harry Minturn's assignment to the UAW are located in WPA, General Subject—Recreation Division, WPA Records, Box 464, Folder 211.6.320. George Lipsitz, *Rainbow at Midnight: Labor and Culture in the 1940s* (Urbana: University of Illinois Press, 1994), 69–86.

37. Nelson Lichtenstein, *Labor's War at Home: The CIO in World War II* (New York: Cambridge University Press, 1982), 189–94; Martin Halpern, *UAW Politics in the Cold War Era* (Albany: State University of New York, 1988), 30–31; Lipsitz, *Rainbow at Midnight,* 87–92.

38. "No Time for Songs of Social Change," *Justice,* August 1, 1941, 12. The Education Department also shifted to greater emphasis on the war, offering instruction that was "directly connected with the Red Cross, first aid, nutrition, air-raid education courses, home nursing etc." "Report of Education Director for General Executive Board Education Committee, June 4–5, 1942," David Dubinsky Papers, ILGWU Collection, Labor-Movement Documentation Center, New York State School for Industrial and Labor Relations, Cornell University, Box 274, Folder 2b.

39. *Justice,* September 16, 1942, 6.

40. "Canteen Popularity Grows," *Justice,* December 1, 1942, 13 (quotation); "Brigade Hostesses Contribute to 'Homey' Feeling at Canteen," *Justice,* February 15, 1943, 12; "Servicemen Flock to Canteen in Ever Increasing Numbers," *Justice,* March 1, 1943, 12.

41. "Local 65 Canteen for Servicemen Opens February 12," *New Voices,* January 30, 1944, 5; "Canteen a Hit as Servicemen Relax at '65,'" *New Voices,* February 27, 1944, 4; "Hurry Girls! Oct. 14 Canteen Tix on Sale," *New Voices,* September 17, 1944.

42. "Next to 65's Social Hall, Soldiers Say USO Is Tops," *New Voices,* March 28, 1943, sec. B, 27; "'65' Library Starts Victory Book Drive," *New Voices,* January 31, 1943, 10; "Victory with Umph: Yvonne Goltry Came Off with Honors in Chicago 'Models for Victory' Contest," *New Voices,* March 14, 1943; "War Bond Sales at '65' on the Rise," *New Voices,* February 13, 1944, 6; "65ers Open Red Cross Fund Drive," *New Voices,* March 12, 1944, 3.

43. "Drammers Planning '20 Grand' Skits in Summer Production," *New Voices,* June 21, 1942, 12; "Dram Group Rehearses Three New Plays," *New Voices,* January 17, 1943, 10.

44. "'Club 65' to Open May 6th—Fun for All!" *New Voices,* April 30, 1944, 7; "Introducing Club 65!" *New Voices,* May 14, 1944, 16.

45. Williams, *Stage Left,* 235–40; interview with Toby Cole, July 13, 1994; Douglas McDermott, "New Theatre School, 1932–1942," *Speech Teacher* 14 (November 1965): 275–85.

46. Harvey Klehr, *The Heyday of American Communism: The Depression Decade* (New York: Basic, 1984), 400–409; Fraser Ottanelli, *The Communist Party of the United States: From the Depression to World War II* (New Brunswick: Rutgers University Press, 1991), 199–202.

47. Interview with Perry Bruskin, December 19, 1985; interview with Henry Corden.

48. Lichtenstein, *Labor's War at Home;* Frank Marquart, *An Autoworker's Journal: The UAW from Crusade to One-Party Union* (University Park: Penn State University Press, 1975), 96–97.

49. On the importance for marginalized groups in society of seeing their lives portrayed in a favorable light, see bell hooks, *Black Looks: Race and Representation* (Boston: South End Press, 1992).

50. Marquart, *Autoworker's Journal,* 119–23.

51. "Be an Actor," *Education Round Up,* January 1947, Local 51 Papers, Box 10, Folder 8; Victor Reuther to presidents and recording secretaries of UAW-CIO locals in Michigan, September 29, 1948, in UAW-Education Department Papers, V. Reuther Files, Archives of Labor and Urban Affairs, Wayne State University, Box 3, Folder 12; "Union Ham," *Recreation Round Up,* May 1949, 1–3, Olga Madar Papers, Archives of Labor and Urban Affairs, Wayne State University, Box 15, Folder 3. I am indebted to Joyce L. Kornbluh for additional insight into the Labor Extension Service and the campaign to close it down.

52. Robert Rogow, "Relationships among the Environment, Policies, and Government of a Labor Union: A Study of District 65," Ph.D. dissertation New York University, 1965, 15–31; George C. Kirstein, *Stores and Unions: A Study of the Growth of Unionism in Dry Goods and Department Stores* (New York: Fairchild Publications, 1950), 153–54; Victor Rabinowitz, "ACA-CIO and Local 65-CIO Refuse to Sign," in Ann Fagan Ginger and David Christiano, *The Cold War against Labor: An Anthology* (Berkeley: Meiklejohn Civil Liberties Instistute, 1987), 264–65.

53. Interview with Milt Reverby, June 24, 1991.

54. Interview with Nettie Harary Shrog, July 14, 1991; interview with Arthur Vogel, October 18, 1985.

55. Robbie Lieberman, *My Song Is My Weapon: People's Songs, American Communism, and the Politics of Culture, 1930–1950* (Urbana: University of Illinois Press, 1989).

CHAPTER 8

1. Telephone conversation with Perry Bruskin, August 22, 1994.

2. Kim McQuaid, *The Anxious Years: America in the Vietnam–Watergate Era* (New York: Basic Books, 1989); Terry H. Anderson, *The Movement and the Sixties* (New York: Oxford University Press, 1995); Alexander Bloom and Winifred Breines, eds., *Takin' It to the Streets: A Sixties Reader* (New York: Oxford University Press, 1995).

3. Henry Lesnick, *Guerilla Street Theatre* (New York: Bard Books, 1973).

4. On the San Francisco Mime Troupe, see R. G. Davis, *The San Francisco Mime Troupe: The First Ten Years* (Palo Alto, Calif.: Ramparts Press, 1975); Theodore Shank,

"Political Theatre: The San Francisco Mime Troupe," *Drama Review* 18 T61 (March 1974): 110–17; William Kleb, "The San Francisco Mime Troupe a Quarter of a Century Later: An Interview with Joan Holden," *Theatre* 16 (Spring 1985): 58–61.

5. Davis, *San Francisco Mime Troupe*, 13–18.

6. Quoted in Lesnick, *Guerilla Street Theatre*, 250.

7. See Beth Bagby, "El Teatro Campesino: Interviews with Luis Valdez," *Drama Review* 11 T36 (Summer 1967): 70–80; Theodore Shank, "El Teatro Campesino: The Farm-Workers' Theatre," in *Theatre for Working-Class Audiences*, ed. Bruce McConachie and Daniel Friedman (Westport, Conn.: Greenwood Press, 1985), 185–95; Yolanda Broyles-Gonzalez, *El Teatro Campesino: Theater in the Chicano Movement* (Austin: University of Texas Press, 1994).

8. Maxine Klein, *Theatre for the 98 Percent* (Boston: South End Press, 1978), 7.

9. Ibid., 19.

10. *Theatrework*, August 1981, special issue on The Gathering; Neala Schleuning, " 'The Gathering' People," *North Country Anvil*, Winter 1983, 8–13. I am grateful to Neala Schleuning for sharing with me these and other materials on The Gathering.

11. Douglas Paterson, "Some Theoretical Questions of a People's Theatre," in *We Are Strong: A Guide to the Work of Popular Theaters across the Americas* (Mankato, Minn.: Institute for Cultural Political Studies, 1983), 2–8.

12. Eugene Van Erven, *Radical People's Theatre* (Bloomington: Indiana University Press, 1988), 5–9; David James Fisher, "Romain Rolland and the French People's Theatre," *Drama Review* 21 T73 (March 1977): 75–90; David Bradby and John McCormick, *People's Theatre* (London: Croom Helm, 1978); Mark Marvin, "An American People's Theatre," *New Theatre*, December 1935, 24.

13. Theodore Shank, *American Alternative Theatre* (London: Macmillan, 1982), 107; Daniel Friedman, "Contemporary Theatre for Working-Class Audiences in the United States," in *Theatre for Working-Class Audiences*, ed. McConachie and Friedman, 197–246.

14. Arlene Goldbard, "The Challenge of Cultural Action," in *We Are Strong*, 10. For a similar analysis, see the periodical *Cultural Democracy*, published by the Alliance for Cultural Democracy.

15. "Join ACD," *Cultural Democracy* 43 (Fall/Winter 1994): 2.

16. Friedman, "Contemporary Theatre," 199.

17. Interview with Maxine Klein, Minneapolis, September 7, 1995.

18. Friedman, "Contemporary Theatre," 212–14; publicity and correspondence regarding Little Flags in files of Labor Heritage Foundation, Washington, D.C. [hereafter LHF]. I am indebted to Joanne "Rocky" Delaplaine, who shared her small office with me as I perused the organization's files while she was in the final stages of preparation for the 1993 Great Labor Arts Exchange.

19. Eliot Norton, "For Labor, Little Flags Theatre Sings of Dissent," *Boston Herald-American*, November 8, 1980, A7. I am grateful to Maxine Klein for sharing with me materials in her possession on the Little Flags Theatre.

20. Letter to author from Joyce Kornbluh, June 16, 1995.

21. "Elise Bryant, Artistic Director, Workers Lives/Workers Stories," inter-

viewed by Perri Giovannucci, *Detroit City Arts,* n.d., 12–13, LHF. Julian Beck and Judith Malina founded the Living Theatre in the 1950s. Although not usually listed among "people's theaters," the Living Theatre performed pieces in Europe and the United States that challenged dominant sexual ideologies, militarism, and the U.S. war in Vietnam. See Shank, *American Alternative Theatre,* 9–37; Pierre Binet, *The Living Theatre,* translated from the French by Robert Meister (New York: Avon Books, 1972).

22. Quoted in "Elise Bryant, Artistic Director," 13.

23. Elise A. Bryant, "Workers Lives/Workers Stories," *Talkin' Union* 13 (December 1985): 4; conversation with Elise Bryant and Joyce Kornbluh, March 7, 1994, Ann Arbor, Michigan. On the work of Workers' Lives, Workers' Stories, see Patricia A. Holm, "Unions and Roses: Alliances between Theatre Artists and Union Activists, 1913 to the Present," M.P.A. thesis, Evergreen State University, 1987. I thank Joyce Kornbluh for this citation.

24. Telephone interview with Elise Bryant, October 6, 1994.

25. Letter from Joyce Kornbluh.

26. Letter to author from Shaun Nethercott, July 5, 1995.

27. Roger Kerson, "Workers Take the Stage," *UAW Solidarity,* November 29, 1986, 11–15; interview with Shaun Nethercott, March 8, 1994, Detroit; Workers' Concept Theatre brochure, ca. 1987, in author's possession, courtesy of Shaun Nethercott.

28. Friedman, "Contemporary Theatre," 218 (quotation); "The Labor Theatre," in *We Are Strong,* 61.

29. I am very grateful to Eric Reuther for providing me with press packets for the productions of his late wife, Jehane Dyllan-Reuther.

30. Brochure for videotapes and audiocassettes produced by Bread and Roses Cultural Project, Inc., in author's possession; interview with Moe Foner, June 17, 1992, New York City; Moe Foner, "We Want Bread and Roses Too: A History of 1199's Cultural Project, Bread and Roses," presentation made at 1992 Great Labor Arts Exchange.

31. Marshall Frank Dubin, "1199: The Bread and Roses Union," Ph.D. dissertation, Columbia University, 1988, 26–34.

32. Peter Rachleff, *Hard-Pressed in the Heartland: The Hormel Strike and the Future of the Labor Movement* (Boston: South End Press 1993); Staughton Lynd, *Solidarity Unionism: Rebuilding the Labor Movement from Below* (Chicago: Charles H. Kerr, 1992); Jeremy Brecher and Tim Costello, eds., *Building Bridges: The Emerging Grassroots Coalition of Labor and Community* (New York: Monthly Review Press, 1990); Dan La Botz, *A Troublemakers' Handbook: How to Fight Back Where You Work—and Win!* (Detroit: A Labor Notes Book, 1991); Toni Gilpin, Gary Isaac, Dan Letwin, and Jack McKivigan, *On Strike for Respect: The Yale Strike of 1984–85* (Chicago: Charles H. Kerr, 1988).

33. Interview with Laurel Blaydes, Washington, D.C., June 28, 1993.

34. Ibid.

35. Labor Heritage Foundation brochure, in author's possession.

36. Lori Elaine Taylor, "The Labor Heritage Foundation: Teaching Labor

Culture to the Labor Movement," paper presented at the annual meeting of the American Folklore Society, October 1991, 8–12 (in author's possession). Various issues of *artworks,* the LHF newsletter, highlight the Great Labor Arts Exchanges.

37. Labor Heritage Foundation brochure, n.d.; Labor Heritage Foundation Annual Report, March 5, 1991, LHF.

38. McCall describes her technique in "Roll the Union On," *Steward Update* 1, 3 (1990): n.p. See also Labor Heritage Foundation Annual Report, March 5, 1991, LHF.

39. Conversation with Julie McCall, June 28, 1993; "14th Arts Exchange 'Diverse, Energized,'" *artworks* (Fall–Winter 1992–93): 1.

40. Joyce L. Kornbluh, *A New Deal for Workers' Education: The Workers' Service Program, 1933–1942* (Urbana: University of Illinois Press, 1987), xi–xii; "Fasanella, Kornbluh Get Joe Hill Awards," *art works* (Fall–Winter 1992–93): 4; letter from Joyce Kornbluh.

41. "Manny Fried Wins Hill Award," *art works* (Fall–Winter 1990–91), 3; LHF Annual Report, March 5, 1991, LHF.

42. "About the Author," in Emanuel Fried, *The Un-American: Autobiographical Non-fiction Novel* (Buffalo: Springhouse Editions/Labor Arts, 1992), n.p.; Emanuel Fried, "Union Life and the Arts," *edcentric* 27–28 (December–January 1974): 19–23.

43. Interview with Moe Foner; Leon Fink and Brian Greenberg, *Upheaval in the Quiet Zone: A History of Hospital Workers' Union Local 1199* (Urbana: University of Illinois Press, 1989), 25.

44. The production attracted the attention of New York theatre critics expecting a new *Pins and Needles:* "A Broadway contingent was there, ready to pounce on another 'Pins and Needles.' Instead the visitors got a strictly intra-mural charade about the occupational hazards of department store workers" ("Store Workers Unit Presents Musical," *New York Times,* November 25, 1947, 37).

45. Interview with Moe Foner.

46. Letter from C. R. Portz, March 17, 1975, Sally Genn Collection, unprocessed, Wagner Labor Archives, New York University; "Songs for the Unsung," newspaper clipping from *UE News,* The Labor Theatre Papers, Wagner Labor Archives [hereafter TLT], Box 3, Folder 7; "Labor Theatre Provides Link to Past and Present," newspaper clipping, TLT, Box 3, Folder 4; "The Labor Theatre Has Toured Productions," n.d., TLT, Box 1, Folder 11.

47. Jerry Lembcke, "A Report on the Portland Labor Players II: An Oral History/Theatre Project," *International Labor and Working-Class History* 19 (Spring 1981): 51–54.

48. Kerson, "Workers Take the Stage," 15.

49. Shaun S. Nethercott and Neil O. Leighton, "Memory, Process, and Performance," *Oral History Review* 18 (Fall 1990): 37–60; Nora Faires, "The Great Flint Sit-Down Strike as Theatre," *Radical History Review* 43 (Winter 1988): 121–35.

50. Shaun S. Nethercott, ed., *Agitprop Workers' Theatre, 1931–1939* (1988) (in author's possession).

51. Clifford Odets, *Waiting for Lefty,* in *Three Plays* (New York: Random House, 1935), 52.

52. On changes in U.S. and global economies that transformed the terrain of labor relations in the 1970s and 1980s, see Kim Moody, *An Injury to All: The Decline of American Unionism* (London: Verso, 1988), esp. chap. 5.

53. Lembcke, "Portland Labor Players II," 52.

54. Nethercott and Leighton, "Memory," 56; "Portrait of The Labor Theatre," clipping, TLT, Box 2, Folder 10.

55. Lembcke, "Portland Labor Players II," 53.

56. Neil O. Leighton and William J. Meyer, quoted in Nethercott and Leighton, "Memory," 41–2.

57. Susan Porter Benson, Stephen Brier, and Roy Rosenzweig, eds., *Presenting the Past: Essays on History and the Public* (Philadelphia: Temple University Press, 1986), xi, xvii.

58. See the collection *Presenting the Past* for essays discussing these projects: Linda Shopes, "Oral History and Community Involvement: The Baltimore Neighborhood Heritage Project" (249–77); Jeremy Brecher, "A Report on Doing History from Below: The Brass Workers' History Project" (267–80); and Sonya Michel, "Feminism, Film, and Public History" (293–306).

59. Marvin Ciporen, "Threads: Humanities in a Union Setting," *Alternative Higher Education* 6 (Fall 1981): 30–39.

60. Shelton Stromquist, *Solidarity and Survival: An Oral History of Iowa Labor in the Twentieth Century* (Iowa City: University of Iowa Press, 1993), ix–xii.

61. Shopes, "Oral History," 249–50.

62. Jeremy Brecher, Jerry Lombardi, and Jan Stackhouse, eds., *Brass Valley: The Story of Working People's Lives and Struggles in an American Industrial Region* (Philadelphia: Temple University Press, 1982), xvi.

63. These phrases are from Moe Foner, Shaun Nethercott, and the Labor Heritage Foundation, respectively (interviews with Foner and Nethercott; Labor Heritage Foundation Mission Statement, LHF).

64. Kerson, "Workers Take the Stage," 14.

65. Conversation with Elise Bryant.

66. LHF Annual Report, 1991.

67. See Lynd, *Solidarity Unionism;* and Rachleff, *Hard-Pressed in the Heartland,* 111–12.

INDEX

Page numbers in italics refer to illustrations.